A TOWN ABANDONED

SUNY Series in Popular Culture and Political Change
Larry Bennett and Ronald Edsforth, Editors

A TOWN ABANDONED

Flint, Michigan,
Confronts Deindustrialization

Steven P. Dandaneau, Ph.D.

STATE UNIVERSITY OF NEW YORK PRESS

Published by
State University of New York Press, Albany

©1996 State University of New York

For information, address State University of New York Press,
State University Plaza, Albany, NY 12246

Production by Kay Bolton
Marketing by Nancy Farrell

Library of Congress Cataloging-in-Publication Data

Dandaneau, Steven P.
      A Town abandoned : Flint, Michigan, confronts deindustrialization
/ Steven P. Dandaneau.
          p.   cm. — (SUNY series in popular culture and political
change)
      Includes bibliographical references and index.
      ISBN 0–7914–2877–X (hc : alk. paper). — ISBN 0–7914–2878–8 (pb :
alk. paper)
        1. Flint (Mich.)—Social conditions. 2. Flint (Mich.)—Economic
conditons. 3. Deindustrialization—Michigan—Flint. 4. Plant
shutdowns—Michigan—Flint. 5. Industrial promotion—Michigan-
-Flint. 6. Capitalism—United States. I. Title. II. Series.
HN80.F54D36 1996
330.9774'37—dc20   95-47289
                                                                                            CIP

10 9 8 7 6 5 4 3 2 1

To Maude and Rick

CONTENTS

LIST OF
ILLUSTRATIONS

PREFACE

A Town Abandoned only appears to be a traditional community study. This book is not, for example, the latest version of Robert and Helen Lynd's classic 1929 *Middletown*, which addressed the whole of a nation's social and cultural experience through a single Muncie, Indiana, microcosm.[1] This book is not even a study of Flint, Michigan, at least not in the sense that it aspires to a comprehensive, ethnographic description of Flint's local institutions and culture. *A Town Abandoned* is instead better understood as a "critical tale" written under the sign of the "critical theory of public life." While grounded in Flint's particulars, *A Town Abandoned* has a dialectical structure and critical, emancipatory intent that make it both something more as well as something less than a straightforward community study.

In his 1988 *Tales of the Field*, John Van Maanen explains that

> Fieldwork studies are often, particularly in sociology, strategically situated to shed light on larger social, political, symbolic, or economic issues. In industrialized societies, and for that matter, in virtually all societies, it is increasingly difficult to argue that fieldwork alone is sufficient to properly grasp the life situation of a studied group.
>
> While among tellers of critical tales there is an appreciation for the unique strengths of fieldwork, there is also a sense that the groups studied need to be selected with more care on the grounds of what they might reveal about larger issues, particularly those concerning the political and economic workings of capitalist society.[2]

It was in this vein that Flint was selected as a strategic site from which to research the workings of deindustrialization, and it is for this reason that *A Town Abandoned* is not simply or straightforwardly about a town that was abandoned. This case study pursues, via Flint, a general critique of key developments in class and culture in late capitalist society. As Van Maanen notes, "critical tales often have a Marxist edge," and this study is no exception.[3]

A Town Abandoned is a revised version of my 1992 Brandeis University dissertation in sociology and is grounded in two years (1990–1992) of field research into Flint's most significant public responses to its deindustrialization. In most cases, this research was conducted in explicitly public contexts (e.g, via government documents, participant observation in public venues, on-the-record interviews with officialdom, analysis of the products of television, film, and various publications and documents). This public-oriented methodology jibes with the book's basic motivation, which is political, at least in the sense that the aim of the book is to reveal and subvert the power of significant ideological forms. *A Town Abandoned* is thus an instance of what, in his 1985 edited volume *Critical Theory and Public Life*, John Forester calls an "applied turn" within contemporary critical theory research.[4] Indeed, as with the Forester volume, this book shares a basic sympathy with Douglas Kellner and Rick Roderick's view that

> If critical theory is to have a future in the English-speaking world it will be through the use of critical theory within various theoretical projects and disciplines and the development of critical theory in relation to contemporary conditions, concerns, and problems. Only then will critical theory be a living force.[5]

A Town Abandoned seeks to contribute to the project of making the critical theory of society a "living force" by reviving and refashioning its often opaque classical formulations for use in criticism of Flint's very contemporary, very tangible, public responses to its deindustrialization. As a text that hopes to further public dialogue about local responses to the devastation that is deindustrialization, it is not too much to say that *A Town Abandoned* is incomplete without a critical public audience.

It is in the reader's interest to note, furthermore, that the original field research on which this book is based was greatly facilitated by the fact that Flint is not only a strategically selected research site but is also the author's hometown. Wary of the potential for bias, it is for this reason also that the author has sought to base claims on objective, accessible materials and recorded events (e.g., tape-recorded interviews, the analysis of films, buildings, documents) rather than to rely solely on participant observation and field notes. This effort to "triangulate" methods in order to reduce the potential for error should not be construed, however, as a claim to the mantle of laboratory science. Rather, to the author's way of thinking, family, friends, and former colleagues are not, as with people in general, sociological guinea pigs, nor is Flint a maze designed in the first instance for learning and study, let alone for anyone's amusement or personal advancement. This book is intended as a work in critical sociology, not as a clinical dissection of abstract social problems.

Finally, there have been new developments in Flint in the several years since this study was first conducted. The observant visitor would, for example, note the city's new and improved airport, changes in several tenants at Flint's Great Lakes Technology Centre (including indication of GM's new Delphi Division), and a sparkling new University of Michigan–Flint library on its downtown campus. Our visitor would also hear Flint's auto factories humming with increased production as a result of a significant upswing in the national economy, and this would include several factories once slated for downsizing and even closure. Less easily noticed would be the anticipated purchase of Flint's defunct AutoWorld themepark by the University of Michigan–Flint, which may eventually raze the site as part of its long-term plans for expansion. Equally ethereal but no less important is the fact that a major portion of Flint was named by the Clinton Administration in 1994 as one of ninety-five national "enterprise communities," a designation bearing a gift of some $2.8 million in Federal monies.[6] In addition to this top-down empowerment, Flint has also seen two area UAW locals wage successful strikes against General Motors, including a major strike action by the New Directions-led UAW Local 599. And Michael Moore of *Roger & Me* fame has parlayed his documentary success into a budding on-camera career, including a new feature film and his own network television series "TV Nation." Indeed, the latter program self-consciously keeps alive as a point of public reflection the continued tough times for many in Flint.

But in 1995, with a popular Republican Governor in Lansing riding the national conservative tide, a new, more agressive president of the UAW taking office, and even with so many local developments suggesting, if nothing else, a more lively, politicized future for the city, this book's original thesis remains unchanged from its initial, dour formulation: conditions of extreme structural dependency in a globalized capitalist system create ideologically soaked local environments that encourage the systematic conceptual distortion of mediated societal relationships, and that, moreover, invite the emergence of a cultural cynicism bent on self-destruction disguised for its own benefit as a survival strategy. Stated more simply and maybe more directly, this book argues that most of America's chief social problems and evident cultural pathologies can be traced, not to our nation's crack houses, unwed mothers, and homeless, but rather to our collective unwillingness to fully appreciate the destructive and corrosive nature of our *capitalist* society.

Importantly, this book itself is a type of response to what Fredric Jameson, for one, calls "the cultural logic of late capitalism."[7] *A Town Abandoned* recommends, and, hopefully, itself exemplifies, a type of mediated self-consciousness appropriate for our times. This self-consciousness emerges out of the critique of prevalent ideological forms, and would, perhaps, if popularly adopted, reverse the slide toward cynicism by encouraging a thoughtful revolution in America's institutions. It is worth repeating: this critical tale, like most, has a Marxist edge.

NOTES

1. See Robert S. Lynd and Helen Merrell Lynd, *Middletown: A Study in Modern American Culture* (New York: Harcourt, Brace & World, 1956) and Maurice R. Stein, *The Eclipse of Community: An Interpretation of American Studies* (Princeton: Princeton University Press, 1960).

2. John Van Maanen, *Tales of the Field* (Chicago: University of Chicago Press, 1988), pp. 127–128.

3. Ibid., p. 128.

4. See John Forester, ed., *Critical Theory of Public Life* (Cambridge: MIT Press, 1985).

5. Ibid., p. xi.

6. My thanks to Nancy Jurkiewicz of the City of Flint's Department of Community & Economic Development for documents describing Flint's successful enterprise community application. It is instructive to note that six U.S. cities, including Detroit, received "empowerment zone" designations, along with a much more substantial $100 million grant. The Flint Area Enterprise Community Zone, for its part, is 10.32 square miles of the most depressed census tracts in the city (including one census tract in Mt. Morris Township). The Zone's poverty rate is 45 percent, while its unemployment rate is 27.5 percent. Over two-thirds of the Zone's nearly 50,000 residents are racial/ethnic minorities. My thanks also to Professor George F. Lord of the University of Michigan–Flint for sharing his insight into the developments in Flint in the period 1992–1995.

7. See Fredric Jameson, *Postmodernism: Or, the Cultural Logic of Late Capitalism* (Durham: Duke University Press, 1991). Also see his brilliant study of Adorno, *Late Marxism: Adorno, or, the Persistence of the Dialectic* (New York: Verso, 1990).

ACKNOWLEDGMENTS

While the author alone bears full responsibility for the content of this book, many have generously contributed to its development. My thanks first go to those individuals who agreed to formal interviews: Victor G. Reuther, Dallas C. Dort, Max Grider, Dave Yettaw, Ken Scott, Russ Cook, Bob Roman, Dennis Carl, James "Cap" Wheeler, Richard Gull, Carl McIntire, John Grimes, Pat Tarver, Mark S. Davis, William J. Donohue, Woodrow Stanley, and Charles R. Weeks. I also gratefully acknowledge those who provided numerous important documents and materials: Dave Yettaw, Richard Gull, George F. Lord, Carl McIntire, Pat Tarver, Mark S. Davis, Nancy Walsh, Irving Kenneth Zola, Phebe Falcone, and friends at Framingham State College.

For de facto support during the fieldwork portion of this project, I wish to acknowledge the Department of Sociology, Anthropology, and Social Work at the University of Michigan–Flint, the Humanities and Social Science Department at Flint's GMI Management and Engineering Institute, and the sociology program at Flint's Charles Stewart Mott Community College. I am especially grateful to Wilfred G. Marston for his influence in securing my transition from Boston to Flint with a visiting full-time faculty position at the University of Michigan–Flint, and to George F. Lord for his willingness to openly share his considerable knowledge of the Flint area social structure.

Initial travel from Boston to the Walter P. Reuther Library of Labor and Urban Affairs at Wayne State University was made possible by a Henry J. Kaiser Family Foundation travel grant. My thanks go to the helpful staff at both the Reuther Library and at the University of Michigan–Flint archives.

As this book is a revised version of my 1992 Brandeis University dissertation in sociology, I am pleased to acknowledge the beneficent influence of my dissertation committee: Maurice R. Stein (chair), Gila J. Hayim, and George W. Ross. Thanks also to Paul Breines of Boston College for serving as an outside examiner, and to the members of my dissertation support group for helping to get the ball rolling. The Brandeis University Department of Sociology is perhaps America's premiere venue for critical sociology. I wish to extend my sincere appreciation to the Department faculty, staff, and students for their challenging intellectual stimulation, support, and for their genuine long-term friendship. Especially dear are my graduate school mates with whom I have been fortunate enough to stay in contact: Betsy, Greg, Ingrid, Johnny, Lawrence, P.J., Rachel, and Will.

I wish to also extend my very special thanks to Ben Agger of the University of Texas–Arlington. No one has provided more support, inspiration, and wise counsel. Popular Culture and Political Change series coeditors Ronald Edsforth and Larry Bennett made countless skillful contributions to the manuscript. Their combined contribution is essential to the quality of the finished book. I thank Ron and Larry most of all, however, for their genuine interest, concern, and patience.

Arthur J. Vidich, Willem Brooke-debock, B. Gregory Wilpert, David L. Harvey, George F. Lord, Dave Yettaw, Michael Moore, and the participants in the 1994 Institute for the Analysis of Contemporary Society meeting and seminar at Marlboro College read all or parts of the manuscript and made many useful suggestions. I especially thank Professor Vidich for his several sets of trenchant criticism and for his advocacy for the resulting manuscript.

For financial support of the revision process, I thank Fred P. Pestello, Chair of the Department of Sociology, Anthropology, and Social Work, former Chair, Patrick G. Donnelly, Paul J. Morman, Dean of the College of Arts and Sciences, and the Research Council, all of the University of Dayton. The staff at State University of New York Press have also been generous and professional. My thanks in particular go to SUNY Press editor Clay Morgan, production editor Kay Bolton, and cover designer Les Bolton. Maude Falcone prepared the index.

I conclude with several especially personal acknowledgments. The original idea for this book was spurred early in my graduate education by Professor Richard Child Hill's formidable instruction in urban theory and documentary/archival research methods at the Michigan State University Department of Sociology. An important additional influence from my years at Michigan State University is my undergraduate mentor, Professor Emeritus Robert A. Solo of the Department of Economics. I wish also to acknowledge a host of good friends (Mike, Alex, Joe, Steve, Scott) and former graduate student colleagues, including Tim Bushnell, who is for me an exemplar of careful and engaged scholarship. While those mentioned bear no direct responsibility for this book whatsoever, I thank them for their endeavors to educate me and for their valued friendship.

I wish also to note the unconditional support received from my family. The years spent in Flint conducting research for this study were made much richer by the chance thereby afforded to maintain, and in some ways renew and extend, intimate family ties. In particular, my love goes to Helen and John Dandaneau, who I adopted as parents when I was still pretty young, and whom I thank for literally everything. Also, and in no particular order, my thanks to my immediate family members: Bart, Carlien, Christopher, Darren, Elaine, Ina, Joe, John, Kristen, Lisa, Marcus, Mary, Nan, Phebe, Renee, Teresa, and Victoria.

Finally, I come to Maude C. Falcone and Richard G. Yuille, to whom this book is dedicated. Maude and Rick shared living space with me through most of the years on which I worked on this book. More than simply domestic companions, however, Maude and Rick gave generously of their time and attention in a sustained effort to assist me in every way imaginable. Their insights, encouragement, and good judgement served as a perpetual check against my own many bouts of fuzzy thinking, occasional despair, and self-doubt. Their many countless concrete contributions, which extended from photographic assistance to shared fieldwork adventures, were of great and enduring influence. Indeed, were it not for their criticisms, editing, and unfaltering patience, this book would simply not exist. Thus, to my spouse and to my best friend, I owe my most profound debts and my greatest appreciation; to Maude and Rick go my heartfelt love and affection; to them, I gratefully dedicate this book.

For kindly granting permission to reprint text and photographs from their publications, thanks to the following publishers and copyright holders:

From the article "And Then There's the Disneyland Solution," by Daniel Zwerdling, in *The Progressive* (July, 1982): pp. 34–35. Copyright © 1982 The Progressive, Inc. Used by permission of The Progressive, Inc.

From the article, "Cynicism—The Twilight of False Consciousness," by Peter Sloterdijk, in *New German Critique* Volume 33 (Fall, 1984): pp. 190–206. Copyright © 1984 Telos Press Ltd. Used by permission of Telos Press Ltd.

From the article, "The Future of Work," by Frithjof Bergmann, in *Praxis International* Volume 3 (October, 1983): pp. 308–323. Copyright © 1983 Blackwell Publishers. Used by permission of Blackwell Publishers.

From the article, "Growth Ideology in a Period of Decline: Deindustrialization and Restructuring, Flint Style," by George F. Lord and Albert C. Price, in *Social Problems* Volume 39, No. 2 (May, 1992): pp. 155–69. Copyright © 1992 by the Society for the Study of Social Problems. Used by permission of University of California Press Journals and the authors.

From the transcript of the DONAHUE® Show #012990 & #013090 entitled "On Location in Flint, Michican." Copyright © 1990 Multimedia Entertainment, Inc. DONAHUE® transcripts courtesy of Multimedia Entertainment, Inc.

From the UAW-GM Local Paid Educational Leave Program's Administrator's Guide and Instructor's Manual. Used by written permission of the UAW-GM Human Resource Center.

From the *Flint Journal Picture History of Flint,* edited by Lawrence R. Gustin. Copyright © 1976 The Flint Journal. Photographs of the Flint Sitdown Strike courtesy of The Flint Journal.

IDEOLOGY AND DEPENDENT DEINDUSTRIALIZATION

The fate of Flint is intertwined with the common fate of all of them. No one can expect a miracle in an isolated city. But you have to study in depth what's going on in *a* city to understand the challenge confronting all of industrial society in the U.S.

—Victor G. Reuther,
UAW-New Directions Movement[1]

Flint is ahead of the rest of the country. The problems that the rest of the country soon will experience exist there now. It is an ideal place to work on new solutions.

—Dr. Frithjof Bergmann,
Center for New Work[2]

Flint would be to life what a cowboy movie is to life or [what] a football game is to life: it is uniquely and usefully simplified. So, we're anything but a microcosm. We are the essence of the issues with all the extraneous stuff stripped away.

—Dallas C. Dort,
GEAR, Inc.[3]

... the dialectic advances by way of extremes, driving thoughts with the utmost consequentiality to the point where they turn back on themselves.

—Theodor W. Adorno,
Minima Moralia[4]

DEPENDENT DEINDUSTRIALIZATION

Barry Bluestone and Bennett Harrison's (1982) *The Deindustrialization of America: Plant Closings, Community Abandonment, and the Dismantling of*

Basic Industry introduced the term *deindustrialization* to a wide American audience.[5] They defined deindustrialization as "the widespread, systemic disinvestment in the nation's basic productive capacity," which, they argued, "can be traced to the way capital—in the forms of financial resources and of real plant and equipment—has been diverted from productive investment in our basic national industries into unproductive speculations, mergers and acquisitions, and foreign investment."[6] Bluestone and Harrison's stated concern for "shuttered factories, displaced workers, and a newly emerging group of ghost towns" struck a responsive chord in a society struggling through a deep recession. Theirs and subsequent studies largely explained the emergence of America's infamous rust belt, defined a series of deindustrialization-related social problem areas, and bolstered critics and activists in their search for political responses to this structural problem in the American economy.[7] Yet, Bluestone and Harrison's pathbreaking, kind-hearted, activist- and policy-oriented approach already appears irretrievably dated. Their call for a "program of democratic socialist reindustrialization," for example, has attracted few supporters in America's rust-belt cities, which, in the 1990s, confront a fundamentally worsened situation than was the case only a little more than a decade ago.[8]

David C. Perry's 1987 "The Politics of Dependency in Deindustrializing America" is less well known than Bluestone and Harrison's work. Perry's essay has had little influence on scholarship and activism. This is unfortunate because it identified the significance of qualitatively lessened local autonomy on the possibility of local economic revival.[9] Writing several years after Bluestone and Harrison, Perry argued that the then dominant conception of "economic restructuring" was far too optimistic a rendering for the "aggregation of powerlessness" that communities experienced when dependent upon "outside market and state forces for [their] economic and social renewal."[10] In other words, the intensified globalization of corporate capital in the 1980s had so increased the levels of external control over local economies that, henceforth, merely local action in defense of a local economy was futile.[11] Thus, there arises *dependent deindustrialization*, a term derived from Latin America-focused dependency theory, but, ironically, now used to identify an emergent periphery *within* the core of global capitalism.[12] In effect, then, Perry argued that America's rust belt was so economically and politically disempowered that it had acquired the chief characteristic of a third world region: dependency on external powers. Perry's correction of Bluestone and Harrison is thus intrinsically unpopular and uninspiring, but, sadly, nonetheless accurate.

The city of Flint, Michigan, illustrates the dimensions of dependent deindustrialization.[13] Thanks primarily to the film *Roger & Me*, Flint has become a notorious example of the phenomenon. Hometown of both the General Motors Corporation, America's largest industrial firm, and the United Auto Workers, America's largest industrial union, Flint was once the mighty "Vehicle City." In his (1987) *Class Conflict and Cultural Consensus: The Making of a Mass*

Consumer Society in Flint, Michigan, historian Ronald Edsforth identified the automobile as the "primary driving force" behind the extraordinary character of twentieth-century America, and placed Flint at the center of the automobile-led second industrial revolution.[14] As Edsforth documents, Flint's (and America's) notable Depression-era class conflict was later muted by the postwar expansion of mass consumer culture. Growing mass production and a broadly distributed surplus produced a stable mass consumer society. In the middle portion of this century, Flint was second only to Detroit as the world's leading automaker and, indeed, was nationally noted for its stability and harmony.[15] What was good for General Motors seemed to be absolutely great for Flint.

Such unprecedented abundance, however, endured for just one generation. By the early 1980s Flint residents seriously wondered whether GM would dare abandon its hometown, and, in particular, its close relationship to the de facto governing local business class. But would Depression-era class consciousness and class conflict reemerge in response to Flint's economic catastrophe?

Edsforth's *Class Conflict and Cultural Consensus* concludes with this telling question, as signs of Flint's permanent decline were already obvious. Most important was the precipitous drop in the Flint area's GM employment—from over 80,000 in 1978 to under 50,000 by 1992—with more plant closings planned for the mid-1990s.[16] Along with the indirect although entirely predictable ripple effects accompanying this devastating job loss, Flint quickly fell from its olympian industrial heights squarely into America's rust belt.[17] The city's singular dependency on GM's $2 billion-plus local annual payroll clearly exaggerated its inability to control its fate. Indeed, Flint is therefore an *extreme* case of dependent deindustrialization.[18] Flint's extreme quality facilitates indepth study of local responses to dependent deindustrialization because the essential factors contributing to decreasing local autonomy are easily identified. Flint's extreme dependency forms the background to this study's inquiry into the changing nature of *ideology in a context of relative local powerlessness.*[19]

IDEOLOGY

Flint residents have not accepted their economic decline passively. Flint is also a place where unique and surprising responses to dependent deindustrialization have already taken shape. *Roger & Me,* for example, is not only *about* Flint's economic ruination, the film *itself* is an extraordinary *response* to this ruination. Flint has responded to dependent deindustrialization in a number of significant ways, and in so doing has implied identifiable competing worldviews.[20] These conceptual frameworks are not, however, politically or culturally neutral, they are instead enmeshed in unequal power relationships and competing interests. In other words, they are encoded with ideological significance.

Ideology is a notoriously ambiguous, and, today, largely old-fashioned concept.[21] A commonsense definition of ideology might be a set of ideas that justifies some situation or relationship, usually economic and political in nature. Although it was not originally so, the term has acquired a pejorative connotation: ideological justifications are seen as typically masking societal contradictions, protecting vested interests, or falsely rendering social and cultural phenomena natural and hence apparently unalterable. In this view, ideologies justify social domination. Yet, ideology may also be defined more poetically, and perhaps more meaningfully, as "systematic error which clings to its own conditions for existence...."[22] This is Peter Sloterdijk's definition in his 1983 *Critique of Cynical Reason*, an exemplary study of contemporary ideological trends. Sloterdijk is concerned with economic decline and the resurgent popularity of politically reactionary thinking.[23] He also provides an exceptional analysis of contemporary cynical reason, a project essential to the revitalization of critical or emancipatory theories of society.[24] This study uses many of Sloterdijk's theoretical insights into the character of contemporary ideology to categorize and describe ideological responses to dependent deindustrialization in Flint.

Specifically, each ideological type is read for its: (a) temporal orientation or relation to history; (b) conception of self or identity; and (c) conception of dependency relationships in capitalist society, or general representations of social structure. In effect, the structure of C. Wright Mills' sociological imagination—with its attention to the conceptual interrelationships between history, biography, and social structure—is imputed to each response.[25] However, instead of holding these dimensions in tension, as we shall see, each programmatic ideology ultimately founders upon the necessarily suppressed realization of its local powerlessness within the global capitalist system. This suppression has produced three falsely collapsed and thus ideologically distorted responses to Flint's dependent deindustrialization.

Analyses of the UAW-New Directions Movement and the film *Roger & Me* (chapters 2 and 5) reveals the first ideological type, termed "enlightenment ideology" (or dissent or critical ideology). Following the Mills-based (history, biography, social structure) method, this orientation is founded on: (a) a mythic perception of American history as a progressive unfolding of democratic-egalitarian ideals, within which the labor movement plays a central role legitimizing the pursuit of unfinished social change; (b) the remembrance and identification with past models of self, where identity is premised upon loyalty to a bequeathed, yet unrealized, heritage, thus producing a consciousness bent on self-sacrifice in a project of redemption; and (c) the rejection of systematic relations of dependency in favor of past models of political-economic organization. Borrowing from Sloterdijk, this is termed "enlightenment ideology" because it is premised on an idealized conceptualization of free dialogue and the free consent produced therein—a central theme, for example, in Jürgen

Habermas' reconceptualization of the unfinished project of Enlightenment.[26] However, Sloterdijk emphasizes, more than Habermas, that, as enlightenment consciousness is rebuffed historically by the determined silence of its would-be conversational partners (who are more inclined to employ power to achieve desired instrumental goals), enlightenment-based responses turn toward what Sloterdijk calls a "miscarried conversation through other means."[27] The UAW-New Directions Movement and the film *Roger & Me* represent exactly this: miscarried conversations concerning dependent deindustrialization.

The Center for New Work and Great Lakes Technology Centre (chapters 3 and 6), are encoded with the second ideological type: a postindustrial ideology or, similarly, an antihistorical or a technoliberal ideology.[28] This orientation is founded on: (a) a utopianism that reestablishes what Ben Agger has dubbed as the apparently liberatory "mythos of scientism and technology" by censoring the experience of its historically realized opposite catastrophe; (b) a rationalist/idealist self-conception suggesting an identification with classical liberal, individualist values; and (c) a conception of an irrepressible postindustrial social revolution that promises the actualization of liberal values through emergent sociotechnological capabilities.[29] This ideology is antihistorical because it rejects the actual historical experience of technological disaster, positing instead a break with this past in order to throw itself into the future. Both the articulation of New Work ideology and its related (though independently conceived) dispersal into the edifice of the Great Lakes Technology Centre represent the one-sided negation of modernist historical consciousness in favor of an outwardly optimistic and liberal portrayal of the limitless possibilities that new postindustrial technologies suggest.

Analyses of the GM/UAW Local Paid Educational Leave Program and Genesee Economic Area Revitalization, Inc. (chapters 4 and 7), uncover the third ideological type, enlightened false consciousness (also termed "cynical" or "organizational" ideology). This orientation is founded on: (a) a self-described mature knowledge that both historical precedent and transcendent future possibilities are irrelevant to immediate efforts dedicated to maintenance of the status quo; (b) an identity that is self-consciously self-interested and survival oriented, even when recognizing the long-term improbability of survival through the pursuit of immediate interests; and (c) a defensive (though acquiescent) posture toward relationships of dependency, specifically manifested in strategic attempts to adapt to social change, regardless of long-term cost, in order to achieve immediate gains in security and power. Again, following Sloterdijk, this response is termed "enlightened false consciousness" because it is a cynical ideology whose "falseness is already reflexively buffered."[30] The acknowledged (thus "reflexively buffered") falsehood of this cynical ideology thwarts traditional methods of immanent ideology critique, which depend upon a notion of possible enlightenment, or increased self-knowledge, through a dialogue based on shared epistemic standards between critic and ideologue.

Sloterdijk's assessment that cynicism represents the "twilight of false consciousness" is empirically assessed here via research into a joint educational program for union members and company managers, and the development of a strategic plan for Flint's economic and social redevelopment.[31] More than the responses organized under the rubrics of enlightenment and postindustrial ideology, this last ideological type carries the weight of institutional power (in terms of economic resources and political influence and authority), and thus represents the dominant local response to dependent deindustrialization. Yet, it is shown equally ineffectual despite its local dominance.

A LOOK BACK, A LOOK AHEAD

Dependent deindustrialization in Flint is largely the product of a fundamental break in the relationship between GM qua transnational corporation and Flint's local business class. Flint is, in this sense, a town abandoned. Edsforth predicted that "such a rupture . . . would surely represent a dramatic new development in American political culture," while Jesse Jackson, for his part, began a campaign in support of Michigan's troubled industrial cities and increasingly impoverished citizenry by stating: "Michigan is the industrial center for the heartland. If Michigan collapses, it's a bombshell for the whole country."[32] While there has been drama and fireworks in Flint's transition from a vibrant industrial center to a largely boarded-up, rust-belt city, analysis of Flint's top-down revitalization efforts—the Center for New Work, Great Lakes Technology Centre, and Genesee Economic Area Revitalization, Inc.—suggests instead the overwhelming dominance of a more sobering reality. Not intellectuals, not postindustrial technologies, not even an increasingly freewheeling local business class, appear capable of reversing the tide against Flint. They lack the power to effect meaningful local change in the ever more globalized capitalist system.

But in Flint as elsewhere, trouble at the helm has not translated into renewed class consciousness below deck, at least not in the vein of traditional Marxian imagery. Whereas Edsforth pointed to the dubious nature of the Quality of Worklife Movement, Flint's Committee for Full UAW Employment, and even the politically conservative effect of "the mass media and especially of Hollywood films," studies of the GM/UAW Local PEL program, the New Directions Movement, and *Roger & Me* suggest new and even novel local responses to Flint's continued decline. However, rather than suggesting the welcome emergence of what Edsforth describes as "an independent, nonhierarchical, politically progressive labor movement in the United States . . . ," these cases instead confirm the suffocation of class consciousness.[33] Indeed, this study of ideology and dependent deindustrialization as a whole is about what is being produced in Flint *instead* of traditional class conflict. This book addresses the ideological formations in America's late capitalist society.

NOTES

1. Interview 1, June 14, 1991.

2. "Brave New Work." *Detroit Free Press*, 18 June 1987, Sec. A. p. 1.

3. Interview 2, August 7, 1991. "GEAR, Inc." is the acronym for Genesee Economic Area Revitalization, Inc., Flint and Genesee County's main economic development organization.

4. 4. *Minima Moralia: Reflections from a Damaged Life* (New York: Verso, 1987 [1951]), p. 86.

5. Barry Bluestone and Bennett Harrison, *The Deindustrialization of America: Plant Closings, Community Abandonment, and the Dismantling of Basic Industry* (New York: Basic Books, 1982). The term *deindustrialization* was first used in Britain, and there in a more technical and less political sense as is the case in Bluestone and Harrison. On the British literature, see Ron Martin and Bob Rowthorn, eds., *The Geography of De-Industrialization* (London: Macmillan, 1986) and F. Blackaby, ed., *Deindustrialization* (London: Heinemann Press, 1979).

6. Bluestone and Harrison, p. 6

7. The literature on deindustrialization, plant shutdowns, and community and worker responses is vast. Especially useful sources include: Jack Metzgar, "Plant Shutdowns and Worker Response: The Case of Johnstown, Pa.," in *Socialist Review* 53, no. 10 (September–October, 1980), pp. 9–49; Dan Luria and Jack Russell, *Rational Reindustrialization* (Detroit: Widgetripper Press, 1981); John C. Raines, Lenora E. Berson, and David McI. Gracie, *Community and Capital in Conflict: Plant Closings and Job Loss* (Philadelphia: Temple University Press, 1982); The Business Week Team, *The Reindustrialization of America* (New York: McGraw-Hill, 1982); Staughton Lynd, *The Fight Against Shutdowns* (San Pedro, CA: Single Jack Books, 1982); Terry Buss and F. Steven Redburn, *Shutdown at Youngstown* (Albany: SUNY Press, 1983); Michael Peter Smith, ed., *Cities in Transformation* (Newbury Park, CA: Sage Publications, 1984); Lawrence W. Rothstein, *Plant Closings: Power, Politics, and Workers* (Dover, MA: Auburn House, 1986); Richard Child Hill and Cynthia Negrey, "Deindustrialization in the Great Lakes," in *Urban Affairs Quarterly* 22 (1987), pp. 580–597; Richard Child Hill and Michael Indergaard, "Downriver: The Deindustrialization of Southwest Detroit," in Scott Cummings, ed., *Business Elites and Urban Development* (Albany: SUNY Press, 1988); Barry Bluestone and Bennett Harrison, *The Great U-Turn* (New York: Basic Books, 1988); Carolyn C. Perrucci, Robert Perrucci, Dena B. Targ, and Harry R. Targ, *Plant Closings: International Context and Social Costs* (Hawthorne, NY: Aldine de Gruyter, 1988); Jeanie Wylie, *Poletown: Community Betrayed* (Urbana, IL: University of Illinois Press, 1989); David Harvey, *The Condition of Postmodernity* (Cambridge: Basil Blackwell, 1989); John Portz, *The Politics of Plant Closings* (Lawrence, KA: University Press of Kansas, 1990); and Jon

C. Teaford, *Cities of the Heartland: The Rise and Fall of the Industrial Midwest* (Bloomington, IN: Indiana University Press, 1993).

8. Bluestone and Harrison, p. 262.

9. David C. Perry, "The Politics of Dependency in Deindustrializing America: The Case of Buffalo, New York," in Michael Peter Smith and Joe R. Feagin, eds., *The Capitalist City: Global Restructuring and Community Politics* (New York: Basil Blackwell, 1987), pp. 113–137.

10. Ibid., pp. 113, 115.

11. The notion of external control is discussed in Paul Knox and John Agnew, *The Geography of the World Economy*, 2d ed. (London: Edward Arnold, 1994), pp 243–245. Also see Stephen Gill and David Law, *The Global Political Economy* (Baltimore: Johns Hopkins University Press, 1988); Richard Child Hill, "Urban Political Economy," in Smith, ed., *Cities in Transformation*, pp. 123–138; and Harvey, *The Condition of Postmodernity*. For more optimistic assessments, see Bruce Nissen, "Successful Labor-Community Coalition Building," in Charles Craypo and Bruce Nissen, eds., *Grand Designs: The Impact of Corporate Strategies on Workers, Unions, and Communities* (Ithaca, NY: ILR Press, 1993), pp. 209–223; *Cities of the Heartland*.

12. The classic statement of dependency theory is Andre Gunder Frank, *Capitalism and Underdevelopment in Latin America* (New York: Monthly Review Press, 1967).

13. This study does not repeat the litany of Flint's many ills. Interested readers might profitably consult the film *Roger & Me*; George F. Lord and Albert C. Price, "Growth Ideology in a Period of Decline: Deindustrialization and Restructuring, Flint Style," in *Social Problems* 39, no. 2 (May, 1992), pp. 155–169; "A City Where Hope Runs on Empty." *New York Times*, 26 February 1992, sec. A, p. 8; or my 1992 Brandeis University dissertation, *Ideology and Dependent Deindustrialization*, available from University Microfilms, Ann Arbor, Michigan.

14. Ronald Edsforth, *Class Conflict and Cultural Consensus: The Making of a Mass Consumer Society in Flint, Michigan* (New Brunswick, NJ: Rutgers University Press, 1987), p. 13.

15. *The World Book Encyclopedia* 1970 edition, "Flint," by Willis F. Dunbar and Homer E. Dowdy; also see Edsforth, especially pp. 191–219.

16. *The Genesis Project*, prepared for Genesee Economic Area Revitalization, Inc., by Price Waterhouse, Inc. (unpublished document source in the hands of the author: hereafter such citations will be labeled "document source"), p. 4. Various sources list somewhat different figures. See James D. Ananich, Neil O. Leighton, and Charles T. Weber, *Economic Impact of G.M. Plant Closings in Flint, Michigan* (Flint: Project for Urban and Regional Affairs, The University of Michigan–Flint, 1989), p. 1, which notes that GM employment in Flint peaked in 1955 at 82,000, and compare to Lord and Price, p. 158, which lists Flint's manufacturing job loss "from a high of about 70,000 in 1980 to slightly over 40,000 in 1989." Also, on anticipated plant closings, see "Flint, Willow Run take hit," *The Flint Journal*, 24 February 1994, Sec. A, p. 1–2; "Hurting: The GM fallout; Thousand still reel from impact of closings," *The Flint Journal*, 25 February 1992, Sec. A, p. 1, 10.; "GM slashes—Michigan bleeds," *Lansing State Journal*, Sec. A, p.

1; "Dupont leaving Flint, affecting 250 workers," *The Flint Journal,* 14 January 1992, Sec. A, pp. 1, 2.

17. See "State of Flint," a 1991 memorandum, State of Michigan Department of Social Services, Flint branch; *The Quality of Life for Children and Their Families in Genesee County,* a June 1991 "Priority 90s" report (document source); "Flint leads state in 1990 per-capita crime rate—FBI," *The Flint Journal,* 11 August 1991, Sec. A, p. 1, 10; "Poverty spreads in Michigan," *The Flint Journal,* 27 September 1991, Sec. A, p. 3; and "FBI figures still place Flint among most violent cities," *The Flint Journal,* 26 April 1992, Sec. A, p. 1, 14. For a general discussion of community impact, see Bluestone and Harrison; and D. Stanley Eitzen and Maxine Baca Zinn, eds., *The Reshaping of America: Social Consequences of the Changing Economy* (Englewood Cliffs, NJ: Prentice-Hall, 1989).

18. "The Facts on Flint" (document source); "Brief Overview of Economic and Community Development," prepared by the Department of Community and Economic Development, City of Flint, Michigan, 1990 (document source); Donald Grimes, "Diversification Trends in Genesee County," Project for Urban and Regional Affairs, University of Michigan–Flint; *Economic Indicator Data Book,* Project of Urban and Regional Affairs, Office of Research, 1990; also Lord and Price.

19. See Maurice R. Stein, *Eclipse of Community* (Princeton: Princeton University Press, 1960); Arthur J. Vidich, Joseph Bensman, and Maurice R. Stein, eds, *Reflections on Community Studies* (New York: Harper & Row, 1971); The Institute for Social Research, *Aspects of Sociology* (Boston: Beacon Press, 1972 [1956]), chapter 10, "Community Studies," pp. 148–167; Joe R. Feagin, Anthony M. Orum, and Gideon Sjoberg, eds., *The Case for the Case Study* (Chapel Hill, NC: University of North Carolina Press, 1991); George E. Marcus and Michael M. J. Fischer, *Anthropology as Cultural Critique* (Chicago: University of Chicago Press, 1986).

20. More precisely: significant, organized actors have acted toward Flint's experience with dependent deindustrialization in various publicly discernable and sustained fashions. This study is not primarily concerned with Flint's many diffuse, random, or individual responses to its decline, a point that is discussed and illustrated in the epilogue.

21. See John B. Thompson, *Ideology and Modern Culture* (Stanford: Stanford University Press, 1990); Raymond Geuss, *The Idea of a Critical Theory: Habermas and the Frankfurt School* (Cambridge: Cambridge University Press, 1981)

22. Peter Sloterdijk, *Critique of Cynical Reason* (Minneapolis: University of Minnesota Press, 1987 [1983]), p. 15.

23. Ibid., p. 8, where Sloterdijk states: "A critique of cynical reason would remain an academic glass bead game if it did not pursue the connection between the problem of survival and the danger of fascism." Also see Andreas Huyssen, foreword, "The Return of Diogenes as Postmodern Intellectual," in *Critique of Cynical Reason,* pp. ix-xxv.

24. Sloterdijk, p. 3. On critical theory, see David Held, *Introduction to Critical Theory* (Berkeley: University of California Press, 1980); Martin Jay, *The Dialectical Imagi-*

nation (Boston: Little Brown, 1973); Richard J. Bernstein, ed., *Habermas and Modernity* (Cambridge: MIT Press, 1985); and Ben Agger, ed., *Western Marxism: An Introduction* (Santa Monica, CA: Goodyear, 1979). Two specific works inform the style of critical theory employed in this study: Ben Agger, *Critical Theory of Public Life* (London: Falmer Press, 1991); John Forester, ed., *Critical Theory of Public Life* (Cambridge: MIT Press, 1985). Also see my "An Immanent Critique of Post-Marxism," in Ben Agger, ed., *Current Perspectives in Social Theory* 12 (JAI Press, 1992), pp. 155–177.

25. C. Wright Mills, *The Sociological Imagination* (Oxford: Oxford University Press, 1959). Also, for further analysis of Mills's conception of the sociological imagination, see my "'Minimalist' Sociology versus 'Taking It Big,'" in Ben Agger, ed., *Current Perspectives in Social Theory* 14 (JAI Press, 1994), pp. 213–239.

26. See Sloterdijk, especially chapters 1 and 2. Also see Jürgen Habermas, *The Theory of Communicative Action*, vols. 1 and 2 (Boston: Beacon Press, 1984 [1981], 1987 [1981]; "Modernity Versus Postmodernity," in *New German Critique* 22 (1981), pp. 3–14; *The Philosophical Discourse on Modernity* (Cambridge: MIT Press, 1987 [1985]).

27. *Critique of Cynical Reason*, especially chapter 2, "Enlightenment as Dialogue: Critique of Ideology as Continuation of the Miscarried Dialogue through Other Means," pp. 10–21.

28. The term *technoliberal ideology* is borrowed from Maude C. Falcone, who originally developed this notion in an unpublished 1991 study of Jean-Francois Lyotard's political philosophy.

29. Ben Agger, "The Dialectic of Deindustrialization: An Essay on Advanced Capitalism," in Forester, pp. 3–21; also see Timothy W. Luke and Stephen K. White, "Critical Theory, the Informational Revolution, and an Ecological Path to Modernity," in Forester, pp. 21–53.

30. Sloterdijk, p. 5.

31. See Sloterdijk, especially chapter 1 entitled, "Cynicism: The Twilight of False Consciousness," pp. 3–9. The reader may be interested to know that empirical research for this study was nearly completed when the author was first introduced to Sloterdijk's work. Therefore, in this instance, data collection and analysis, as it were, preceded theory.

32. Edsforth, p. 225. "Jackson, governor will eschew politics, discuss jobs for state," *The Flint Journal*, 15 January 1992, Sec. A, p. 5. Note that Michigan's rate of poverty was 10.4 percent in 1980 and 14.3 percent in 1990. Also see "Poverty spreads in Michigan," *The Flint Journal*, 27 September 1991, Sec. A, p. 3.

33. Edsforth, pp. 225, 228. It should be noted that Edsforth was not himself optimistic about the realization of such a labor movement. Quite the contrary: *Class Conflict and Cultural Consensus* concludes on a clearly pessimistic note.

PART I ∾ *Class*

In what historians generally regard as the single most important labor battle in American history—Flint's 1936–37 Great Sit-Down Strike—money was not, as might have been expected, the main issue pitting the nascent United Auto Workers in its struggle against the General Motors Corporation. Rather, it was the speed-up: the ever more exhausting pace of work that made weariness and violent retching a commonplace experience after a stint in the factory. It is no exaggeration to say that this is what industrial work once meant in Flint. As Henry Kraus, a strike leader and, later, an astute analyst of Flint's Great Sit-Down Strike, has suggested: the "oppression of incredible working conditions, the effects of the implacable speedup . . ." and the "deaths in the state's auto centers" were crucial, bodily factors driving rebellion from below.[1]

Hegel might well have felt at home in Depression-era Flint. The bondage that was industrial labor was experienced both as self-destructive and, as it were, motivating: the physical pain of alienated labor served as a necessary pre-condition for the struggle for recognition that ensued. In December 1936, members of Flint's industrial work force went on strike against General Motors by occupying key Flint factories. They broke their work-induced silence in the face of a sometimes violent reaction by placing themselves before clubs, tear gas, and bullets: the risk of life-and-death struggle was worth it, and class consciousness meant realizing that.

Marx, too, would have been intrigued: the rhetoric of union organizers in 1936 and 1937 owed much to his work. Wyndham Mortimer, then UAW First Vice President and chief union organizer in Flint, stated in one of his open letters to Flint's auto workers:

ALL THE EXPLOITERS OF LABOR HANG TOGETHER. THEY ARE
CLASS CONSCIOUS. They are aware of the fact that the interests of
their CLASS is (sic) involved, and all this patriotic blah blah is for the
consum[p]tion (sic) of fools, and they are hoping we are the fools. We
as workers must too become aware of CLASS INTEREST. It is only in
this way we may get the true picture and understand all the move being
made on our political and economic checker board. Under our present
economic system, we as workers can only improve our condition by
improving the condition of the entire working class.[2]

The Strike's local meaning was unquestionably articulated within a vision
of a larger class struggle. Indeed, when several thousand workers finally came
to occupy strategic points of production—that is, when they literally sat down
in the "tremendous industrial establishments that mark the points of the com-
pass from the center of the city"[3]—they sought to integrate their workplace lives
with their lives *as such*, asserting their status as human beings of intrinsic worth
living as members of a community. It is not romanticizing to say that Flint's
Great Sit-Down Strike was a struggle precipitated by an alienated *existence*, not
simply in Hegel's realm of *Spirit*, but in Marx's more sobering realm of materiality. This, in fact, is how social class was experienced in Flint: it was *lived*.
        And though this specific struggle was centered in a handful of apparently
ordinary workplaces—within the boundaries of a nondescript, midsize, mid-
dle-west industrial city—Flint's GM factories were actually the core capital
assets in an expansive, interdependent network of automobile-centered mass
production and consumption. The illegal seizure of *this* property could not
have cut any faster to the quick of American capitalist society: from Flint to
Detroit to Wall Street in a heartbeat. It sliced through the community, and, to
a degree, divided the nation, as though questioning the legitimacy of the entire
industrial-capitalist system in the midst of America's Great Depression. This
strike certainly had enormous repercussions. As Leighton, Meyer, and Pendrell
remind us:

> Within a year of the sit-down strike, wages in the auto industry
> increased by $300 million; the UAW had grown from 30,000 to
> 500,000 members; and the union had written agreements with 4,000
> automobile and auto-parts concerns. Throughout the nation sit-
> down strikes became the way to organize: teachers, WPA workers,
> artists, busboys, bellboys, municipal employees, clerks, and stenogra-
> phers joined with cooks, steel workers, longshoremen, garment
> workers, fur workers, lumberjacks, and share-croppers in such
> strikes.
>   Black workers began to be organized, and working women were
> admitted into industrial unions other than textile and needle trades,

where they were already accepted. Today virtually all labor historians recognize the centrality of the Flint sit-down strike to subsequent labor and corporate developments.[4]

In short, the Flint sit-down strike served as an empowering catalyst, a spark that ignited a firestorm of industrial militancy across the United States.

But, for several notable reasons, the historical significance of this strike is, and has been, easily forgotten. In itself this strike achieved nothing more than the mere "recognition" of the UAW as the sole bargaining agent for the striking workers. For risking everything, the strikers realized in practice only their abstract, legal right to form a union that would represent them in collective bargaining. As one striker explained to his comrades when initially confronted with the official strike settlement:

> What's the use of kidding ourselves? All that piece of paper means is that we got a union. The rest depends on us. For God's sake, let's go back to work and keep up what we started here![5]

Of course, even though this struggle established a powerful industrial union in a previously open shop industry, it did not, however, expand to a more ferocious plane such as could precipitate a social or class revolution to alter the basic property relations of American capitalist society.

The second reason the Strike's meaning has been largely forgotten by contemporaries follows from this first reason: the UAW and its kindred industrial unions have themselves developed into great bureaucracies enmeshed in what William Serrin famously describes as "civilized relations" with corporate America.[6] For various reasons (which shall be discussed below), the moment of potential radical struggle was compromised. Today, Flint's Great Sit-Down Strike is part of the union bureaucracy's official origins myth, not a living part of a people's history.

Third, the state's monopoly on the legitimate means of organized violence was not wholly and ruthlessly employed in this struggle to defend the status quo—although, legally, it might well have been. In 1937, New Deal Democratic Governor Frank Murphy placed Michigan National Guard Troops *between* local police and the sit-down strikers. If the Strike did not incite revolution per se, neither did it illicit a violently unforgiving and morally unforgettable repression of dissent. Charles Stewart Mott—an early founder and long-time GM board member, as well as three-time Flint mayor—later complained to Studs Terkel:

> [Frank Murphy] was the Governor during the sit-down strikes, and he didn't do his job. He didn't enforce the law. He kept his hands off.

He didn't protect our property. They should have said [to the strik-
ers], "Stop that thing. Move on, or we'll shoot." And if they didn't,
they should have been shot.[7]

Some *were* shot, not by National Guardsmen, but by Flint police. Still, unlike
the Tiannamen Squares of the world, no one was killed. The repression that
Mott desired and expected was circumvented by the politics of the New Deal
compromise, including President Franklin Delano Roosevelt's discreet personal interventions.[8] In Flint in 1937 a new, more stable political-economic
order, in which the welfare state and industrial unions worked in concert with
corporate America, came of age. This apparently was lost on Mr. Mott, who, in
his 1970 interview with Terkel, still remembered F.D.R. as "the great destroyer."[9]

Finally, it may be that the larger implications of this specific moment in
American history are today mostly forgotten—except as union lore—simply
because ordinary people generally do not feel the *need* to remember. Although
the United States has experienced many economic downturns since the 1930s,
it has since never suffered a comparably widespread, sustained, nor such a
socially volatile economic depression as the still aptly named *Great* Depression.
Of course, it is also true that there are minority groups, cities, regions, and
whole industries and occupational categories that have witnessed Depression-
like conditions and decline, even as the nation as a whole has progressed. Deindustrialization has certainly created great depressions in specific localities.
Indeed, nowhere has this been more true than in Flint, birthplace of GM and
the UAW, and still the location of the single largest concentration of GM
employees in the world.

Flint has recently witnessed a new national movement within the UAW
developing important local roots. Significantly, *this* organized, self-conscious
response to dependent deindustrialization remembers the initial meaning of
Flint's Great Sit-Down Strike. Its name is the UAW-New Directions Movement.

NOTES

1. Henry Kraus, *The Many and the Few: A Chronicle of the Dynamic Auto Workers*,
2d ed., with an introduction by Neil O. Leighton, William J. Meyer, and Nan Pendrell
(Urbana, IL: University of Illinois Press, 1985 [1947]), p. 23. Also see Sidney Fine, *Sit-
Down: The General Motors Strike of 1936–1937* (Ann Arbor, MI: The University of
Michigan Press, 1969); Victor Reuther, *The Brothers Reuther and the Story of the UAW*
(Boston: Houghton Mifflin, 1976); Frank Marquart, *An Auto Worker's Journal: The
UAW from Crusade to One-Party Union* (University Park, PA: Pennsylvania State Uni-
versity Press, 1975); and Ronald Edsforth, *Class Conflict and Cultural Consensus: The
Making of a Mass Consumer Society in Flint, Michigan* (New Brunswick, NJ: Rutgers
University Press, 1987).

2. Letter from Wyndham Mortimer, October 6, 1936, in the Henry Kraus Collection, Archives of Labor History and Urban Affairs, Walter P. Reuther Library, Wayne State University, Detroit, Michigan.

3. Charles Stewart Mott, introduction in Clarence H. Young and William A. Quinn, *Foundation For Living* (New York: McGraw-Hill, 1963), pp. v–ix, v.

4. Neil O. Leighton, William J. Meyer, and Nan Pendrell, introduction to the 2d ed., Kraus, pp. xiv–xv. Also see "Sit-down an effective tool world over," *The Flint Journal*, 9 February 1992, sec. A, pp. 1, 10.

5. Kraus, p. 287.

6. William Serrin, *The Company and the Union: The "Civilized Relations" of the General Motors Corporation and the United Auto Workers* (New York: Vintage Press, 1974).

7. Studs Terkel, *Hard Times: An Oral History of the Great Depression* (New York: Pantheon, 1970), p. 135.

8. An indication of President Roosevelt's popularity in Flint is given in *The Flint Journal Centennial Picture History of Flint*, edited by Lawrence R. Gustin, 1976, where F.D.R.'s October 15, 1936 visit to Flint is recorded in photographs. According to this source, Roosevelt "was greeted by an estimated 150,000 people—the largest crowd in local history. . . . People were packed 4,500 to a block between Court Street and Atwood Stadium, where 20,000 more were packed in to await FDR's speech." For a scholarly treatment of F.D.R.'s role in the strike, see Fine, p. 233, where Fine notes that F.D.R. "played a larger role behind the scenes than was evident at the time."

9. Terkel, p. 135.

Chapter 1

NEW DIRECTIONS

I love to speak about the *unfinished* American Revolution.

—Victor G. Reuther,
UAW-NDM Retiree Representative[1]

Quite frankly, I share a lot of the convictions of the early Flint sit-downers and the Reuther Brothers, who were quite often called "socialists" at that time.

—Jerry Tucker,
UAW-NDM National Organizing Coordinator[2]

The capitalists control this country, control the media, and, I think, control a lot of the masses who aren't willing to think for themselves, who are afraid to look at alternatives, who are distrustful of anybody who doesn't like the word *capitalist*. I'm sure as hell not communist: far, far, from it. But I cringe at the word *capitalism*. I see its failures, and I would like a more just society than what capitalism provides.

—Max Grider,
UAW-NDM National Trustee[3]

You have to be a leader to belong to New Directions. I don't care if you're the guy on the factory floor who runs a machine, if you're on the assembly line, or if you're pushing a broom, to be New Directions is to more or less wear a badge of courage.

—Dave Yettaw,
UAW-NDM National Co-Chair[4]

The New Directions Movement (NDM) addresses America's dependent deindustrialization through its attempt to mobilize a confrontational ideology among UAW rank and file and, by extension, the whole of the country's working people. As birthplace of a once-radical working-class movement and today home to a successful local NDM organization, Flint serves this movement as a key political and symbolic center. Founded in 1989, the NDM speaks to the late-century crisis in America's industrial heartland using the imagery and sentiment of its early-century labor movement predecessors. Indeed, in its most radical moments, the NDM seeks mass mobilization in the pursuit of historically compromised working-class goals. Through their support for this movement, thousands of UAW members are tacitly redefining their present condition as material for yet another chapter in America's "labor wars." In effect, then, the NDM is decentering the status quo by articulating a form of internal union dissent that stands in sharp and critical contrast to the mainstream consciousness of contemporary American organized labor.

I. THE NEW DIRECTIONS MOVEMENT IN FLINT

Walter Reuther died in 1970 in a suspicious plane crash.[5] He had been President of the UAW since 1947, and, by the time of his death, he was perhaps the nation's most prominent, respected, and powerful labor leader. His passing stunned the UAW, leaving it without a leader of equal experience or national stature.

The time of transition in top UAW leadership coincided with the beginning signs of long-term decline in the U.S. auto industry, which is symbolized by the fate of the once-dominant GM. Between 1971 and 1991, GM lost roughly 30 percent of its U.S. market share, cut its U.S. work force in half, and posted record financial losses.[6] The story of the American automobile industry in this period is replete with corporate bailouts and bankruptcy, alienated work and frustrated workers, engineering tragedies and poor product quality, demands for trade barriers, Japan bashing, and, importantly, the UAW's staggering loss of over 700,000 members.[7]

It was from this long decline that a historically unique type of intra-UAW dissent emerged. While factionalism or political infighting is as old as the UAW itself, the New Directions Movement was new because it was articulated by retiring members of the de facto founding UAW leadership, and, moreover, because the object of their criticism was not a particular political faction within the UAW (as had typically been the case), but instead was the UAW itself, in toto, as a viable industrial union. At this turning point in the union's history, representatives of the UAW's old guard began to publicly question the ultimate result of their years of union building, openly and critically comparing the UAW of the 1970s to their original vision.

The NDM had several intellectual precursors. In his 1975 book *An Auto Worker's Journal: The UAW from Crusade to One-Party Union*, Frank Marquart tells the story of how a once-radical working-class social movement developed into an undemocratic bureaucracy solely committed to the perpetuation of its hierarchy.[8] At the time of the union's founding (as when writing his memoir),

Marquart was a committed and independently minded socialist, with his "bottom up . . . outlook . . . shaped by close contact with the rank and file and not in the union bureaucracy far removed from the rank and file."[9] In 1936 and 1937, for example, he and his auto worker comrades were in Flint:

> helping out in the kitchen, passing out leaflets, marching before the plants to show solidarity with the sit-downers, ready at the drop of a hat to battle police or even National Guardsmen if the sit-downers were attacked.[10]

Marquart's 1975 criticism of the UAW as a "one-party union" anticipated many of the ideas that would, by the 1990s, return to Flint in the perspective and platform of the NDM.

Marquart was especially concerned with working conditions. With the infamous early 1970s strikes at GM's Lordstown and Norwood, Ohio factories as points of immediate reference, Marquart wrote in strong opposition to the initial top-down, joint company/union efforts aimed at "humanizing working conditions," efforts that would later blossom into the full-fledged union/company emphasis on pursuing Quality of Work Life reforms. Instead of truly cooperative or "joint" company/union decision making and genuinely "humanized" working conditions, Marquart indicts UAW leadership as complicitous in profit-oriented corporate efforts to achieve a general speedup. Union officials maintained a tacit policy of trading off demands for improved working conditions for marginally higher wages because these union bureaucrats were too distanced from the everyday world of the factory to appreciate the significance of workplace issues.[11] For Marquart, a bureaucratized union had silenced the voices of ordinary workers, whereas the radical labor movement that he idealized considers the emancipation of the worker from alienated work its raison d'etre.

A significant portion of Marquart's own union career, interestingly, transpired away from the shop floor in various worker education roles. As an educator, Marquart valued critical scholarship and free political dialogue. In *An Auto Worker's Journal*, he criticized contemporary UAW worker education programs as exercises in "thought control," contrasting them to the early labor movement's emphasis on radical "political education." In his view, contemporary UAW educational courses routinely sought to "indoctrinate" their participants into believing in the sanctity of the UAW itself, as well as the value and necessity of participation in mainstream politics via the Democratic Party. Marquart described a speech before a UAW education conference by the sociologist Robert S. Lynd, where Lynd stressed the importance of "class struggle" and the need for a "class party or labor party," to the cheers of the UAW's older socialists in attendance. Marquart wryly notes: "needless to say, Professor Lynd was never again invited to address a UAW education conference."[12]

The broad character of Marquart's critique is succinctly summarized in the introduction to *An Auto Worker's Journal*:

> Time was when the American labor movement was respected as a force for social justice. Certainly this view was widely held in early CIO (Congress of Industrial Organization) days.
>
> Today, however, even liberals regard unions as bureaucratized self-interest establishments that no longer identify, as the labor movement once did, with the oppressed and underprivileged sections of the working class.[13]

Marquart blames Walter Reuther, Reuther's younger brothers, Roy and Victor, and their ascendent "right-wing social democratic" (and thus antisocialist and violently anticommunist) allies in the post-1947 union hierarchy for having set in motion these fundamental tendencies.[14] Given Marquart's democratic-socialist political sensibilities, such top-down manipulation represented the negation of the labor movement's original radical social and cultural significance.

The second of the NDM's intellectual precursors followed quickly after *An Auto Worker's Journal*. With the 1976 publication of *The Brothers Reuther and the Story of the UAW*,[15] Victor G. Reuther—the long-time union activist and leader (and, much like Robert to John Kennedy, his brother Walter's trusted political confidant)—initiated criticisms of the UAW from above like Marquart's from below that questioned the union's overall development and future trajectory. Like Marquart's apparently humble journal, Reuther's memoir is organized around systematically applied sociological and political theory. However, whereas Marquart focused on the bureaucratization of the UAW and the betrayal of its origin as a democratic-socialist "crusade," Reuther's story pays closer attention to the shape of antiunion right-wing ideology, especially in its manifestations as political repression. In a word, Reuther's focus is the larger politics of the modern, capitalist-industrial epoch. He is less ideologically partisan than Marquart: fearing fascism more than a strong advocate for socialism, his critical fulcrum is the high ideals of a modern liberal.

Reuther's extraordinary biography made him particularly well suited to play the role of a sage for the New Directions Movement. As he recounts in *The Brothers Reuther*, this Wheeling, West Virginia, youth was taken by his activist father to meet a close labor movement ally who had been jailed: the prisoner was Eugene V. Debs. The young Reuther also experienced Nazi Germany and Stalinist Russia first hand, and was an important leader in Flint's Great Sit-Down Strike. Like his brother Walter, Victor Reuther was the victim of a near-fatal assassination attempt in postwar Detroit. He served for decades in top UAW positions, especially as the UAW's International Representative. This work brought him in close contact with European labor and social-democratic political leaders, as well as world political figures like J.F.K. and Khrushchev. Upon his official retirement from the UAW in 1972, and with the memory of Walter's death still fresh, Reuther eschewed a life of passive contemplation to instead actively analyze and critically assess the UAW and its times. His 1976 book does just that.

Recalling, for example, a moment of reflection that came upon him during his last official speech to UAW National Convention delegates, Reuther writes:

> What a flood of unresolved problems flashed before my mind's eye—unemployment and runaway inflation, the decay of urban centers, the rise of crime and racial tensions, the waste of lives and resources while nations squander their wealth on arsenals of destruction.
>
> Must our aimless drift as a people continue?
>
> The progress of our union developed from clear guidelines held firm by years of struggle in pursuit of social justice. This heritage is a compass that can hold us on a steady course now and in the days ahead.[16]

With these words, Reuther held out hope that his union would renew its struggle for an abstract, as yet unrealized social justice; that the labor movement would not, through inaction, prolong "our aimless drift as a people." By articulating an historical standard to which they were accountable, Reuther's reflections were presumably intended to prod the UAW's younger leadership into renewing what, for this founder, was the union's original commitment to progressive social change.

In the book, Victor Reuther describes Flint's Great Sit-Down Strike:

> [The Flint strikers] endured what seemed an unending nightmare; they suffered terror, broken heads, their families' hunger, and extreme risk, not just for another nickel an hour, but for the dignity and individuality denied them by an arrogant corporation.
>
> They won a richer life for millions of industrial workers in other towns and cities. They exhibited the most selfless quality men can possess: the ability to sacrifice immediate material security for desirable but as yet unrealized goals for humankind.[17]

This notion of "sacrifice [of] material security for desirable but as yet unrealized goals for humankind" represents, as we shall see, a fundamental aspect of NDM ideology.

Reuther also addressed himself to the up-and-coming leaders of a post-Reuther UAW:

Where is the leadership to meet this challenge? My thoughts returned quickly to the sea of delegates I was addressing. In that audience were many young leaders I had come to know and respect.

They are the response to our urgent need.

More than a torch has been passed to this new generation of leaders: what they have is a clearer vision of a better world, more productive tools with which to fashion it, and the will and determination to settle for nothing less.[18]

Already by 1976, in other words, Victor Reuther was sounding a note of "urgency" and appealing to "young leaders" for help in a project dedicated to rekindling the original "heritage" of the labor movement.

Together, Marquart's and Reuther's books form a large part of ideological basis of what would become NDM's official self-consciousness. A decade later, when dissatisfied UAW members and a younger, bolder leadership started looking for an articulated intellectual precedent for their inclination toward radical intraunion dissent, Reuther's and Marquart's mid-1970s ideas were available and easily disseminated.

But while ideas are important, it is essential to stress that the NDM's organizational base coalesced more from below than from above. Widespread and growing dissatisfaction with the deteriorating power of the UAW to deliver the goods, as it were, and to conduct its own internal affairs legally and fairly, contributed more to the genesis of the NDM than did the sheer appeal of visionary ideals or the force of forward-looking argument. Construction of the NDM's organizational base was in fact first initiated by a relatively small group of grassroots union activists and local union leaders in the UAW's "Region 5" headquartered in St. Louis, Missouri. The NDM organization grew directly from this group's support for Jerry Tucker's 1986 candidacy for Region 5 director, and the surprising response that this mobilization elicited from a wary mainstream leadership.

At the time, the UAW was divided into fifteen roughly equal districts or regions. Regional officers exercise authority at a level below the union's top "International" leaders and above the local union leadership who most directly represent the rank and file. While Jerry Tucker is today recognized as *the* leader of the NDM organization, in 1986 he was simply a noted union activist holding a middle-level post as Assistant Director of UAW Region 5.[19] This changed when he was asked by a coalition of local leaders and activists to challenge his mainstream union boss for the job of Region 5 director. Tucker believed that the support of this militant and unusually powerful group assured him victory. Thinking he had the commitment of more than enough UAW National Convention delegates to easily win, Tucker accepted this grassroots draft and prepared to become the spokesperson for intraunion dissent in the UAW.

But he did not win. Instead of smoothly riding this wave of local political mobilization to a position of national UAW prominence, Tucker was first summarily fired from his union post by UAW International President Owen Bieber, who claimed that within the constitutional structure of the union an assistant director could not run for a directorship. Disturbed but undaunted, Tucker went to the 1986 UAW National Convention and put himself forward as a candidate, only to lose by less than one-fifth of a vote out of 650 votes cast from Region 5.[20] It seemed as though the mainstream would prevail, with the incumbent retaining his position for three more years.

But Tucker's election had been stolen from him. As alleged at the time of the vote and as subsequently upheld in a U.S. Department of Labor suit against the UAW, twenty-eight votes had been illegally cast for the incumbent, just enough votes, that is, to tip the scales in the incumbent's favor. The lengthy investigation and court battle that produced this finding meant, however, that the mainstream director would serve nearly his entire term of office before the court's ruling forced the UAW to allow Tucker to assume his post. Tucker thus faced a new round of elections soon after taking office.

Despite the reprimand implicit in this ruling, Tucker alleges that the UAW International leadership continued to violate labor law and UAW bylaws in an effort to thwart his already attenuated activities as regional director and prevent his reelection at the 1989 UAW national convention. With only an estimated 10 percent backing among the delegates, Tucker did in fact lose his reelection bid, by a substantial 197.727 votes. Owen Bieber wasted no time in declaring that the nascent New Directions Movement was thus "dead in the UAW."[21] Even though this election was also investigated, none of the alleged violations were proven. Still, the NDM did not die, as Bieber and his "Administration Caucus" allies wished.

Thwarted in their effort to obtain a voice at the national level of the union hierarchy via conventional means, Tucker and his grassroots supporters sought to organize their own chartered political caucus within the UAW. As Tucker has said concerning the impact of his disputed election bids:

> A lot of people from around the country began to pay attention to what was happening in our region. . . . There was a general widening of the impact not only of the election but the ideological questions that were being raised here about the role of internal democracy and accountability.[22]

One person who began to pay attention was Victor Reuther. From this time forward, Reuther became an active and publicly acknowledged supporter of Tucker's cause. When activists from around the country met in St. Louis in October 1989 to officially form the UAW-New Directions Movement, the seventy-seven-year-old Reuther was there to return to work as the NDM's Retiree Representative.

The influence of Reuther's (as well as Marquart's) ideas is evident in the NDM's Preface to its Constitution & By-Laws:

> The New Directions Movement in the UAW is rooted in our union's founding tradition of democracy, accountability, and solidarity.
>
> In recent years the almost total lack of accountability of the UAW leadership has thrown us into a tragic, costly, and false relationship with corporations who think nothing of exploiting our membership and our communities. We have traded away the only true means of gaining and exercising power in the workplace and community—our solidarity as workers. The need for new directions dictates the creation of a viable, rank and file directed alternative.
>
> Our union must defend workers from corporate attacks. Only a strong democratic union can coordinate this struggle to regain past concessions, and prepare the membership to resist future exploitation. We need a union controlled by an informed membership, not one under the domination of a one-party political caucus concerned primarily with its own political self-preservation.
>
> We need a union leadership that understands that "an injury to one is an injury to all." We need leaders committed to develop strategies and work with like-minded allies to stand up against all assaults on people's basic rights, whether in the workplace or in the society. They must have the courage and commitment to fight racist and sexist violence and discrimination.
>
> The struggle to create a socially and economically just society can not be won without such a labor leadership. Through New Directions our union can once again be in the forefront of that struggle.[23]

This statement of political philosophy and organizational purpose was adopted at the founding NDM convention and remains the organization's official declaration of purpose.

With Jerry Tucker and Victor Reuther its two most recognized leaders, the NDM has since developed steadily as the UAW's chief dissident group. It is difficult, though, to precisely gauge the organization's overall national shape and potential. For example, even basic estimates of rank-and-file support vary considerably. Tucker himself estimated that in 1990 the NDM had a presence in 600 to 700 of the UAW's 1,800 locals, although by 1991 he had revised this figure to an active presence in 204 of 1,200 active UAW locals, with 7,000 individual UAW members on NDM mailing lists.[24] Apparently, even Tucker recognized that a better measure of the NDM's support was needed. In 1991, he declared his intention to challenge Bieber for the job of UAW International President, and the results from this election among delegates at the 1992 UAW National Convention are indeed telling: Bieber 7,647.317 votes (or approximately 95 percent); Tucker 408.652 votes (or approximately 5 percent).[25] These figures suggest that the NDM's support may have in fact diminished between 1989 and 1992.

On the other hand, the 1992 convention also saw roughly a quarter of its delegates support the NDM-led "one-member, one-vote" policy initiative designed to end the UAW's weighted, delegate-centered election system. This is a significant issue for the NDM as it was a (government-ordered) one-member, one-vote system that made possible Ron Carey's surprising 1991 election as Teamsters' President. After serving for years as the leader of the dissident Teamsters for a Democratic Union, the U.S. government's interventions allowed Carey to bypass the administered and largely corrupt Teamster delegate-centered system to appeal *directly* to the union's rank and file. Carey's election buoyed the NDM's prospects, just as did dissident success in various key UAW locals during this period.[26] Indeed, by 1993, the New Directions Movement was again able to win a significant and, to an extent, reinvigorating victory, this time in Flint, where this background sketch concludes.

The NDM formally entered Flint's UAW politics in 1989 when Dave Yettaw, President of Flint's UAW Local 599, became one of the three NDM National Co-Chairs. Local 599's support for New Directions is significant because of its prominence within the UAW. The approximately 13,000 UAW members who work at Flint's Buick Complex make Local 599 not only the numerically largest local in the UAW's hometown, but also the largest UAW auto assembly local in the nation. Local 599's profile is also heightened by the fact that it is the home local of Stan Marshall, one of only four UAW International Vice Presidents. Yettaw's personal involvement with the UAW and the NDM is of special interest because his experience is typical of many at the local level.[27]

Like many of his generation, Yettaw was hired into the Buick Complex in 1965 fresh out of a Flint area high school. After a tour of duty in the Vietnam War, he returned to the factory and became involved in union activities in 1970. Though a self-described "redneck" prior to his military service, educational and work-related experiences transformed him into a self-described "militant" by the time of his first election to union office in 1972. After twelve years as a committee man on the shop floor, he became Local 599's Education Director in 1984, and then its President in 1987. Yettaw's initial involvement with what would later develop into the New Directions Movement began at the 1986 UAW national convention, at a time when, in his words, he "wouldn't have known Jerry Tucker from Adam."

Yettaw's description of his initial encounter with the NDM helps to explain its appeal:

I'll never forget the tremendous turmoil. This group came up to me, and because I had taken some literature from one of the activists, a sergeant-of-arms tells me that I shouldn't be taking that stuff, that "they're communists and socialists."

I kind of recoiled at that, and I thought, "it doesn't matter if they're black, brown, or white, or what they are, I'm not afraid to read what someone's ideas are."

That was my first experience with the "Administration Boys," as I call them, who have no mind of their own or, if they do, they sell their principles to keep their jobs.[28]

In Yettaw's view, the union principles that he believed in were grossly contradicted by the election fraud and the repression of political dissent that he personally witnessed at the 1986 convention. For someone who had accepted the UAW's own self-congratulatory rhetoric, these events were disillusioning. Yettaw thought, "This can't be."[29]

These same events led Victor Reuther to conclude that the subtle criticism proffered in *The Brothers Reuther* was no longer sufficient. Reuther describes the stolen election in Region 5 as "the final blow for me; I could no longer remain silent."[30] When these two leaders joined forces—the president of Flint's most prominent UAW Local, and a man who played an integral role in the Flint Sit-Down Strike—together they practically and symbolically brought working-class militancy back to Flint.

Reuther's reflections on Flint indicate his strong personal and symbolic connection to the city's history and people:

I feel close to the people of Flint because it is a microcosm of the struggle that's going on in the whole country.

I care about the people of Flint, by God. They're real heros, they really are. They built a tremendous industry and they made tremendous changes in that city. And now they're paying the price. They're being shoved aside, and I don't like it.

And I don't like it when the leaders of my own union are palsy-walsy with the corporate structure that turned its back on Flint. They just walked away from it! And they're doing it to dozens of other cities across the country.[31]

Flint's reciprocal sense of connectedness to Reuther is also noteworthy. He was, for example, invited to the city for the dedication of a downtown monument to Flint's Great Sit-Down Strike that features his words as well as his image as part of a mosaic mural. Having thus been memorialized—in effect, written into Flint's official history—it is interesting that Reuther continues to play an important role shaping the city's future. The continuing bonds between Reuther and Flint's labor activists is exemplified by the thoughts of Local 599's Max Grider, a National NDM Trustee:

> Victor Reuther is the greatest living trade union leader remaining in America. With all due respect to Walter Reuther—who I think was a wonderful, dynamic leader—I think Victor was the real brains in the Reuther family.
>
> I'll tell you, one of the reasons that I'm against this International union is the way that they have treated this man. For them to say that he's a senile, feeble old man, who doesn't know what he's talking about, who's turned against the Union! He hasn't turned against the union. He may have turned against the leadership, but that's because the leadership has turned against the membership. The membership is the union.
>
> I think he's a great man. I admire him. I love him, you know? He's the inspiration. He challenges us.[32]

Grider's feelings for Reuther suggest the degree to which the latter is an inspiring and legitimizing presence for the entire NDM, a relationship that is especially strong in Flint.

Still, Dave Yettaw remains Flint's principal New Directions leader. His 1987 election to Local 599's presidency was conducted on a de facto New Directions platform, even though he and his supporters were not then officially and unequivocally affiliated with the St. Louis base of the movement. Indeed, Yettaw's subsequent formal affiliation with the NDM quickly resulted in the disintegration of the 1987 political alliance. In Yettaw's diplomatic understatement: "It created friction among us."[33] Yettaw has also experienced conflict with other members of the NDM leadership. In 1992, for example, Yettaw was "selected" to join Jerry Tucker as a national candidate for the UAW's Secretary-Treasurer position, but without his foreknowledge or permission. Offended (but also out of basic concern for his family), Yettaw refused to put himself forward as a candidate. Such internal wrangling aside, however, Yettaw has remained firmly committed to the NDM since his participation at the St. Louis convention in 1989.

Yettaw's main battles are with his political opposition over local rank-and-file support. Indeed, support for his NDM affiliation has been tested several times in heated local union elections. In May 1990, Yettaw ran for reelection as Local 599's President, this time officially as a National Co-Chair of the most controversial political group currently active in the UAW. Yettaw's reelection bid was widely regarded as a significant test of the NDM's strength nationwide, and the UAW leadership quickly mobilized against Yettaw and his fellow Local 599 "Reuther Slate" candidates (the political caucus name Local 599's NDM group adopted in honor of *Walter*, not Victor, Reuther). Close attention to the rhetoric generated by this election is suggestive of the wider ideological split between the dissident NDM and the UAW's mainstream.

Local 599's "Unity Caucus" (the name, ironically, of the 1946–1949 Walter Reuther-led caucus) is the NDM's primary local opposition, with their criticism of Yettaw and his supporters mirroring the International's criticism of the NDM as a whole.[34] As early as 1988, one mainstream leader (who later became the Unity Caucus' 1993 candidate for Local 599 President) published a strident critique of Yettaw and his allies in *Headlight*, Local 599's weekly newspaper. Although New Directions is never named, the target of the critique is unmistakable:

> As you know, we have another U.A.W. National Convention next year. Is it only a coincidence that another group of political parasites and scavengers are beginning to circle in the skies above our Union?
>
> These groups will call themselves dissenters or they will call themselves the vanguard of the workers. They may choose to identify themselves with some of our Union Heros like Walter Reuther. They will tell us . . . what they are against. [But] the direction they wish to take is "old directions," as if they have learned nothing from the history of our movement at all.
>
> They seem to have some methods in common with some of the most dangerous people in history. Adolf Hitler, in the beginning of [his] reign of terror, verbally assaulted anyone that happened to disagree with him. As we all know, he and his gang, in the final analysis, had no dissenters to be concerned about.
>
> Joseph Stalin, the Dictator of Russia, the Leader of a group that had, ironically, called themselves the vanguard of the working class, felt compelled to cannibalize his own political organization. And this was done for one simple motive, the attainment of power over the very workers and their organizations he was elected to serve.[35]

Leaving aside the question of its historical accuracy, this piece suggests the poisonous flavor of the mainstream leadership's rhetorical counter-offensive against the NDM. It is nothing for them to engage in ad hominem criticism, red baiting, and innuendo.

In a 1991 interview this same individual repeated his disdain for the NDM, but by this time his critique had developed an analytical, if no less paranoid, formulation:

> There's two things they want to do. Number one, they want their goddamn names in print, personally. The leaders, Okay? And number

two, if I had a chance to see secret documents, if there are any, about what their real goals are and everything, [it] is to, again, supplant the labor movement with themselves, and let them be dictators of the working class.

Even though they don't say those things, they say those things. To me, they say those things.[36]

These sentiments were widely shared. In the words of another top Local 599 official, who insisted on referring to Yettaw simply as "him":

They believe in going back to the old Reuther days. [Walter] Reuther had a foresight of changing things as he went in each contract. And that's what the UAW is about as a union: [it] is to better improve every contract, not go back to the old. Why should you go back and beat on something that ain't there no more?[37]

A third mainstream official said of the NDM's support among Local 599's rank and file:

I think that's a natural reaction of people not wanting to change, [who] are accustomed to militancy . . .

They're not trying to change anything. They want to go back in history. The change has already happened.

Some of the New Directions leadership is communist in nature, as far as how they act. I'm not calling them communist, but their only interest is self-serving, and that's it.[38]

Occasionally criticism is less dramatic. In the words of a fourth Local 599 official:

New Directions goes public with their arguments more than in-house. That's not good for an organization, in my opinion.

I get along all right with Dave [Yettaw], but I just don't happen to agree with his philosophy of what's best for our membership here.[39]

When these same leaders were asked to comment on Victor Reuther's role in the NDM, they typically suggested that NDM leaders are "pseudo-intellects," with Reuther:

a nice old man . . . that you can listen to and possibly learn some things from for today's world. But to lead me? I don't know.

> If he has a personal axe to grind . . . because he wasn't allowed to do things back in the 30s and 40s, or something like that, that's fine. We all do that.
>
> But I think that [New Directions] organization is using him, using an old man, and I think it's sad. Rather than revering him, they're going to try and work him to death.[40]

With views of this sort current among Local 599's elected leadership, it is not surprising that many held out little hope for Yettaw's May 1990 reelection bid. How could the same membership that elected these leaders elect such a militant New Directions candidate?

But Yettaw over came his opposition's criticism, and received just over 50 percent of the votes (4850 out 9650 ballots cast), for a close but significant reelection victory. No other Reuther Slate candidate, however, succeeded in their respective bids for union office. Yettaw would remain the lone NDM representative among Local 599's elected leadership until the next election in 1993. Indeed, he was the only NDM member among all of Flint's UAW leadership. Since only a single NDM candidate was elected, the mainstream leaders assumed that the NDM itself did not enjoy much support among their membership in Flint. Yettaw was seen more as mere "watchdog," as a kind of lone ombudsmen who represented a membership wary of putting all of its eggs in one basket.

Yet this watchdog and his NDM political allies were able to gain strength during the 1990 to 1993 period. Over this time, New Directions' dissident stand was supported and energized by a number of factors, including the high-profile politics generated by Michael Moore's widely discussed, Flint-based film, *Roger & Me*; the 1992 Presidential election season, which saw Yettaw—eventually elected as a Brown For President national convention delegate—introduce Democratic Presidential hopeful Jerry Brown to an enthusiastic Local 599 and C-SPAN network audience; and the fact of the UAW national convention this same year, which Yettaw attended as the top vote getter in Local 599's delegate election. In his 1993 bid to capture his third consecutive three-year term as Local 599 President, Yettaw stunned his opposition by *easily* defeating the mainstream challenger and capturing over 57 percent of the vote.[41] More significantly, perhaps, Yettaw's coattails were finally broad enough to secure two key positions for his NDM allies—Gary Mattson, Recording Secretary, and Dean Braid, Education Director—thus further establishing Flint and Local 599 as a major base for NDM support.

Commenting on the period before Yettaw's 1990 reelection, Victor Reuther had observed:

> I saw the incredible [union] staff that was sent in to destroy Dave Yettaw in Buick because they couldn't tolerate *one voice* [of dissent] in the local leadership.[42]

By 1993, NDM electoral success forced the UAW mainstream in Flint to deal with multiple voices of dissent, as the New Directions Movement showed no signs of simply disappearing, not the least in the UAW's hometown.

II. NEW DIRECTIONS MOVEMENT IDEOLOGY

New Directions Movement ideology is rooted in a teleological belief that historical events are somehow arranged and progressive, as in Victor Reuther's particular historicism, where "the American revolution is still going on." Reuther's vision of a perpetual American revolution is, in fact, so composed as to read like a book still being written:

> The thirties was a brilliant chapter in the continuation of the American revolution. The Civil Rights Movement, a brilliant chapter. Women, now, in their efforts to win more than just frills in terms of equal consideration, but *genuine* equal rights, is another chapter that is evolving.[43]

For Reuther, this process of America's unfolding revolution has not only served to "invigorate American society," but also distinguishes America's political history from those of the Soviet Union and France, whose own revolutions were "aborted in midstream." His sense for America's exceptional revolutionary potential notwithstanding, Reuther believes that Americans today have good reason to "hope" for continued progressive change. He states, "if in my short lifetime I've seen those changes [noted above], there's reason to believe it can happen again, and that leads me to New Directions."[44]

As indicated by its focus on equal and civil rights, the NDM conceives its revolution as democratic-egalitarian in quality. An example of this emphasis is found in the NDM's proclaimed alliance with members of various minority groups in the union and wider society. The NDM's Preamble cited above states that New Directions members "must have the courage and commitment to fight racist and sexist violence and discrimination." Jerry Tucker also suggests this theme in what amounts to a parable about the mainstream UAW:

> One night at a St. Louis CAP meeting—our community action program—a group of [UAW] administration loyalists came to that meeting with bags of raw eggs and attacked my supporters. They called them Tucker suckers and not only threw eggs but physically attacked them. One fellow had cracked ribs, another fellow had a broken nose, another had a concussion.
>
> There was a racial overtone to it. It was principally white males— which tends to be the core of the International's support—who went

after my supporters, a number of whom were women, black, and minority.[45]

NDM leaders have a self-understanding as defenders of nondiscriminatory democratic ideals.

The NDM's fight for democratic-egalitarian rights takes several additional forms, including a concern for workers' welfare regardless of race, ethnicity, or nationality. The NDM has repeatedly, for example, spoke out against the exploitation of Mexican workers by U.S. corporations. Indeed, the NDM is committed to a solidarity that includes all fellow workers (whether they are unionized or not). The NDM is also self-conscious about the potential for cities and communities to become dependent on local UAW jobs. In Flint, Dave Yettaw has successfully fought the internal UAW censorship of his articles in Local 599's newspaper, but he has also appeared before Flint's City Council to demand public disclosure of tax abatement documents potentially embarrassing to GM and to the city. It is not uncommon in Flint for the debate between NDM advocates and mainstream union leaders to spill out of the union hall and into the pages of the daily newspaper, or for Yettaw to state his position on various local issues during slotted editorial time on Flint-area television or radio stations. The NDM even expresses concern for the well being of future generations. For example, the NDM advocates ecological policies that would be detrimental in the short term to the U.S. auto industry and its own supporters and potential supporters. In Max Grider's words:

> One of the differences between us and those at the Administrative Caucus [is] we *do* try to look at the bigger picture. We aren't just concerned about our jobs. We aren't willing to let our world suffer to keep jobs for a moment [or] for a few years. We are concerned about emissions, about pollution, the sort of things that the companies that we work for really haven't addressed, any more than what they've been forced to address by the government.
>
> And New Directions people probably realize that some of our goals, in terms of looking a the bigger picture, can cost us jobs over the short run because we don't want to see our companies pollute. We'd like to see higher standards for gas mileage, and so on. These are things that in the short run hurt the industry and impact our work force. But we would like to believe that, with an effort at correcting these problems, that maybe there'll be some jobs in a world for our children and their children, and so on, to live in the future.[46]

The NDM consistently advocates for democratic-egalitarian rights for all in its efforts to build solidarity with local groups beyond the shop floor and union hall.

Writ large, the heritage of the American Labor Movement is also deemed central to the NDM's conceptualization of America's "unfinished revolution," not only as the historical predecessor of later progressive "chapters," but, interestingly, because the labor movement directed mass attention to the power of democratic citizenship. Victor Reuther suggests that the "rise of industrial labor" in the thirties led "millions of citizens ... to exercise their citizenship rights in the political field, and not *just* at the bargaining table." For the NDM, the labor movement is conceived as inherently dedicated to economic *and* social reform. The NDM is thus in large part, as Reuther continues, an "effort to get the labor movement to be true to its historic obligations." This is carried forth today in the NDM's support and advocacy for Labor Party Advocates.[47]

As its name implies, Labor Party Advocates is a group that is dedicated to building support for the formation of an American Labor Party. This organization was established by Tony Mazzocchi, then Secretary-Treasurer of the Oil, Chemical and Atomic Workers International Union. Believing that "democracy requires equality," this ongoing "organizing committee" seeks for the United States a political party whose ideological orientation would parallel traditional European Labor parties, or, perhaps, an American political party similar to the once-powerful Canadian New Democratic Party. Its political goals are exemplified in their stated notion that "we need another New Deal." As a Labor Party Advocates position paper suggests:

> Two hundred years ago, the American Revolution resulted in a system of government—founded upon the principles of majority rule, democratic representation, and equal rights—that has been a model for the world.
>
> Unfortunately, even the promise of majority rule, democratic representation and equal rights is now homeless in the country of its birth.[48]

This type of imagery—equally familiar to 1992 Brown for President supporters as to H. Ross Perot backers—jibes with the NDM's particular vision of history.

The NDM ideology of American history is thus mythic, not necessarily in the sense that it is false or fantastic, but in that American history is conceived of as unfolding, with immanent possibilities that call for their contemporary realization. In this ideology the present thereby becomes, in Reuther's words, a "crucial moment," or a "golden opportunity," for change, while the future is rendered full of anticipation. Or as Yettaw speculates:

> I've always been a visionary, I guess, a visionary whose visions are a hell of a long way off. But I believe that now I'm starting to see occur

in this country [a phenomenon in which] the 90s are going to be a
gelling like in the 60s.[49]

Pointing to the mobilization of the Labor Advocates Party and Carey's election
as Teamster President, among other factors, Yettaw senses social change in the
air.

If the NDM is premised upon self-conscious participation in a progressively unfolding American Revolution, how, then, do its members construct
their identities as actors in this social movement? Even though Yettaw believes
that every member of the NDM is "leader," it remains important to consider
the contrast between the NDM's official leaders and the members whose participation is limited more or less to supporting NDM candidates.

Results from a 1988–89 factorywide opinion survey conducted by the
Local 599 Commission on the Future suggests that Local 599's membership as
a whole is dissatisfied with their union leadership.[50] For example, in response
to the question "Is the International U.A.W. headed in the correct direction?"
only 31 percent of respondents answered in the affirmative, while in response
to the question "What is the confidence level you have in the national leadership?" 56 percent answered that they were "not" or "not very" confident in their
national leadership. On the other hand, when asked whether or not the UAW
should continue the mainstream leadership's "joint," or cooperatively administered corporate/union programs, such as the Quality of Work Life initiative,
approval clearly outweighed discontent for each of the twenty-seven separate
programs evaluated. With regard to QWL, for example, only 25 percent of the
respondents explicitly favored the program's *dis*continuation. On the whole,
then, Local 599's membership would appear to be disgruntled, but willing to
accept the cooperative policy orientation advocated by the mainstream union
leadership.

Max Grider, who helped conduct this survey, suggests a similar interpretation of specifically NDM supporters at Local 599.[51] Whereas New Directions
leadership tries to "balance and weigh" the "big picture" and the "small picture," in Grider's view the rank and file are more concerned with "What can
New Directions do to make my job, my life in this plant, better today and
tomorrow?" This includes "the little things," such as "getting the help they need,
having a relief person in their area so when they gotta take a leak, they can take
a leak." But rank-and-file concerns also include the ever omnipresent pace of
work. With recent changes in factory work rules designed to debureaucratize
the shop floor and increase productivity, Grider believes that "over half the
work force is overworked," and that workers are being treated as "disposable
goods." Here, he echoes the NDM's strong stand against Japanese-style, so-
called team concept management practices and work rules, which, following
authors Mike Parker and Jane Slaughter, are collectively called "management by
stress."[52] NDM support is rooted, it would appear, in the personally experi-

enced trials of factory work itself, a consideration reminiscent of Marquart's perspective.

The story of the NDM leadership is different. Their sights tend to be set on comparatively abstract goals, and their relationship to the Movement, not surprisingly, is far more conceptually mediated. Although they, too, recognize the cardinal significance of the world within the factory walls, their self-conception escapes these walls through a hole called the "heritage of the labor movement." This identity is formed, in part, through remembrance of and identification with the spirit of seminal labor leaders who are understood to have faced challenges similar to those the NDM faces today. As noted, Local 599 NDM candidates run on the Reuther Slate in honor of Walter Reuther. Yettaw believes that being a part of the NDM means "that you believe in the goals of traditional organized labor that [Walter] Reuther taught." Walter Reuther's portrait hangs prominently on the wall behind Yettaw's desk, whereas a large picture of Local 599's boy who made good—the mainstream UAW Vice President Stan Marshall—is kept face down on the floor of Yettaw's office closet.

Of course, though he would eventually preside over a bureaucratic UAW for over twenty years, Walter Reuther's was initially a very difficult world. Organizing a union from scratch often meant battling corporate goon squads and their loyal police allies. It sometimes also meant stool pigeons and even fanatical demagogues within one's own ranks. When, in the 1920s, American corporations hoped to subvert independent unionization by advancing their own brand of company unionism, labor leaders like Walter Reuther also had to resist a false reconciliation of their particular interests and the universal good of industrial working people everywhere.

New Directions' remembrance and identification with this period is no doubt greatly aided by Victor Reuther's presence. Consider his own formulation:

> [I am led] to a comparison of the situation that existed in the late '20s, when the corporate structure was so arrogant and so blind to its social responsibilities, and an old bureaucratic segment of the labor movement got suckered into a partnership mentality. The old leaders of small and puny A.F. of L. unions were invited to dine with corporate leaders and wear white ties, and they thought they had arrived.
>
> And so-called industrial labor experts in the late '20s wrote that we were on the threshold of a "great new era of partnership between capital and labor." The ink was hardly dry on these pontifications when the great industrial upheaval took place—the rise of industrial unions—because there was an underclass that no one had bothered to listen to or to talk with.
>
> And I have a feeling today we're entering an era much like that, where those without vision and foresight and the courage to face real

problems, pretend we are on the threshold of a great "new world order."[53]

As is generally recognized, the very meaning of *New* Directions becomes ironic given this identification with the situation, courage, and vision of their union forbears. NDM ideology might well be concisely defined as a redemption of the old directions once embarked upon by the brothers Reuther. The NDM leadership values its loyalty to this heritage, and they are willing to accept personal sacrifices in its service. This is more true of the middle-aged leaders than of Reuther, who, since he is long officially retired from union politics, sacrifices only the peace of mind that should perhaps be his in his later years. But for those such as Tucker and Yettaw, leadership in the NDM means that their careers within the mainstream union cease where they stand. Observing the growth of dissident movements within large international unions around the country, Yettaw finds hope, because, in his words:

> it's not because these people want to climb to the [top] leadership, because who in their right minds would go through such penalizing sacrifice and punishment to get to the top? You can join the administration boys and weasel your way right up there.[54]

Personal sacrifice is the price of conviction to the larger goals of social unionism.

New Directions leaders not only value progressive labor's heritage, they judge others by this standard. Yettaw and his supporters see themselves as the true heirs to Walter Reuther's teachings. They hang banners at UAW rallies in Flint proclaiming themselves the heirs of this city's Great Sit-Down Strike. They mock their opponents as little more than "administration boys" and "clipboard warriors." Victor Reuther plays his special role with grace, speaking of "praetorian guards" instead of "administration boys," never giving in to the temptation to personalize his dissent even in the face of the many personal attacks against him.[55] Still, to the mainstream union leaders' claim that they carry on the traditions of Walter Reuther, Victor retorts, "That's a contemptible lie, and they know it!"[56]

The mainstream response to Victor Reuther and the NDM from former UAW President Douglas Fraser contests NDM's claim to Walter Reuther's legacy. Fraser contends:

> Walter Reuther, more than any other single individual, forged and molded the ideas and principles of the UAW. Those things became institutionalized, and now the institution forms people like Owen Bieber . . . as they come up through the ranks.[57]

But where NDM leaders learn from Walter Reuther's life, Fraser turns over the task of instruction to Reuther's union; where NDM leaders seek to embody and live Walter Reuther's legacy, Fraser's view suggests that the guardianship of this heritage is better left to those who were forged and molded in their climb through the union bureaucracy.

Overall, NDM leaders sacrifice their immediate interests in order to claim the right to participate in the redemption of the industrial union. But to what end? What type of social change is intimated by an historical consciousness structured around America's "unfinished revolution"?

Although Grider "cringes" at the word "capitalism," NDM ideology is not opposed to capitalist society's property relations *as such*. When Reuther speaks of "revolution," he does not mean a radical overturning of such basic social relationships. And, though Tucker shares convictions with those who were called "socialists" in their time, the NDM does not advocate the nationalization of industry or the elimination of the private ownership of social capital in any form, nor do this movement's leaders wish to be called socialists. New Directions does not constitute, and does not wish to constitute, a revolutionary movement in the vein of classical Marxian imagery. It is an intraunion movement first, and only thereafter a social movement. The NDM seeks to revitalize the UAW as the first step in a larger project of revitalizing American society. They call this the project of social unionism.[58]

At issue for New Directions is the renewal and extension of New Deal politics. The NDM supports the universal provision of health care as a right of citizenship, the preservation of key environmental resources, and legal restrictions on capital investment decisions, including greater government regulation of international trade (advocating what they call fair as opposed to free trade). Of course, the NDM also seeks the empowerment of unions in the traditional adversarial collective bargaining framework in which unions would be solely responsible for protecting the interests of workers and corporations responsible for profitable production. In general, the NDM sees our society's "greatest challenge" as how to "take the capitalist system as we know it and change the bottom line from profits to people." However, its ideal of a "social unionism" remains premised upon a profitable capitalist economy from which "workers extract from the corporations their gains." Social unionism thus fits within the framework of New Deal ideology because it seeks to ameliorate capitalism's socially detrimental effects while the key structural feature of capitalism—private ownership of the social means of production for private ends—remains intact. It is fitting, then, that NDM leaders seem to prefer liberal or social democrat to socialist as a political label, which also jibes with their identification with reformist European Labor and Canadian New Democratic political parties.

Indeed, in the last instance, the NDM's criticism of American social structure really boils down to concern for the comparatively diminishing role of adversarial industrial unions in a deindustrializing period. In contrast to the

Canadian Auto Workers, for example, who are recognized as having strengthened their position in Canadian society by rejecting concessionary contracts and jointness relationships in the workplace, NDM leaders see American unions as losing strength by following a much more conciliatory course. And whereas the Canadian Auto Workers have, in Victor Reuther's words, "exploited to the hilt their association with the New Democratic Party," particularly in their struggle against a North American "free trade zone," the political ambitions of American organized labor have foundered with the weakening of the Democratic Party's ties to organized labor, a phenomena that many see confirmed in President Clinton's support for a North American Free Trade Agreement (NAFTA). The NDM struggles against declining union power because this is understood as the unnecessary result of a union leadership unwilling to strike a militantly, fiercely independent pose vis-a-vis unsympathetic government and corporate interests. The NDM sees the mainstream UAW International leadership as "selling its membership down the drain" by acquiescing to corporate power, and, in effect, accepting the union's dependent relationship with corporate America. The mainstream leadership's policy is viewed as appeasement designed, in Grider's words, to "save a piece of [the union], and more importantly, to save the bureaucracy of the union."

NDM proposes to imitate the Canadian model by adopting a similarly oppositional stance to wage and work rule concessions, and to seek the rejuvenation or replacement of the Democratic Party in order to form a political organization that is committed to realizing the wider social goals of working people. Grider imputes this oppositional sentiment to Canadian Auto Worker President Bob White: "'Damn it, we might lose, but we're gonna go down fighting like heck.'" The NDM defiantly adopts this last-ditch stance toward economic and political relations of dependency.

What is the NDM's vision for its role in the future? Victor Reuther advances a novel response to this question, implicitly turning New Directions away from the perceived rearguard (save-the-union bureaucracy) politics of the mainstream International UAW leadership. For Reuther, the people of the world still need and want automobiles and other industrial goods. In his words:

> It is sad at this crucial moment in U.S. history—with the great industries that we helped unionize becoming increasingly parts of rust belts, with vast resources lying there unutilized, more plants being closed—[that people speak] of over-production, never under-consumption—*over capacity* while millions hunger, you know, for the very products that flow from these industries.[59]

In other words, greater attention to systems crises denoted by the Marxian focus on over-production misses, for Reuther, the relatively more crucial social crises denoted by the Keynesian term *underconsumption*. Because of unions' redistributive effects on national income—from corporate surplus to wages and benefits—Reuther credits unions with having created "the great U.S. market," and with this having solved capitalism's chief inherent contradiction. Again, in his words:

> The corporate structure has lost sight of the fact that it has an obligation: if it wants to seek an expanding market, then it has to assist in the growth and expansion of a consumer market that will keep pace with the rise in the industrial capacity to produce things. Otherwise, an inevitable gap will develop between the inability of people to purchase what they have already produced.[60]

Beyond workplace and internal union democracy, then, lies the larger political-economic goal of balancing supply and demand through negotiated (and non-inflationary) redistribution, and the larger moral goal of meeting basic human needs worldwide.

Given the scope of these concerns, it is possible to appreciate the significance that the NDM attaches to social unionism. It is also possible to appreciate the strain resulting from the need to conceptualize the relationship between the problems of the shop floor, comparative economic systems, and global ecological crises. In conceptualizing the structure of society, it seems that the NDM starts within the immediate confines of the factory walls, proceeding to the larger issues of social structure, and back again. That the NDM leaves the essential structure of capitalism and other fundamental features of contemporary society intact is perhaps a result of the sheer arduousness of this conceptual journey; intellectuals do not often fair much better. Nevertheless, the NDM stakes out a clearly defined territory of dissent: capitalism is acceptable, but industrial rust belts are not; a capitalist class is perhaps acceptable, but the impoverishment and disempowerment of the working class is not. The structure of a New Directions-inspired American society would resemble that of societies organized by the principles of social-democratic compromise, or, equivalently, what Roosevelt's New Deal once represented to American working people. In a word, the NDM's social unionism stands for a new, New Deal society.

When Dave Yettaw first came into contact with New Directions ideology at the 1986 convention, he thought, "It sound[s] rational and reasonable to me."[61] As we have seen, the NDM is guided in its dissent by the UAW's founding principles. Theirs is an immanent critique of the UAW symbolized and literally embodied in Victor Reuther's ongoing leadership. Struggling with opponents that ignore, debase, or otherwise attempt to silence them, New Directions instead seeks free dialogue concerning the higher purpose and meaning of America's Labor Movement, and not, that is, mere power *as such*. As Reuther says:

I would be very happy tomorrow if suddenly the leadership of the UAW, even under Owen Bieber, were to accept the fact that they've been going down the wrong road, and [that] they've got to shift gears, [that] they've got to change directions.[62]

But in practice there is no direct dialogue between the NDM and the UAW leadership, nor is there conversation with the wider rank-and-file majority. If the NDM ideology is in fact "rational and reasonable," rationality and reason have not received an enthusiastic welcome from the UAW's membership. Given the mainstream's view of the NDM as reactionary and self-interested, it is not especially surprising that they reject it as a preferred conversational partner. This sentiment was symbolized by one Local 599 leader who said simply of his relationship with Dave Yettaw, as he sat in an office adjacent to Yettaw's: "I ignore him."[63]

NOTES

1. Interview 1, June 14, 1991, original emphasis.

2. Personal letter from Jerry Tucker to Linda Barnhart, November 24, 1990, p. 2. I thank Ms. Barnhart for making this letter available for this research.

3. Interview 3, July 17, 1991.

4. Interview 4a, May 28, 1991.

5. See Victor G. Reuther's account in his *The Brothers Reuther and the Story of the UAW* (Boston: Houghton Mifflin, 1976). "Union leader Reuther's family questions cause of fatal crash," *The Flint Journal,* 7 May 1995, Sec. A, pp. 1, 12.

6. John Greenwald, "How GM Broke Down," in *Time* 140, no. 19 (9 November 1992), pp. 42–50.

7. Jerry Lee Lembcke, "Regional Distributions of Corporate and Union Power: A Case Study of the UAW," in *Labor Studies Journal* 19, no. 2 (forthcoming); David Halberstram, *The Reckoning* (New York: William Morrow, 1986).

8. Frank Marquart, *An Auto Worker's Journal: The UAW from Crusade to One-Party Union* (University Park, PA: Pennsylvania State University Press, 1975).

9. Ibid., p. 1.

10. Ibid., p. 71.

11. Ibid., pp. 137–138. See Harry Braverman, *Labor and Monopoly Capital: The Degradation of Work in the Twentieth Century* (New York: Monthly Review Press, 1974).

12. Marquart, p. 123; also see pp. 144–148; 132; 122; 153.

13. Ibid., pp. 1–2.

14. Ibid. Although this is a factional critique of the origins of these bureaucratic trends, Marquart's main target is their result, the UAW in the 1970s, as an entire entity.

15. Victor G. Reuther, *The Brothers Reuther and the Story of the UAW* (Boston: Houghton Mifflin, 1976).

16. Ibid., p. 475.

17. Ibid., p. 21.

18. Ibid.

19. Sources for this section include: "New Directions for the UAW: An Interview with Jerry Tucker," in *Multinational Monitor* (January/February, 1990), pp. 27–33; "NDM National Conference Points the Way," in *The Voice of New Directions: UAW National Edition* 1, no. 3 (December, 1989): 1, 8; "500 Workers Vote to Set Up Group for Tougher UAW," *St. Louis Post-Dispatch*, 22 October 1989, Sec. 1, pp. 1, 3; "Biographic Information On: UAW Presidential Candidate—Jerry Tucker" (document source); Jeff Stansbury, "A Reporter's Notebook on Jerry Tucker" (document source); Eric Mann, *Taking on General Motors* (Los Angeles: Center for Labor Research and Education, Institute of Industrial Relations, University of California, Los Angeles, 1987), pp. 368–372.

20. This election figure is made possible by the UAW's peculiar system of weighing votes. All votes are reported to the third decimal (e.g., 510.678 votes).

21. Pro-New Directions Delegates numbered approximately 200 from the 2000 total. See "Spirited Debate: Dissidents Are Heard, But 'Jointness' Reigns," in *Ward's Auto World* (July, 1989): p. 103. The 1989 Anaheim, CA, convention also saw political ally Don Douglas lose his own bid for the directorship of UAW Region 1–1B by nearly 260 votes of 1170 cast.

22. "New Directions for the UAW," p. 28.

23. UAW New Directions *Constitution & By-Laws: Preamble*, approved 21 October 1989, St. Louis, MO. (document source).

24. See "New Directions for the UAW: An Interview with Jerry Tucker," and "UAW Dissidents Mounting Challenge to Bieber," *The Flint Journal*, 2 November 1991, sec. A, p. 12.

25. "Convention Summary," UAW Local 599 *Headlight*, 23 July 1992, p. 4. Also see "Dissident UAW Candidate Picks Flint to Kick Off Campaign," *The Flint Journal*, 29 January 1992, Sec. E, p.1; "UAW Dissidents Mounting Challenge to Bieber," *The Flint Journal*, 2 November 1991, Sec. A, p. 12, and "New Directors Opens Campaign for UAW Presidency," *Labor Notes* 156 (March, 1992): pp. 8–9.

26. See "Carey's Teamsters Win May Start Trend for Unions," *The Flint Journal*, 13 December 1991, Sec. D, p. 8; "Ready or Not, Reform Coming to Teamsters: Convention Outcome May Spark Democracy in UAW, Other Unions," *The Flint Journal*, 23 June 1991, Sec. E, p. 1; Interview 4c, January 17, 1992; "Cooperation still key at GM-Toyota Plant: Despite Victory By UAW Insurgent, Union Shunning Confrontation at Joint Venture," *The Flint Journal*, 23 June 1991, Sec. E, p. 1; Interview 1, June 14, 1991.

27. Sources for the following discussion of Dave Yettaw's union career include Interviews 4a, 4b, and 4c, as well as back issues of Local 599's *Headlight* (from 1968 forward) stored in the Genesee Historical Collections Center at The University of Michigan–Flint.

28. Interview 4a, May 28, 1991.

29. Interview 4a, May 28, 1991.

30. Interview 1, June 14, 1991.

31. Ibid.

32. Interview 3, July 17, 1991.

33. Interview 4a, May 28, 1991.

34. Primary sources for this section include Interview 5, June 20, 1991; Interview 6, July 3, 1991; Interview 7, July 5, 1991; Interview 8, July 10, 1991; Interview 9, July 26, 1991; Local 599's *Headlight*; and field notes from observation at official UAW gatherings in Flint.

35. Russ Cook, "Shop Committee Report" in *Headlight*, 8 December 1988, p. 2.

36. Interview 6, July 3, 1991.

37. Interview 6, July 3, 1991.

38. Interview 5, June 20, 1991. Perhaps this implied definition of communist tendencies as manifest in self-interested political factionalism is rooted in the history of internal union struggles between self-interested communist party cadre and sympathizers and the forces that supported Reuther's more moderate and independent social unionism.

39. Interview 8, July 10, 1991.

40. Interview 6, July 3, 1991.

41. Yettaw received 5108 votes (58 percent) to his mainstream opponent's 3231 votes (38 percent). New Directions' relationship to *Roger & Me* is discussed in greater detail below. It should be noted also that Yettaw was elected to represent Local 599 at its 1992 national convention in San Diego, and was elected to serve as a Brown for President delegate at the Democratic Party's 1992 national convention in New York City.

42. Interview 1, June 14, 1991.

43. Interview 1, June 14, 1991.

44. Ibid. All Reuther quotations are from Interview 1 unless otherwise indicated.

45. "New Directions for the UAW," pp. 28–29.

46. Interview 3, July 17, 1991. Also "UAW National New Directions 1992 Convention Platform" (document source).

47. The following discussion of "Labor Party Advocates" is based on membership materials, including *Labor Party Advocates* Newsletter, 1, 3 (August 1991); Labor Party Advocates *Questions and Answers* (document source); *An Open Letter from Tony Maz-*

zocchi, Secretary-Treasurer, Oil, Chemical and Atomic Workers International Union (20 August 1991); as well as interview 4b and 4c.

48. *Questions and Answers*, pp. 2–3, 15.

49. Interview 4a, May 28, 1991.

50. Report by "Local 599 U.A.W. Commission on the Future," *Headlight*, 12 January 1989. 632 union members responded to this survey, which includes both quantitative and qualitative responses to an extensive array of questions.

51. Interview 3, July 17, 1991.

52. Mike Parker and Jane Slaughter, *Choosing Sides: Unions and the Team Concept* (Boston: A Labor Notes Book, South End Press, 1988). A foreword by Victor Reuther is included in this volume.

53. Interview 1, June 14, 1991.

54. Interview 4a, May 28, 1991.

55. See Robert Weissman, "Solidarity Forever?: The UAW's Harassment of Victor Reuther," in *Multinational Monitor*, January/February, 1990, pp. 34–36; "Factions Grasp for Walter Reuther's Legacy," *Detroit Free Press*, 5 May 1990, p. 12A ; and "Organizers Say UAW Ruined Bash for Reuther," *The Flint Journal*, 13 February 1992, Sec. A, p. 2.

56. Interview 1, June 14, 1991.

57. "Factions Grasp for Walter Reuther's Legacy."

58. Note Yettaw's explanation of "social unionism" to the Local 599 membership: "Walter Reuther knew that this union did not need leadership in pure trade unionism as in the AFL . . . but SOCIAL UNIONISM . . . *a union in which it would be in harmony with and in tune with the social goals and objectives (sic), such as education, full employment, proper health care, protecting democratic process, raising wages, bringing about free democratic unions, elsewhere in the world,*" *Headlight*, 2 March 1989, p. 6, emphasis in original. For Yettaw, "pure" or what he sometimes calls "business," trade unionism is the lesser relation to a union as a social movement.

59. Interview 1, June 14, 1991.

60. Ibid.

61. Interview 4a, 28 May 1991.

62. Interview 1, 14 June 1991.

63. Interview 7, July 5, 1991.

Chapter 2

NEW WORK

Speaking of this mythical past, a lot of workers say what you have to do is get tough in the spirit of '37 and '38 and all that. There's a kind of tension between that and utopian thinking. They're not at a utopian level. They're reviving the past. Like New Directions: What is the *new direction* that we're going to go?

—Richard Gull,
Co-Director, Center for New Work[1]

People wonder why anybody in GM management would listen to someone who looks like me and talks like me. But people are so desperate, they're willing to listen to a philosopher.

—Frithjof Bergmann,
Director, Center for New Work[2]

As Dr. Bergmann says, "Is it ever good to think that you can lift a door handle eight to ten hours for the rest of your life?" His words parallel Plato's statement that "an unexamined life is not worth living."

—Josie Kearns, *Life after the Line*[3]

We all know that General Motors Corporation will close six plants in Michigan, that three will be in Flint alone, and that this will layoff a total of 7,000 workers. We also know that this is only the beginning. Robots are becoming cheaper every year, and wages in the third world are not rising. The question is: What does it make sense to do about this? For the last four years we at the Center for New Work have researched and evolved ideas that we now propose as an intelligent response.

—*New Work Ideas*[4]

The Center for New Work (CNW) was founded in 1984 by Flint's "autotown philosophers," University of Michigan professors Frithjof Bergmann and Richard Gull.[5] The CNW nonprofit community education initiative sought a "solution" to the city's unemployment predicament that "could lead to a renewed and better city of Flint," and which, once "worked out in Flint," could be "a model for [Michigan] and the nation."[6] The CNW's self-described "intelligent response" to Flint's dependent deindustrialization was based on the idea that structural unemployment could be conceived of as "job-free time," that is, as an opportunity to engage in innovative forms of life-fulfilling "new work."

While the New Directions Movement remains a going concern, Flint saw the Center for New Work close its doors in 1988. This does not mean, however, that the CNW's ideology has lost its significance. Regardless of its ultimate failure to facilitate Flint's transition to a liberating postindustrial future, analysis of the Center for New Work's ideas about work and technology, education and jobs, and philosophy and practice, provides the means to assess from close range the meaning of postindustrial ideology in America's deindustrializing heartland. It turns out, however, that the CNW's postindustrial vision was so out of sync with the realities of Flint's deindustrialization that even the local elite found insufficient reason to nurture its potential ideological value.

THE CENTER FOR NEW WORK IN FLINT

The story of Flint's Center for New Work begins with its founder, Dr. Frithjof Bergmann. The Austrian-born Bergmann is a student of the renowned philosopher Walter Kaufmann, and he is (as he was throughout the period under discussion) Professor of Philosophy and Anthropology at the University of Michigan at Ann Arbor. Bergmann's philosophical analysis of freedom, as espoused in his 1977 book *On Being Free*, led him to the idea of "new work."[7]

In *On Being Free*, Bergmann develops a metatheory of freedom, or "a theory about other *theories* of freedom."[8] The main substance of this metatheory may be expressed thusly: freedom is not found in an objective societal or presocietal state of anarchy, nor under conditions sans restraint on individual volition and choice; rather, in Bergmann's words, "the primary prerequisite of freedom is an impulse, is a self possessed of something that wants to be acted out."[9] In other words, freedom is best conceptualized as a practice of the self. Bergmann continues:

> The primary condition of freedom is the possession of an identity, or of a self—freedom is the acting out of that identity.
>   Tell me a man's identity and I will tell you his freedom, tell me his limits and I will tell you when his is coerced.[10]

This type of conceptualization requires "a shift in focus from the outside to the inside of a person."[11] Bergmann's is an argument for a change in commonsense thinking concerning the meaning of freedom: from the traditional emphasis on the presence and absence of constraining external conditions to a concern with individual self-growth.

Near the end of *On Being Free*, Bergmann examines the meaning of work and freedom in human society. If freedom is realized in practice by doing, as Bergmann says elsewhere, what "[one] identifies with—what [one] *really* wants to do," then uncoerced work is the essence of a life lived freely.[12] If free work is the essence of a free society, then the modern capitalist labor market and capitalist workplace must be modified to amend or eliminate their respective work-or-starve and authoritarian structure. In other words, as long as human labor power is bought and sold as a mere factor of production, and human work is determined by and controlled for profit's sake in alienated workplaces, then there is little freedom in capitalist society. What, Bergmann asks, could liberate us from this "job servitude"?

Bergmann's answer is, in a word, technology. In his view, "the basic purpose of technology from its beginnings was the elimination of human labor."[13] The ongoing Western technological revolution is the force that has perpetually changed society by replacing human labor, first in the realm of agriculture, then in manufacturing, and finally, today, in the provision of services. Bergmann suggests that the implementation of contemporary technological capabilities could immediately reduce the market demand for human labor by as much as half. He further argues that such a massive technological displacement of work and workers, so often considered a social problem, is in fact the means whereby people might be freed at long last from the capitalist labor market. Structural unemployment of this type could allow sufficient time for substantial, creative, meaningful, and self-directed work projects, what Bergmann also calls "pursuits," or, simply, "new work."

Bergmann sees great significance in these ideas, which he means to forcefully convey. Invoking biblical and Athenian points of reference in what amounts to a sage's epic tale of humanity's self-becoming, this celebrant of modern technology often writes as a latterday Hegel:

> If we could really cut in half the clock-punching and spirit-breaking grind-work that many must still do, does this not . . . represent a quite astonishing achievement? Do not even the first pages of the Bible describe laboring "in the sweat of one's brow" as a penalty that was incurred for a transgression?
>
> Why then is . . . [our modern growth in technological capacity] not the long-awaited commuting of that sentence? Why do we not experience the fact that we can produced as much as or more than we did in the past, but now with only half the effort, as a liberation? Why can we not celebrate this triumph with months-long public festivals, as they would have in Athens?[14]

Bergmann also reaches for a Nietzscheian aura, as in *On Being Free*, where he teaches through the literary conceit of a Zarathrustraesque yoga instructor. Bergmann's is intentionally a utopian and idiosyncratic philosophy, exploring the aesthetic dimension of human existence through a myriad of unusual didactic literary forms. His is also a humanist philosophy of self and work, which, in the end, rests on a technologically determinist social theory. As a CNW flyer would later proclaim:

> New Technology comes toward us like a large wave: if we do nothing
> it could drown us, but if we move with intelligence and skill, the wave
> could lift us higher than we ever were before.[15]

In comparison to Professor Bergmann's efforts, Dr. Richard Gull's contribution to the founding of the CNW was of a more practical nature. Gull was then as he is today Professor of Philosophy at the University of Michigan's Flint campus. From this position he was able to greatly facilitate the translation of Bergmann's philosophy into Flint's particular experience with deindustrialization. Even though his own scholarship has diverged significantly from Bergmann's original formulations, Gull readily admits that he "grew up," intellectually at least, on Bergmann's work.[16] It was Gull's initial excitement with *On Being Free* that led him to invite Bergmann to Flint to give several videotaped public lectures on its themes. This coming together in the late 1970s eventually led him to join with Bergmann several years later as codirector of Flint's Center for New Work.

Before there was an actual standing "Center for New Work" to codirect, however, new work ideas first received a televised airing. During a 1980–1981 stint at the University of California at Santa Cruz, Bergmann produced a ten-part television series entitled "Culture after the Elimination of Labor." A year later, this series was broadcast on Michigan Public Television, with Bergmann hosting several community television discussions. This effort received an encouraging reception, and soon thereafter Bergmann decided to return to his University of Michigan post. He and Gull's close working relationship quickly resumed. Indeed, inspired by Bergmann's television successes, the CNW made its Flint debut with "Workers without Work: The Future of Labor and the Future of Flint," which aired in March 1984 on Flint public television.[17]

With over $18,000 in University of Michigan seed grants and locally donated space, the CNW finally opened its doors in Flint in November 1984. Bergmann's statement of purpose announced the center's arrival:

> The mission of the Center for New Work is to develop practical solutions to the present crisis in the world of work.[18]

Gull recalls the practical facets of the center's early years:

It wasn't a "center" in the sense that people could come there every day, like an office. But we had lunches there once a week, and we had events there. We began to formulate ideas for doing a television series called "The Future of Work." A lot of people from the union [UAW] came to the Center for New Work, including Dave Yettaw, and he got to know our ideas.

At that point we tried to figure . . . how were we going to make this go? How could we change things in Flint? The idea was, if you could do it in Flint, then you could do it anywhere. Flint was pretty hard hit, and it was obvious that you had to do something.[19]

Initially, the CNW organized several conferences: one in late 1984 and another in 1985. Another early project, noted by Gull, was the production of "The Future of Work," a Flint-based ten-part television series that introduces high-school and college-age students to New Work ideas. (This program aired in 1987, and remains available to the public through the University of Michigan–Flint.) In this period Gull also produced and hosted a local "New Work" radio program. Still, despite the extraordinary industry implied in such efforts, they were subordinate to the center's evolving goals.

As a CNW document entitled *Strategies for the Future* suggests:

The [CNW] project was initially designed to assist Flint during a time of dramatic change in the automotive industry. It has grown to encompass a much wider response to the crisis currently affecting the American worker and workplace.[20]

This "wider response" included: (1) development of "high school curriculum modules" to supplement the educational value of the "Future of Work" video series, which were piloted in Flint schools in 1986 and 1987; (2) "workplace implementation" consulting, which included especially the promotion of the CNW's "Six months/Six months" job rotation and job sharing plan (where workers would "work normal production schedules" for six months and be "freed from job responsibilities" the rest of the year); (3) "programs for the poor," including "strategies designed to assist the poor in becoming more self-providing through the use of new technologies," such as through the use of "a space-age 'foam' in innovative home building systems"; and (4) "research and development" for "new, practical productive responses to the crisis that faces American workers and employers."[21]

Of course, the CNW—based on the "most basic belief that every human being must do meaningful and serious work"—also envisioned and enumerated practical examples of the sort of labor that might fill the city's expanding job-free time.[22] The CNW clearly realized that "programs must be established

that will enable people to do *new work* in the hours that are cut."[23] In this
regard, the CNW proposed various "permanent self-education" and "community improvement" programs, as well as what they called "variable time entrepreneurship." This latter program was based on the idea that "there are plenty
of people in Flint who can start up businesses of their own," if only GM would
see its "responsibility . . . to help provide the venture capital that is needed. . . ."
Addressing itself to temporarily laid-off, and un- and under-employed workers, the CNW ultimately suggested that:

> Many workers could teach. They already do it now. Many could
> develop new inventions. Many could pursue a talent for writing or for
> painting or martial arts. Many could become consultants to farm
> communities in Third World countries that are now learning how to
> use machines, many could work with infants or aging [sic] and many
> more are needed to work with our youth.[24]

One thing was clear: the practical realization of these self-described "innovative
and ambitious projects" would require the committed support and financial
backing of Flint's dominant institutions, namely, GM, the UAW, and the
Charles Stewart Mott Foundation. There was initial reason for optimism.

With its 1984 founding the CNW immediately received an official affilia-
tion with the University of Michigan–Flint through the latter's "Project for
Urban and Regional Affairs," a university research bureau supported largely by
Charles Stewart Mott Foundation funding. The CNW also received a joint letter of endorsement signed by the heads of Flint's GMI Engineering & Management Institute, C. S. Mott Community College, and University of Michigan–
Flint.[25] And money did pour in. The CNW received $25,000 from Michigan's
Department of Commerce and an additional $60,000 from the Michigan
Department of Education. These sums appear substantial, but they were not
nearly enough; not nearly enough, for instance, to fund the center's proposed
quarter of a million dollar first-year budget.[26]

An "Advisory Council" was also formed to aid in the CNW's development,
and it counted among its number significant community leaders. Local 599's
Dave Yettaw served on this council. He was joined by such unlikely partners as
Paul D. Newman, director of labor relations for the Flint-headquartered General Motors AC Spark Plug Division, and Don Peters of the Flint Area Chamber
of Commerce. This council helped attract significant attention for New Work
ideas. For example, UAW President Owen Bieber stated that: "in a number of
respects, we're in agreement [with Bergmann] on where we think things are
going in the long range"; a former AC Spark Plug General Manager agreed, saying: "[The center's] ideas may well represent the direction in which we should
be moving"; the Co-Director of UAW Region 1-C and its current Director, said:
"[The center's] ideas are revolutionary, but that's what we need"; the UAW

Region 1-C Director and current UAW Vice President Stan Marshall lent his support by appearing in "The Future of Work" videos; then-President of UAW Local 599 Fred Meyers and then-Education Director Yettaw requested funding for the CNW from Don Ephlin, the UAW Vice President for General Motors.[27] Also, the UAW "approved" a $50,000 grant that was meant to provide the CNW leverage with other funding sources (but which itself was never actually dispersed).

Bergmann and Gull were themselves fairly bold in their attempt to cultivate local recognition and support. In June of 1984, for example, the two achieved a degree of local notoriety when they coauthored an Op-Ed piece in the *Flint Journal* that addressed the volatile issue of unemployment and overtime work in the area's auto industry.[28] This particular debate was sparked by a vote at Local 599 on whether to cede overtime pay and agree to a four-day, ten-hour-per-day work schedule so that 1,700 laid-off workers could be recalled at Flint's Buick complex. The plan was rejected, and many in the community concluded that this result stemmed from worker greed overriding union solidarity. Flint's autotown philosophers weighed in on the side of the workers, arguing that management had not given Buick's workers reasonable assurances of job security and that the workers were thus justified in their reluctance to accept pay losses to make gains in active union membership. Bergmann and Gull supported the UAW's call for "a shorter week, earlier retirement, and job security," as this meshed with the CNW's emphasis on collectively sharing both a reduced amount of paid work and *increased* opportunity for new work. They concluded by lecturing GM: "if in some fashion an increase of security could have been offered in exchange for fewer hours of overtime, the outcome [of the vote] might not have been the same."[29] Their moxie motivated one *Flint Journal* reader to write to the editor: "My God, GM public relations doesn't control the news media after all. Our side is being told."[30]

Yet, these successes notwithstanding, the fatal blow for the CNW's organizational efforts came in 1988. After a year of extensive negotiation with executives at the GM Willow Run factory in Ypsilanti, Michigan, local management decided against implementing New Work programs.[31] GM's support—even for only a trial period at a single facility—would have meant a great deal. The CNW had tried to walk a fine line between GM and the UAW, appealing to "win/win" or mutually beneficial strategies, but never ultimately to either side's satisfaction. The frustration this caused remained evident in Gull's recollection of the Willow Run decision four years later:

> [I knew] this was going to turn into a gigantic failure, that [the GM management was] going to just jack us off, bullshit us all the way, and I saw that a year before Frithjof did.[32]

There were additional meetings and further attempts to secure funding, but after five years of struggling for a tangible vote of confidence, and despite initial funding, endorsements, and local notoriety, the end for the Center for New Work had come.

Compared to the grand scale of the CNW's initial ambitions, new work ideas are today a slight presence in Flint, regularly renewed only through Professor Gull's scholarship and instruction and the continued distribution of "The Future of Work" video series.[33] Analysis and criticism of the center's postindustrialist ideology remains, however, an important task: What better place than in Flint to reveal postindustrial ideology's internal theoretical and political contradictions?; What better way than through critical explication of the CNW's practical intervention?

CENTER FOR NEW WORK IDEOLOGY

In his 1987 front-page *Detroit Free Press* article entitled "Brave New Work," James Ricci captures the optimistic spirit of New Work ideology's historical dimension:

> Through his philosopher's eyes, Frithjof Bergmann looks at the economic gloom over suffering Flint and sees the dawn glimmerings of a new phase in human history.
>
> In the tradition of seers of new light, he has been working tirelessly to get Flintites and, by extension, everyone in industrial America, to look up from their despond and read the skies.[34]

As this characterization suggests, New Work ideology conceives history as epic and the future bright with utopian possibilities. Indeed, with the coming of postindustrial technology, the dawning of a richer human freedom is at hand, if only we could see it.

Note Bergmann's own scholarly formulation, as presented in his 1983 *Praxis International* article:

> At the moment we have no picture of a future—certainly we do not have an image of a more attractive, better, maybe even nobler social order that we could aim for, for which it would make sense to exert ourselves, let alone to struggle. One by one, like lights, the visions have gone out.
>
> The intellectual failure to invent and to conceptualize a worked-out alternative undercuts the very possibility of any opposition. Coercion need no longer be invoked. Everyone will go along, for a really different course has not even been imagined.

Naturally this also has its other side: if this intellectual lapse has momentous consequences then the urgency to repair it is proportionately great. This could thus also be a long-awaited crack in a closed door, especially for those who are still haunted by the ineffectuality of mere words: for the present also might be one of the in-estimately rare occasions where the mere thinking—or writing—of something could by itself alter the configuration of the mundane world: for as soon as an alternative were even just invented—it would exist.[35]

Bergmann suggests that mere words, thinking, and writing—that is, mere intellectual invention—could on their own "alter the configuration of the mundane world." This mundane world is important because it is here, among those enslaved in a nine-to–five workaday existence, that "alternatives" are needed that could animate a mass society and culture gone sour on itself.

Gull agrees. His "imaginative utopian thinking" is needed to reveal the immanent possibilities of contemporary technology. The path toward the new work utopia must be demystified by positing, in the first place, a viable utopia. Gull argues that it is essential for utopian consciousness to battle the fearful and sometimes reactionary inertia that haunts modern mass culture. This is why he also sees imaginative utopian thinking as a type of "revolution from the top."[36]

The steps in New Work's historical reasoning are recapitulated by the following (admittedly, mildly sardonic) if-then statements: If utopia is a state in which freedom would reign, and if freedom requires liberation from coerced labor, and if postindustrial technology could serve precisely this purpose, then utopia is a postindustrial society. If the material force of history is technological development, and if technological development is assumed an autonomous, progressive, and rational force, and if culture hinders technological development, then History is an epic battle between technology and irrational stasis rooted in culture's "mundane world." If an outdated industrial culture stands between utopia missed and utopia realized, and if such a "mundane world" is susceptible to "imaginative utopian thinking," and if Flint is a nearby exaggeration of such a world, then one must go to Flint and disabuse the people there of their industrial self-consciousness in order to fill up their heads with the mythos of a technological utopia.

The CNW's utopian futurism stands in sharp contrast to the more common pessimistic characterizations of late twentieth-century historical consciousness, so much so, in fact, that it is instructive to juxtapose them. Sloterdijk's provocative historical analysis provides a representative contrast. In his *Critique of Cynical Reason*, he writes:

since the technical atrocities of the twentieth century, from Verdun to the Gulag, from Aushwitz to Hiroshima, experience scorns all optimism. Historical consciousness and pessimism seem to amount to the same thing. And the catastrophes that have not yet happened, which are waiting in the wings, nurture the ever-present doubts about civilization. The late twentieth century rides on a wave of negative futurism. "The worst was already expected," it just has "not yet" happened.[37]

Bergmann, as we have seen, must disagree that "historical consciousness and pessimism ... amount to the same thing"; to any such so-called negative futurism, he responds:

> The last 200 years represented perhaps only a transition or rather a tooling-up period—which are notoriously wasteful and cumbersome—but now that full-grown technology has finally arrived there is no presumption whatsoever that forty hours of every week for forty-five years of everybody's life would be filled by a job.[38]

Where Sloterdijk describes concrete historical experiences, Bergmann's idealist dialectic requires that he speak only of a "tooling-up period"; where Sloterdijk notes "technical atrocities," Bergmann's submission to technological determinism allows only him to bear witness to an ultimately glorious (if initially "wasteful and cumbersome") arrival of a "full-grown technology." Ignoring Marx's previous intervention, Bergmann again rights Hegel so that new work Ideas may blithely step over the body of twentieth-century history.

The CNW's conceptualization of history is thus so constructed to meet its overwhelming concern with the utopian future, this, at the expense of empirical or experienced history. The notion that Flint—Flint!—was "*ahead* of the rest of the country" underscores the CNW's airy futurism. This aspect of its ideology led the CNW to disregard Flint's past as anything other than an obstacle to the realization of its postindustrial future. By positing a history that is rooted in a utopian future, Bergmann could reverse the signs of Flint's experience with a deindustrializing "negative futurism," at least in the realm of mere words. The CNW's program represented an attempt to do the same in practice. But Flint's overwhelming facticity as an industrial city proved too recalcitrant a reality: the CNW's immaculate postindustrial promise was itself never real enough to overcome the reverberating din of disbelief and dismissal caused by its initially having had the "intelligence" to dub unemployment "job-free time."

That New Work ideology conceived itself an intelligent response to Flint's deindustrialization also suggests much about its own reflexive self-understanding. In effect, the CNW project rearticulated liberal values in a posited postindustrial context.[39] Premised upon a self-referential social analytic that projected academic life onto a utopian plane, New Work ideology called for, not Economic Man *as such*, but the apparent contemporary counterpart, Post-

Industrial Man. New Work's intelligent response was further rooted in a rationalist bias for value-neutrality, realism, and dialectical insight.

The Enlightenment's liberalism was above all concerned with the individual: individual freedom and autonomy are posited as humanity's highest values. The individual in the Age of Reason was the true and highest seat of Reason, even as it was recognized that the realization of free and autonomous individuality was premised on and constrained by various social conditions. For Locke, these conditions were defined primarily in terms of the ownership of private property. For Smith, the ownership of property provided adequately for the community of individuals only when properly mobilized within a freely competitive market economy. For Rousseau, there was the matter of a social contract; for Hobbes, the state. While the valuation of the inherently reasonable individual focused their common ground, debate over the social conditions that would best provide for autonomous, rational individuals divided classical liberal theorists.

New Work's contemporary version of liberalism—what might be called its "technoliberalism"—is also infused with the value of individual autonomy and freedom. The CNW, after all, was premised on the belief that the advent of postindustrial technology makes possible the sociohistorical realization of individual freedom and autonomy, if only we are prepared to exploit this situation to pursue—through "new work"—our inner freedom. "Technology comes at us like a large wave." Will we sink or swim?

Enter education. If New Work's utopian society is an aggregation of individuals pursuing intrinsically meaningful "pursuits," then what would constitute intrinsically meaningful work? How does one know what one "*really* wants to do"? In this regard, the CNW's many educational programs paid special attention to high school-level education, where an inner life full of creative and sophisticated desire might reasonably, if given the chance, be nurtured. "The Future of Work" video series, for example, included a lengthy session in which Flint area students discuss the future of work and the challenges posed to their generation by postindustrial society. Bergmann and Gull stress three points to this audience, one as a threat, another as wise counsel, and the last as a prophecy.

First, the threat. In his most professorial, Moseslike Austrian accent, Bergmann assures these students:

> People really have to get into their heads that lack of education from
> here on in will mean poverty. And the only way you can have any kind
> of assurance of some decent standard of living is with education.[40]

If postindustrial jobs require ever more extensive formal education, failure or even low-level educational achievement means condemnation to material poverty. Dramatizing this point, Gull and Bergmann enlist the help of these students in naming jobs that will be eliminated as a result of technological innovation. The narrator concludes:

> With a little research and a little imagination, these students have eliminated a lot of jobs, possibly even their jobs. This group is aware of the ramifications and are thinking toward the future. They're looking for challenging careers and seeking the correct path.[41]

"Possibly even *their* jobs" drives home the motivation for seeking "*the* correct path."

Second, the counsel: obtain the *correct type* of education. As Bergmann pleaded to these students:

> Above all, get an education that teaches you a kind of imagination, a kind of flexibility, a kind of intuitive sense, that teaches you how to adjust to new situations.[42]

In other words, in a postindustrial world filled with flexible manufacturing, demands for quickly changing skills and styles, and floods of over-information, an autonomous existence requires "a kind of flexibility," or a kind of plasticity. This type of self is nurtured through traditional "liberal education," which, once acquired, allows the broadly educated to perpetually float from one specific job and even from one occupational or professional category to another.

Third, the CNW's end-of-work-as-we-know-it prophecy. Bergmann, again, took the honors:

> The whole age of jobs is slowly coming to a close. The way people talk about sunset industries? Jobs are sort of in a sunset condition.[43]

Bergmann suggested to these (apparently not the least incredulous) students that, within their lifetimes, there may be no paid work at all. They must therefore prepare themselves for some type of "mission" or "calling."[44] Bergmann promises these students a kind of spirited vanguard status as the first members of a humanity that at long last will get to do what it *really* wants to do. Overall, then, these students were given fair warning: prepare your inner selves for the job-free time that will follow inevitable technological advance; in this task, failure means material *and* spiritual poverty.

The essential meaning of New Work ideology revolves around this sink-or-swim dynamic. The notion that new technology "could *lift us higher* than we ever were before" stipulates that postindustrial technology provides the basis upon which humanity could yet realize its liberal values. Bergmann's philosophy of freedom supplies the second part of this formula. In shifting the focus from "the outside of a person to the inside," his humanistic approach counsels self-actualization via new work. Bergmann has stated:

> People get the idea I'm in favor of working less, and I'm not. Most people get their greatest satisfaction out of their work.
> I would look forward to a society in which everybody does fulfilling, satisfying, and socially useful work, and gets paid for it.[45]

The CNW's programs thus stress the attainment of autonomous "self-sufficiency" in the pursuit of "meaningful and serious work." Between humanistic philosophy and technological determinism there lies technoliberalism.

Interestingly, Bergmann's and Gull's own self-conception as intellectuals speaks to these liberal orientations. As professional philosophers, they are free from the mundane world of work inasmuch as technology has already liberated them from the fields, the factories, and, to a large extent (i.e., when not teaching their university students), from the service sector as well. In their studies, they already do, so to speak, what they "really want to do."

Moreover, *what* they do—imaginative utopian thinking—is considered of cultural significance. In their homage to the power of the Word, Gull advocates for revolutions from "the top" while Bergmann is optimistic that "as soon as an alternative were just invented—it would exist." New Work's intellectual practice was essentially designed to bring their world—the academic world of sabbaticals, grants, and the free pursuit of ostensibly meaningful projects—to the mundane world. In this sense, their conception of *themselves* was that of a vanguard: not only do they have the power to make the future for others, they also see it in their mirror. The academic-philosopher lifestyle emerges as the model for "Post-Industrial Man," as the epitome of technoliberal freedom.

There is a not-so-latent elitism implicit in this aspect of New Work's postindustrial ideology. The proposed development of a "kind of intuitive sense" needed for true new work tends to privilege abstract intellect over sentient skills,[46] intelligent consumption over muscular production, even reflective inwardness over expressive display. If in the immanent postindustrial future we are all to live Plato's examined lives, then those presently who generally do not—industrial auto workers?—represent an obstacle to our collective transformation.

In this regard, note a telling set of interactions between an older auto worker and members of a Bergmann-led discussion group, abstracted from a scene in the last of the ten-part "Future of Work" video series. After nearly forty-five minutes of discussion, the auto worker began speaking in a slow and depressed tone:

> I see this issue as more far-reaching than education or advanced technology. . . . I think it's an outgrowth of our whole Western cul-

tural heritage. And so it's appropriate that the Philosophy Department is dealing with this issue.

It's something to robotize the manufacturing process, but men and women were robotized all along in this process. And the educational system has been an automation; they've been captured by the technology and the economic-social system that we live in. So it's sort of futile to talk about reeducating people when the educational system under which we're doing it is sort of a robot to begin with.

And so I think it's a religious issue also. I mean, the Protestant work ethic: we think that it's sinful to not work . . . to just loll away the time without doing anything that's productive in an economic, monetary sense. . . . So, maybe we should become more philosophic and realize that education isn't going to help us alone. Economic structures—like large corporations—are not going to help us. The media is not going to help us. We have to begin with ourselves, I think.

And so maybe what we should do is try to encourage each other as individuals to read. One of my favorite philosophers is Friedrich Nietzsche.

Soon after introducing Nietzsche to the conversation, the auto worker is interrupted by an apparently irritated participant. The following interaction ensued:

SPEAKER 1   What does Nietzsche say to you on this kind of an issue?

SPEAKER 2   In what sense? You mean in a religious context?

SPEAKER 1   I mean in terms of restructuring work? In our attitudes toward it?

SPEAKER 2   I think Nietzsche would say that we need to be free from our religious biases, for one thing. I think that he would encourage us to rid ourselves of the past—of past traditions—to become artists in the sense that we're willing to explore and transcend our own culture. And it takes a lot of courage to deny those social values that we live by.

The auto worker is again interrupted, this time by Dr. Bergmann, the student of the renown Nietzsche scholar Walter Kaufmann. Clearly agitated and taken aback by what he is hearing, Bergmann is anxious to refocus the discussion:

I certainly sympathize with the profile. I have tremendous (stop, lengthy pause).

I think that somebody listening to us would say: "Okay, great, wonderful, people should be artists about their life." But how does that relate to people? As [another participant] was saying, "walk around this block, on this block you can see ten houses, just on this block, that are boarded-up." How does what we're talking about relate to people who are really poor, who are really down, who are really depressed?

At this point, the conversation moved on—as if spurred by a sudden release of repressed energy—to discussion of previously ignored but essential topics, including a frank if tacit acknowledgment of the relative powerlessness of as small an organization as the "Center for New Work" vis-a-vis corporate America.

From the perspective of Gull and Bergmann's self-conception as academic philosophers engaged in social reform, this impromptu and evidently unplanned role reversal—the auto worker cites Nietzsche and recalls the significance of the Protestant ethic, and the philosopher demands that attention be directed to immediate, local, and pragmatic concerns, as in Bergmann's "this block" refrain—suggests that the CNW founders were more interested in maintaining status boundaries than in empowering those considered in need of an "intelligent response."

The CNW's intelligent self-understanding is first rooted in its posited disinterestedness in the pursuit of truth, a liberal virtue. The Center for New Work billed itself to the community as an objective observer, armed with a "win/win" vision of what needed doing that transcended all vested interests. Furthermore, as Flint's postindustrialization was considered inevitable, CNW ideology was intelligent precisely because it counseled the use of "skill and intelligence" in the project of adaptation to an inescapable future. As Gull saw it: "Flint was an amazing, amazing study in denial."[47] Against denial, New Work ideology presented social facts as social fate. Where others saw only the obvious signs of decline in Flint, the CNW turned disaster into utopia through dialectical insight: because of its severe decline, Flint could be a "model" in the "advance of the rest of the country"; because of its massive unemployment, more of Flint's citizens could take advantage of their job-free time to pursue self-actualization; the more the United States deindustrialized, the more it neared its postindustrial utopia, and so forth. "In the tradition of seers of new light," the Center for New Work could turn water into wine. New Work's response was self-consciously intelligent, then, because its ideology was deemed superior to that articulated by those actually living in Flint. New Work's identity, as a whole, then, was rationalist: ideas were assumed powerful enough to overcome irrational short-term interests, denial, and mundane social reality. Since the CNW was established and directed by career philosophers, perhaps these qualities are not very surprising.

The CNW's ideology also conceptualized social structure. For Bergmann and Gull, two essential social relationships determine a society's structure: on the one hand, autonomous, rational, and progressive technology determines the means of production; and, on the other, visionary intellectuals battle social inertia and cultural reaction to determine the relations of social production. As in a crude cartoon form of Marxism, crisis occurs when the social relations of production fetter the potential development of the means of production. CNW ideology suggests that the crisis in Flint is exacerbated by the community's denial of the fundamental changes in technology that have altered the means of production, particularly in automobile manufacturing. The most significant change, of course, is the technological displacement of human labor. Since Flint's social relations depend upon its industrial working class, the future well being of the city is imperiled.

Four main ideological results follow from the CNW conceptualization of social structure: dependency relations are assumed; deindustrialization is not theorized as such; crisis tendencies are depoliticized; and blame for Flint's social crisis is placed on the shoulders of Flint's citizens. New Work ideology paints a picture of a social process that might be called "dependent *postindustrialization*," as opposed to dependent deindustrialization, and the CNW's practical intervention may be seen as a response to the question, What is to be done with the surplus people made redundant by postindustrial technology?

In CNW ideology, dependency relations are not seen as *capitalist* dependency relations: the CNW did not directly address itself to class relations, property relations, nor Flint's dependency on private capitalist investment. Rather, dependency is cast first and foremost as a relationship between people and the autonomous, rational, and progressive force of technology. This technological determinism means that the practical mechanisms and choices that lie behind the *social* development and deployment of technology are concealed from thought.[48] Capitalist dependency relationships, however, *are* tacitly recognized in New Work's assumption that a capitalist labor market will continue to operate in a postindustrial society, thus requiring that "new work" be heavily supplemented with "old work" (e.g., "variable-time entrepreneurship") to earn life-sustaining wages. Furthermore, the private ownership of capital and the system of production for private profits are also assumed as key facets of a postindustrial society inasmuch as the CNW appeals to capitalist self-interest in its solicitations for New Work projects. In tacit recognition and acceptance of societal dependency upon privately held wealth and power, the CNW repeatedly told General Motors, for example, that new work programs would

> give people security and hope. That would improve the quality of their work and that in turn would improve the quality of the cars made. The company would be more competitive, and the workers would have a higher standard of living.[49]

It was further emphasized that a fully instituted New Work program would eliminate worker resistance to labor-displacing technological innovation in the workplace, as well as eliminate the rationale for "built-in obsolescence" since the unimpeded application of technology could result in higher quality products that could so successfully dominate foreign markets as to escape the problem of domestic market saturation. Bergmann adopts the perspective of corporate management when he writes of "better morale, fewer burn-outs, greater flexibility in relation to one's personnel during high and low work seasons, and more of the like."[50] He is unafraid to raise the specter of fascism (describing the "'South Americanization' of the United States," for example) when discussing the political implications of sustained massive unemployment and Third World levels of inequality.[51] Political crisis and the deterioration of the physical and social infrastructure are clearly not, on the whole, good for business. There is an additional implicit dependency relationship worth noting in New Work ideology. CNW ideology assumed that their intelligent response to Flint's deindustrialization was needed; a similar organic response from within Flint was apparently seen as unlikely. In this way, local actors were assumed dependent upon extrinsic intellectual enlightenment, as in Gull's "revolution from the top."

In New Work ideology, major sociohistorical periods are conceived in terms of the changing dominant technical means of production (e.g., agricultural, industrial, postindustrial society), allowing the significance of *relations of production* to fall by the wayside. The notion of "deindustrialization" is thus essentially irrelevant to New Work's concerns, as this concept calls special attention to capitalist interests and disinvestment decisions as structured within the power relations of a global capitalist economic system. A legion of theoretical and empirical lacunae result from New Work's assumptions. The CNW ideology virtually ignores, for instance, both the globalization of production and the international division of labor. While it recognized that the unimpeded incorporation of new technologies into the system of production could help domestic firms compete in international markets, the multinationalization of "domestic" firms was never addressed. During the same time that GM reduced its Flint work force by over 30,000, it also established over thirty-eight production facilities in Mexico, and became Mexico's single largest private employer. Members of GM's Mexican work force are paid, not surprisingly, substantially less than their American counterparts, even though both contribute in essentially equal terms to the corporation's productivity. While New Work ideology cited a concern with the "South Americanization" of North America, it was not equally concerned with the reverse process, nor the systematic capitalist relationships that lie behind such processes.

Both the deindustrialization and postindustrialization models recognize the existence of a social crisis in America's industrial heartland. As a result of their differences in perspective, however, the former directs responsibility onto the capitalist economic system, while the latter directs blame onto the clash between the immaculate development of technology—which, of course, cannot really be blamed at all—and those affected by its posited irresistible force.

In the case of Flint, CNW ideology implicitly pins responsibility for the city's decline on the citizens themselves for not being willing to adapt to technological change. It is *people*, after all, who must adapt or be drowned. Failure to adapt is attributed to "decadence" and "denial."

Although intellectual "ideas" are assumed to have the power to reconfigure the "mundane world," the CNW ideology implicitly recognizes that this power is not necessarily sufficient to overcome countervailing forms of societal inertia. This is recognized only *implicitly* because, for example, Gull holds out the possibility that the ideas in question are simply not refined and detailed enough; perhaps, after further intellectual work, they will be powerful enough to spur cultural change. Gull also suggests, however, that grand ideas may not be useful at all if the members of a society are not even mature enough to carry out the most simple and obvious beneficial changes.

The Center for New Work attempted to address America's dependent postindustrialization. That Flint was the home of many thousands of newly redundant people made it an attractive site in which to engage in a New Work reeducation program. These now technologically superfluous people—the former core of America's industrial working class—were recast as vanguard members of what would inevitably become a nationwide surplus population. Whereas Marx might have called this proletarian group the "reserve army of the unemployed," New Work ideology saw them simply as having been freed from job servitude, and thereby enriched with loads of job-free time.

NOTES

1. Interview 10b, August 2, 1991.

2. "Brave New Work," *Detroit Free Press*, 18 January 1987, Sec. A, p. 1.

3. Josie Kearns, *Life after the Line* (Detroit: Wayne State University Press, 1990), p. 12.

4. *New Work Ideas* (document source, c. 1984), p. 1.

5. Alice Garrison, "Autotown Philosophers: Seeking to Make the Leisure Class a Reality" (document source, c. 1984), produced by the Office of University Relations and Development, The University of Michigan–Flint.

6. Ibid., p. 2.

7. Frithjof Bergmann, *On Being Free* (Notre Dame: University of Notre Dame Press, 1977).

8. Ibid., pp. 37–38.

9. Ibid., p. 39, emphasis in text.

10. Ibid., p. 37.

11. Ibid.

12. "Brave New Work," p. 1, emphasis in original. Bergmann's use of the gendered pronoun *he* has been replaced in this quotation with *one*. Also see *On Being Free*, pp. 177–230.

13. Frithjof Bergmann, "The Future of Work," in *Praxis International* 3 (October, 1983): pp. 308–323, 311.

14. Ibid., pp. 308–309.

15. *Center for New Work: Strategies for the Future* (document source, c. 1988).

16. Gull eventually questioned Bergmann's conceptualization of technology and "new work." In addition, with Richard Rorty, he has also questioned the meaning of philosophy itself, especially for a viable, holistic social theory. In Interview 10a, July 19, 1991, Gull stated: "Forget all these huge ideas, and, in some sense, let's keep this sort of obvious and small, and do it. There may be a lot of theoretical power behind an idea, [but] it doesn't help very much." Gull continued: "Frithjof used to talk about Hegel in Flint, and, I think, philosophically, that's very interesting, but, practically, [it's] deadly." See Richard Rorty, *Contingency, Irony, and Solidarity* (Cambridge: Cambridge University Press, 1989), and Interview 10b, August 2, 1991.

17. "Press Release," WFUM Channel 28, Public Television of The University of Michigan–Flint (document source, February 20, 1984).

18. *Center for New Work: Strategies for the Future* (document source, c. 1988).

19. Interview 10a, July 19, 1991.

20. *Center for New Work: Strategies for the Future.* Note that the approximate date of this document was confirmed by Dr. Gull (Interview 10a, July 19, 1991).

21. See *Center for New Work: Strategies for the Future.*

22. "The New Work Ideas."

23. Ibid., emphasis in original.

24. Ibid.

25. An "open letter" from Clinton B. Jones, chancellor, the University of Michigan–Flint, William B. Cottingham, president, GMI Engineering & Management Institute, and Robert N. Rue, president, C. S. Mott Community College, 27 November 1984 (document source), "to endorse the proposal for a NEW WORK CENTER by Professors Frithjof Bergmann and Richard Gull."

26. "Brave New Work"; an "open letter" from Frithjof Bergmann and Richard Gull, 24 May 1984 (document source); and "Proposal for a New Work Center" (document source, c. 1984), including "First Year Budget," which details proposed expenses for $237,950.

27. "Brave New Work"; *Center for New Work: Strategies for the Future,* "The Future of Work" video series; letter from Fred Meyer, president, and Dave Yettaw, education director, UAW Local 599, to Donald Ephlin, vice president, International Union UAW, 16 November 1984 (document source).

28. "That Buick Vote: Reasons Many for Rejection of Proposal to Recall 1,700," *The Flint Journal,* 17 June 1984, Sec. E, pp. 1, 5.

29. Ibid.

30. Dan Davis, "Buick Vote Article Overdue," *The Flint Journal,* 24 June 1984 (document source).

31. Interview 10b, August 2, 1991.

32. Ibid. As reasons for the center's ultimate demise, Professor Gull also emphasizes that "people weren't ready to change because they didn't think the downturn was permanent." "What stopped us," he continues, "was a reluctance to do anything new." In addition, Gull progressively became disillusioned with Bergmann's original philosophical and theoretical vision for the center's activities. Both of these issues are further discussed below.

33. See, for example, Richard Gull, "New Work, Leisure, and Decadence," in *Leisure and Ethics* (mimeograph source) pp. 117–139. Professor Gull's regularly offered course "Philosophy of Work and Economic Freedom" helps to maintain the presence of CNW ideas in the community. "The Future of Work" is available through the University of Michigan–Flint's Project for Urban and Regional Affairs (PURA).

34. "Brave New Work," p. 1.

35. "The Future of Work," p. 308.

36. As Gull says, "sometimes, I think, as Aristotle said, people have a tendency to live like cows, meaning that there's a kind of stagnancy that sets in. . . . I think it's a fear of modernism, a clinging to a kind of fundamentalism, an unwillingness to change very much, to do something about these large disasters that keep happening." Interview 10a, July 19, 1991. Gull also cites approvingly the notion of "decadence" developed by Lawrence Haworth in his book *Decadence & Objectivity* (Toronto: University of Toronto Press, 1977), where Haworth states: "A decadent person is one who lacks an animating vision of an ideal state of affairs. . . . In this sense most people are decadent: they live largely in private spheres and value the public domain for the contribution it makes toward enhancing their private lives" (p. 3).

37. Peter Sloterdijk, *Critique of Cynical Reason* (Minneapolis: University of Minnesota Press, 1987), pp. 11–12.

38. "The Future of Work," pp. 310–311.

39. See Jean-Francois Lyotard, *The Postmodern Condition: A Report on Knowledge* (Minneapolis, MN: The University of Minnesota Press, 1984). Also helpful has been Maude Falcone, "Habermas and Lyotard on Legitimation Crisis," an unpublished manuscript that develops the idea of a "technoliberalism" as a legitimating ideology for contemporary times.

40. "The Future of Work" (1987), video tape program 108.

41. Ibid., program 104.

42. Ibid., program 108.

43. Ibid.

44. Ibid., program 109.

45. "Brave New Work," p. 1.

46. This notion is from Shoshana Zuboff, *The Age of the Smart Machine* (New York: Basic Books, 1988). For competing visions, see Harry Braverman, *Labor and Monopoly Capital* (New York: Monthly Review Press, 1974) and Robert Howard, *Brave New Workplace* (New York: Penguin Books, 1985).

47. Interview 10a, July 19, 1991.

48. Richard Gull later found this aspect of New Work ideology disturbing. Interview 10a, July 19, 1991.

49. *New Work Ideas,* p. 2.

50. "The Future of Work," pp. 321–322.

51. Ibid., pp. 314–315.

Chapter 3

NEW COMPETITORS

This is where labor stands: there are labor leaders who are running labor unions, most of them along the main drift; there are left intellectuals who are not running labor unions, but who think they know how to run them against the main drift; and there are wage workers who are disgruntled and ready to do what must be done. It is the task of the labor leaders to allow and to initiate a union of the power and the intellect. They are the only ones who can do it; that is why they are now the strategic elite in American society. Never has so much depended upon men who are so ill prepared and so little inclined to assume the responsibility.

—C. Wright Mills,
The New Men of Power[1]

The UAW, and organized labor as a whole for that matter, has taken some hard cracks from big business and big government. [This] has a tendency to force us to focus on our immediate needs and our immediate survival versus long term, whereas, in better times, when things were going better for organized labor, we had the opportunity to look long term and set some objective goals for the future. But when they put the crunch on you and things are impacting you *now*, you don't have that luxury.

—Dennis Carl,
Education Director, UAW Local 599[2]

I see the purpose of PEL as awakening the membership to reality.

—Ken Scott,
Shop Committee Chairman, UAW Local 599[3]

In order to survive, one has to attend the school of reality.

—Peter Sloterdijk,
The Critique of Cynical Reason[4]

Local Paid Educational Leave (Local PEL) is Flint's latest "school of reality." This joint UAW/GM program is a week-long educational forum that introduces GM's middle to lower management and union employees to the history, economics, politics, and sociology of the U.S. automobile industry. The Local PEL program is a condensed version of the four-week National PEL program designed exclusively for senior company and union officials by leading American scholars. The National PEL program began in 1985, and the Local PEL programs followed a year thereafter. By 1991, over seventy Local PELs were in operation nationally, three of these in Flint. Indeed, it is projected that every willing Flint area GM employee will eventually graduate from a Local PEL program.

The Local PEL program represents another ideological enigma in Flint's exaggerated experience with deindustrialization. For Flint's mainstream labor leaders, the luxury of Mills' main drift has long since vanished. The Local PEL program helps these leaders exorcise the spirits of both Flint's mythic past and future mythos in favor of forcing attention to the very present-oriented aspects of strategic planning. In between the redemption of the labor movement and technoliberal rationalism, Local PEL inserts an ethos of organizational survival. Instead of deindustrializing or even postindustrializing society, Local PEL sees only a hostile "environment" filled with "new competitors." Together, these qualities represents a perilous collaboration with a new sort of main drift, one that poses serious questions concerning the long-term viability of America's industrial institutions.

LOCAL PEL IN FLINT

Harry Katz calls it "shifting gears."[5] U.S. industrial relations are shifting gears, and the UAW/GM Local PEL program plays an important role in this transformation. Not itself a reform of workplace organization or of collective bargaining arrangements, nor even a structural reform that directly links workplace organization to business strategy, Local PEL is best understood as a type of educational grease gun for these and similar changes in America's industrial relations. Given that UAW/GM industrial relations have historically been trend setting, the development of Local PEL takes on added importance.

Local PEL is a "joint program," which means that it is financially supported and administered by both the company and the union. GM and the UAW have many joint programs, but Local PEL stands out for four significant reasons. Local PEL is an open educational forum without any specific training objectives. In a sense, Local PEL offers week-long fellowships to management and union employees for the sole purpose of educational attainment. Local PEL is also designed as a mass program intended to include *all* interested employees. In addition, Local PEL involves the "third party" participation of academics, including both the scholars who created the National and Local PEL syllabuses as well as the local academics who are paid as Local PEL instructors. Lastly, Local PEL's supporters conceptualize this program as being in direct contrast to the first generation of joint programs that emerged out of the "Quality of Work Life Movement" that swept through America's industrial relations in the 1970s and 1980s. Local PEL is touted as a new, "new beginning" for union/company relations. Closer examination of these factors places Local PEL in the context of cutting edge developments in America's industrial relations.

Local PEL is not only perceived as an advance over the now relatively unpopular joint reform efforts associated with the Quality of Worklife Movement, it is, in fact, a type of last-ditch effort to save the concept of company/union jointness altogether. Broadly defined as cooperation in the pursuit of common interests, "jointness" has been a part of auto industry industrial relations since the early 1970s, when depressed economic conditions, worker dissatisfaction, increasingly aggressive and successful foreign competition, and a host of other similarly dubious developments, encouraged the perception on the part of both the mainstream union and the company that a more cooperative and constructive relationship was desirable and needed.[6] The most well known of these early efforts—Quality of Work Life or, simply, QWL—was supposed to increase the average worker's sense of belonging and responsibility by encouraging their participation in shop-floor decision making. It was thought that this would benefit the company's bottom line through increasing product quality and productivity, whereas union officials expected improved working conditions and the job security promised by the perpetual retraining of the work force to keep pace with the introduction of new production technologies. As in so many other respects, Flint was in the vanguard of this program.

First negotiated in 1973 with the strong backing of Irving Bluestone, the UAW Vice President for GM, the QWL program quickly found its way to Flint's increasingly desperate auto industry. For example, according to Ronald Edsforth, UAW employment at Flint's Buick complex had by 1975 fallen by nearly two-thirds from its postwar peak. At the behest of Buick's general manager, UAW Local 599 president Al Christner began instituting the QWL program at various factory sites. Still described today by mainstream Local 599 leadership as a "visionary," Christner and Buick management vigorously pursued the implementation of QWL, gaining substantial support from the once relatively militant Local 599 membership. The Buick program was "the first of its kind at General Motors."[7]

Yet, neither the motivation coming from the threat of continued increases in unemployment nor the prestige gained from being out in front with this innovative program were enough to prevent Local 599's membership from souring on the QWL Movement by 1984. This change of heart resulted from the perception that corporate management had gained undue control over the QWL programs to the detriment of the unionized work force, a feeling that was

only intensified with the wide-spread layoffs and announced plant closings in
Flint during the early 1980s recession. Edsforth describes these developments:

> As rank-and-file discontent rose throughout Flint in the fall of 1984,
> unhappy Buick workers voted Local 599 President Christner out of
> office. Four other local union presidents, who had been involved in
> starting QWL experiments, suffered a similar fate in the same elec-
> tions.[8]

Since the mid-1980s, QWL has lost much of its symbolic value as the promise
of true company/union jointness.

When asked to compare Local PEL to the early QWL Movement, John
Grimes, UAW Region 1-C Education Director, stated:

> This PEL program, in my opinion, is probably the best thing we've
> done in a long time because it's not what I call "warm and fuzzies." I
> used to go out and do these Quality of Work Life [programs], which
> was the first phase of jointness, and I never understood why I had to
> go out and teach a supervisor how to say "good morning." That baf-
> fles me. I never understood that. Still don't.[9]

When Grimes was asked to comment on criticisms of joint programs like Local
PEL, he responded thus:

> Criticizing some of these programs goes way back. They go back to
> the Quality of Work Life programs because those, in my opinion,
> were a waste of time and money.
> They basically, in my opinion, tried to cement something into
> our brains, to prepare us . . . (pause). You know, it kind of reminded
> me of being doped up before you go to the slaughterhouse. I used to
> tell them that. They used to tell me: "well, you got to go through this
> 'process.'" And I'd say: "you know, when you guys tell me that I feel
> like lying down in this butcherblock paper and rolling myself up and
> let you tie the ends up."[10]

As these comments suggest, the Local PEL program is generally understood as
part of a second phase of jointness, in which it is hoped that strong and vigilant
union participation will prevent a repetition of the "warm and fuzzy," vaguely
insidious, QWL "process."

Local PEL's integrity as a joint program is also bolstered by the unique participation of third party academicians.[11] The National PEL program counts
among its core group of instructors such leading American academicians as

Charles Sable (MIT), David Cole (University of Michigan), Harry Katz (Cornell), and Barry Bluestone (University of Massachusetts–Boston). First negotiated into the 1984 UAW/GM contract, National PEL students typically spend their four weeks traveling to cities around the United States to hear these and other scholars lecture in their various specialties. National PEL has also attracted the attention of political representatives, making Washington D.C. a favorite stop for this high-flying program.

The second aspect of PEL's third-party academic participation comes at the local level. Local PEL instructors are approved by the UAW/GM Human Resource Center, which manages and organizes both the National and Local PEL programs. Local PEL instructors are not typically widely recognized experts in their fields. Instead, they are more often faculty drawn from universities and colleges situated near Local PEL sites who have an interest in one or more of the PEL topic areas, and who agree to follow the syllabus developed by the National PEL instructors. According to the UAW/GM Human Resource Center, the chief "function" of Local PEL instructors involves:

> establishing the credibility of the curriculum as a fact-providing program aimed at giving participants unbiased information and guidance in making their own decisions.[12]

Armed with "facts" and "unbiased information and guidance," "third-party" academics are thus asked to play the role of reality brokers and discussion moderators.

Local PEL's extraordinary scope also needs to be underscored. While the National PEL program has been in operation since September of 1985, the Local PEL program first began in 1986 at the Willow Run, Michigan, Hydra-Matic Plant. As noted, over seventy Local PEL programs are in operation nationally.[13] With Flint's major GM facilities either participating or planning to participate, it is possible that all willing Flint-based GM employees—that is, nearly 50,000 people—could pass through this program. Because employees receive full pay for the week spent at Local PEL, response is expected to be high. For example, at the first Flint facility to begin its Local PEL program—GM's AC Rochester Division-East, in October of 1989—current applications for participation will keep it in operation until the year 2005. With full participation, this program would continue until the year 2010. At Flint's Buick Complex, which itself is roughly one-third larger than Flint's AC Rochester Division, Local PEL could run well into the second decade of the next century.[14] Local PEL is a uniquely massive undertaking.

Perhaps the most significant factor making Local PEL a unique joint program is that education—not training—is its sole focus. While the UAW, like most labor unions, has always stressed the importance of educational forums, PEL is the first joint program to do this. Whereas past programs have traditionally served either to promote "union awareness" or productivity-enhancing training objectives (depending upon whether the union or company was the sponsor), Local PEL is more analogous to a university course in that the presentation and discussion of empirically grounded knowledge is its only manifest objective. Both GM and the UAW have agreed, in other words, that their employees and members should receive a course in the unbiased facts about of their industry.

Local PEL's unique educational content is closely tied, however, to the program's overall purpose and objectives, which are themselves necessarily subordinate to GM's and the UAW's overarching organizational interests. In this light, consider Local PEL's official statement of purpose:

> The immediate purpose of the Local PEL Program is to provide you with greater understanding of the issues facing the industry as a whole as well as your own specific location. More generally, it is hoped that achieving this goal will encourage those who participate to take a more active role in initiating and carrying out joint decision-making activities.[15]

This organizational focus is further emphasized in Local PEL's five official objectives:

1. Understand the basic changes occurring in the auto industry

2. Understand GM's strategic response to these changes at the corporate level

3. Understand the strategic implication for the UAW of these changing conditions

4. Understand strategy at the Divisional level

5. Understand the implications for the local union and the division strategy.[16]

From these objectives, it is clear that *strategic planning* is the central concept at the heart of the Local PEL curriculum. According to Local PEL's official syllabus, strategic planning is defined as the process of "understanding and managing change," and is offered as "an overall conceptual framework for the [educational] material" otherwise contained in the program.[17] The centrality of strategic planning in Local PEL's educational content is further indicated by the official description of the program's week-long structure:

> A brief introduction to strategic planning is provided on the first day. Most of the rest of the week (Monday afternoon through Thursday

morning) consists of the environmental analysis that is one of the foundations for formulating plans. The last day and a half includes discussion of the strategic planning process, both at the level of the Corporation and International Union, and at the local/divisional level.[18]

That the content of the Local PEL syllabus is organized in these terms has four main implications.

First, the educational focus of PEL is limited to the development of what might be termed an "organizational imagination." Although the social sciences are well represented among PEL course topics and authors of choice, their works are *not* presented in order that participants might gain, for example, an interrelated understanding of Mills' "history and biography and the relations between the two within society."[19] Rather, the purpose of PEL is to encourage participants to locate themselves within the structure of GM and the UAW, not society as whole or *as such*. Achieving such a self-consciousness requires, then, knowledge of the respective histories of these organizations, and also information depicting the so-called environments in which these organizations operate.

Second, Local PEL's educational content is further defined by the three basic questions of strategic planning: Where are we? Where must we be? How do we get there?[20] Given the origin of this program, it is not surprising that the goals are preset; indeed, they are nothing less than the goals outlined in the Preamble of the UAW Constitution and GM's corporate mission statement. Participants are encouraged to identify their individual self-interest with their respective organization's goals. Because the overriding purpose of Local PEL is to encourage participation in decision-making activities, the question of "means" is put off. That better means will eventually be developed through a joint decision-making process stands as Local PEL's chief assumption.[21] The only question left open for the week-long session is thus: Where are we? In strategic planning terms, as a "realistic, unemotional look at the current situation," Local PEL is the "first step" in the planning process.[22]

The third implication of Local PEL's strategic planning focus is closely related to these first two: the Local PEL curriculum necessarily places its participants in a passive relationship to "the current situation." This may appear ironic, given, that is, Local PEL's stated intention to encourage participation in decision-making activities. But this passive relationship is predetermined by the program's empirical focus. Each of the program's five objectives involves "understanding" phenomena that are presented as factual. In this context, the mental operation of "understanding" thus becomes synonymous with internalizing an official representation of reality. The role of the expert National PEL instructors is to "establish the credibility" of this reality, while the role of the Local PEL instructors is to transmit this reality to the local level in an unbiased, dutiful, machinelike fashion.

Finally, the nature of Local PEL's educational content is further clarified by what is excluded from its purview. If the mutual self-interest of one corporation and one industrial union form the curriculum's raison d'etre, and if the educator's latitude is limited to the presentation of an strategically conceived reality to a passive audience, then a Local PEL education excludes all forms of what may be termed transcendent thought, or thought that, in Herbert Marcuse's words, "'overshoot[s]' the established universe of discourse and action."[23] Formed around strategic planning, Local PEL's educational content is untinged by any revolutionary or even wishful thinking. As will be emphasized below, even where the Local PEL program presents conflicting prospective options for UAW/GM joint action—such as, Is Japan or Sweden the exemplary model for U.S. labor relations?—these alternatives are always drawn from actually existing cases in point. This necessarily excludes from Local PEL's educational content the realm of nonactualized concepts, desires, hopes, or actions; that is, excluded are all goals that are by definition irreducible to strategic patterns of thought. In Local PEL, then, thought is disciplined by the pregiven acceptance of reality: strategic planning is all about "understanding and managing change," and nothing about creating and initiating "change" that is unmanageable.

Within these parameters, the social sciences contribute the bulk of the program's content. These contributions include specific lectures that are dedicated to the following topics: "History of the Auto Industry," "The Auto Industry in Transition," "The New Competitors," "The Economic Environment," "New Technology and Work Organization," and "New Patterns in Industrial Relations."[24] Also included are a "simulation" of the American "political process" and several films dealing with technological change, industrial relations, the history of the auto industry, as well as the so-called new competitors.[25] While a detailed analysis of Local PEL's content is beyond the scope of this study, it is nevertheless important to describe its chief intellectual parameters.

Local PEL's history of the auto industry is based on the intellectual work of Hal Stack, director of Wayne State University's Labor Studies Program. The central lesson of Stack's presentation is that a business strategy that is successful "in one period might not work once conditions change." To this end, Stack places special emphasis on what is commonly described as "Fordism" and "Sloanism." For example, while Henry Ford exploited a "mass market" for standardized automobiles, GM became the dominant automotive company under Alfred Sloan's leadership because it exploited "an increasingly differentiated market." Stack organizes the history of the auto industry in terms of such changing conditions, placing emphasis on structural factors that have contributed historically to business success and failure.[26]

Industry experts David Cole of the University of Michigan and Daniel Luria of Michigan's Industrial Technology Institute are jointly responsible for the "Auto Industry in Transition." The main objective of this material is to emphasize that not only is the auto industry's current situation characterized by fundamental structural changes, but also that these structural changes are occurring at an increasing rate. The changes that are given special focus include "product and process technology, and market and industry structure." As stated in the Local PEL instructor's manual:

> the material presented in this section is sobering, but it should be emphasized that any realistic strategy has to take into account the fact that the auto industry of today is fundamentally different from the industry of the '50s and '60s.[27]

Where history teaches the critical importance of "conditions," this section on the "Auto Industry in Transition" draws attention to the fact that "any realistic strategy" today has to take into account the nature of current structural conditions. The section on history thus serves the purpose of laying the foundation for the structural mode of analysis that follows it.

The Japanese auto industry is the case study in "The New Competitors," a lecture developed by the University of Michigan's Center for Japanese Studies that emphasizes "the seriousness of the current international competitive challenge." While nationalistic and even racist overtones seem a general rule in discussions involving American and Japanese economic competition, there is none of this in the Local PEL presentation. Instead, the analysis of Japanese auto industry competitiveness is presented from a "total system's view" that stresses how various elements in Japanese society interrelate with Japan's auto industry to produce an integrated and coordinated "market strategy." The central aim of this presentation is to indicate that, because "members of the U.S. auto industry are faced with the challenge of developing and implementing strategies that will enable them to match and surpass Japan in the competitive arena," the American auto industry will also have to adopt a "total system's view" of themselves in order to make the changes necessary for successful economic competition.[28] This lecture represents a pivotal turning point of the Local PEL curriculum as the final four substantive lectures describe key elements in such a "total system's view."

Barry Bluestone's intellectual work is the basis for "The Economic Environment." The main point of this presentation is to focus attention on those aspects of the "economic environment" that most directly impact the auto industry. Particular weight is given to describing the rise and decline of America's post-World War II international economic dominance, this, in combination with instruction in basic economic jargon such as GNP, productivity, and profit. This provides for discussion and debate of various economic policy questions, particularly those related to industrial and trade policies and the impact of these on the American standard of living. Participants are taught that changes in the global system of capitalist economic relations constitute an important set of parameters within which they must develop competitive strategies.

There is no official lecture that accompanies the discussion of the "Political Process," but its focus is clearly derived from a pluralist theory that emphasizes how "competing interest groups" divide power in an ongoing coalition-building process. Program participants role play their way through a mock U.S. legislative process: some as senators, some as congressman, some as lobbyists. Through this simulation, as it is called, Local PEL participants are taught that they have interests that are debated within America's governmental process, and that their participation in this political process could potentially further these interests. Emphasis is laid upon the importance of voting and lobbying. The significance of this political participation is connected to the economic policy issues previously discussed, suggesting that changes in the economic environment are to be achieved through active participation in the institutionalized political process.[29]

The next element within the total system's view is the lecture on "New Technology and Work Organization," based on the work of MIT economist and historian Charles Sable. Three points are emphasized: the specific results of technological innovation are unpredictable; nevertheless, together, new technologies will surely have an extraordinary impact on work and society; and Local PEL participants can influence the implementation of new technological innovations and thus help to shape the future structure of society in accordance with their values and interests.[30] This last point is crucial. Past forms of authoritarian "Taylorist" or "scientific management" strategies are contrasted with an alternative "sociotechnical" approach that substitutes worker participation for managerial authoritarianism in the implementation of new workplace technologies. Local PEL participants are encouraged to envision their participation in the implementation of new technologies within their workplace, throughout the auto industry, and in society as a whole.

This discussion is followed by the last element in the total system's view. The lecture on "New Patterns in Industrial Relations Systems," which is based on the work of MIT's Thomas Kockan and Robert McKersie, Harvard's Charles Hecksher, and Cornell's Harry Katz, asks the key question: Is a fundamentally new industrial relations system emerging, or is the old system merely operating under new conditions? One view, which is associated with the corporation, holds that the old adversarial system of labor and management relations is outdated for three reasons: power sharing and jointness are possible because of historically achieved mutual acceptance and "maturity"; the newly emerging world economic system forces labor and management to work together for their common interest of survival; and the evolution of society into a postindustrial economic system is leading to the development of flexible automation, requiring heightened levels of worker participation to maintain maximum effectiveness and flexibility.[31] This overall view emphasizes the possibility and necessity of jointness resulting from various environmental changes.

A second view, associated with a union perspective, holds that the adversarial system of labor and management relations continues to obtain for three counterreasons: instead of "maturity leading to cooperation," it has rather led them to a more "sophisticated" level of "conflict"; the world economic system does not expand mutual interests because corporations can now simply "move operations all over the world" in an effort to bypass union power; and a new postindustrial economy, primarily composed of "service jobs" that are low paying and difficult to unionize, is not in the union's interest and thus should be opposed.[32] This view emphasizes the danger of jointness in a context of uneven labor/management power.

As the PEL program describes it, an industrial relations system is divided into three analytically distinguishable levels: the workplace, collective bargaining, and the level of the firm's relationship to the marketplace, or what is called the "strategic" level.[33] Because American labor law codifies only the middle (or collective bargaining) level, the PEL authors point out that the workplace and business strategy levels are thereby open to experimentation. They suggest, in fact, that these latter areas are precisely where changes in technology and the competitive marketplace have created the most disruption. Therefore, the primary arenas for labor/management struggle are the workplace and the strategic level, with the management-oriented view of the new industrial relations system encouraging cooperation in the workplace, and the union-oriented view fearing cooptation both in the workplace and at the strategic level.

The Local PEL curriculum deals extensively with these issues. Although the authors of this lecture repeatedly emphasize that they "cannot give any final answers" to the questions that they pose, they do suggest that "one possible road out of this dilemma is for unions to expand their strategic range to include questions that have previously been seen as purely business decision"; that is, expand their participation into the realms of workplace organization and strategic planning.[34] As the authors say, "such involvement has its own risks of course, but it may be that the labor movement finds it has little choice."[35] Given Kochan's, McKersie's, Hecksher's, and Katz's prior scholarly work, and the fact that they themselves are participating in the Local PEL program—a program dedicated to this very goal—it can be assumed that this get-involved advice constitutes a positive recommendation to the Local PEL participants. It is also important to note that, whatever the perspective of the Local PEL participants regarding the two competing views of the industrial relations system, the Local PEL program frames the debate *within the context* of an "industrial relations system." Such a system is thus, as it were, *a given.*

This lecture on industrial relations completes Local PEL's total system's view, thus capping its answers to the strategic planning question, Where are we? Overall, the answer provided is that the UAW and GM are in changing systems environments, and that these environments may be influenced in various ways. For example, the economic environment may be influenced through participation in the political environment, and the technological environment may be influenced by participation in the industrial relations environment. Participation in these various systems is considered crucial. Indeed, it is participation and involvement that are again emphasized in the last day and a half of the program's curriculum.

The lecture involves a discussion of "UAW/GM's Mission," which addresses the Where must we be? question of strategic planning. This is immediately followed by a "WOTS-UP" analysis, where Local PEL students engage in a mock strategic planning exercise. In the WOTS-UP analysis, participants identify the main Weakness, Opportunities, Threats, and Strengths (WOTS) of the UAW and GM at both the national and local levels. At this point, their newly emerging "organizational imagination" is put into practice with the help of the GM-authored strategic planning section of the Local PEL curriculum. Subgroups are directed to develop strategic plans for their workplace. These amateur WOTS-UP analyses are then presented to the group at large. This exercise is followed by professional business-strategy presentations from representatives of local GM business units. Finally, regional and local union leadership arrive to guide question-and-answer sessions, just before the Local PEL participants go through their "graduation" ceremony.

Together these lectures and discussions constitute Local PEL's educational substance, which the program's purpose and objectives frame in strategic planning terms. However, as is the case with many programs that are organized from on high, Local PEL's actual implementation and practice is often more complicated than official documents would indicate. This is the case with Local PEL in Flint. Flint's practical experience with Local PEL raises two important issues that shed light on the meaning of Local PEL in general. First, all of Flint's UAW leaders are not in favor of the program; the New Directions Movement opposes it. Second, while Local PEL instructors are given stylistic license and are permitted to offer viewpoints and opinions, their primary official role is to act as a third party: disinterested, value neutral, expert. That the actual role of Local PEL instructors is more complicated should not be surprising. These two points are considered in turn.

In the section of the Local PEL curriculum that describes the competing perspectives on contemporary industrial relations, it is stated that the union-based judgement on these "new" relations is, first, skeptical that "employers have learned to use psychology and group motivation techniques" to manipulate employee attitudes against employee interests, and, second, that "the integration of the world economic system . . . creates more serious problems for labor as corporations move operations all over the world. . . ."[36] These concerns parallel New Directions' skeptical interpretation of the National and Local PEL programs. In Dave Yettaw's words, for example, Local PEL is a "behavior modification program" that "puts forth management's arguments of why we must help management achieve their goals," and it "also justifies the job loss of hundreds of thousands of auto workers' jobs while the Big Three build plants in Mexico."[37] These statements are indicative of the NDM's main criticisms of PEL: PEL uses psychological manipulation techniques; and PEL is biased toward GM's, and the mainstream UAW's, joint interest.

In explaining his opposition to PEL, NDM's Max Grider describes his experience with psychological manipulation at a special two-week PEL program designed for representatives from GM's Hydra-Matic Division:

> It was a real gut-wrenching experience for many of the people there. [It was a] roller coaster ride—highs and lows, workshops and experiments—which concluded the night before we left with a big group circle where each person took their turn in the limelight, on a chair, surrounded by all the other people. And those people proceeded to stroke you, to say good things about you: God, I mean there were people crying during this whole experience![38]

Grider contrasts this gut-wrenching experience with his experience at a regular one-week Local PEL:

> The one-week PEL that I went to at Hydra-Matic Headquarters was much more to the point. They didn't have the . . . (pause), they didn't play the psychological games that became a big part of the Corporation's grand design—the behavior modification and all that.
>
> It was nuts and bolts. It was: "we had never shared this information with union people before, and this shows our commitment to you, and this is why we've got to eliminate 4,000 jobs in your plant."[39]

For Grider, even though Local PEL "took some of the skeletons out of the closet," the bottom line remained that the company made the key decisions and the union people were expected to acquiesce.

Given Local PEL's "nuts and bolts" style, NDM criticism focuses on the program's content. For example, PEL's emphasis on competitiveness is, in Yettaw's words, "a treadmill that we just don't get off of." In other words, the NDM suspects that PEL's focus on the union's need to "be competitive" is intended to justify wage cuts, job reductions, and the curtailment of work rules that were initially won by the union in order to protect workers from exploitative and inhumane workpaces. The NDM views PEL's encouragement of union participation in changing workplace and business strategy relationships as ultimately benefiting GM at the expense of the workers. In support of their perspective, they often point to the unsatisfactory experience of workers at experimental factory sites (Saturn), to continued GM disinvestment in the U.S. industrial base in favor of foreign direct investments (Mexico, Europe), and to corporate mergers and joint ventures with ostensible competitors (GM-Toyota).[40]

More importantly, perhaps, the NDM also sees PEL as part of the mainstream UAW International's strategy to justify their own concessionary and cooperative relationship with GM. In Yettaw's words:

> The leaders that choose to can say: "Gee, what can I do, my hands are tied, you see right there?" They bring the union guys in on the last day, and they say: "Well, now have you seen why we had to combine classifications? Have you seen why we had to increase your workload? Do you see we're confronted with all these things? Well, that's just the way it is, and we're doing the best we can."[41]

At Local 599, Yettaw and his supporters unsuccessfully opposed the implementation of a Local PEL program. Prior to Local PEL, Local 599 operated what they called a "union awareness" program that was organized strictly by and for UAW members. At the behest of Buick management and mainstream Local 599 leadership, this program was cancelled, or at least put on indefinite layoff, in favor of Local PEL. Examining the mainstream leadership's perspective on Local PEL helps illuminate the program's significance in internal union politics.

While the mainstream UAW leadership rejects the NDM because they believe that it is out to "destroy the union" in order to "supplant the labor movement with themselves," they tend to see themselves as doing "the best they can" to lead a declining "organization *within* a corporation" into an uncertain future.[42] Local PEL serves two important functions for this leadership.

First, Local PEL redirects the responsibility for the UAW's decline away from the leadership and back on to the rank and file. As a mainstream Local 599 official explains:

> We have what we call a mini-PEL program where they focus on letting people know how the free trade [agreement] is going to relate to you as far as competitiveness is concerned, how these different issues that are coming up can actually affect you on your job.
>
> And at the end of that . . . we'll come in as local union leaders, and then they'll fire back what they've learned: "We have learned this can be a problem; What is our union doing to address it?"
>
> [This] gives us the opportunity to say: "Now wait a minute, *you're* the union. We are only the elected leaders . . . and anytime [that you want to change that,] all you got to do is elect someone else. You're the union."[43]

At face value, this interpretation of PEL's function can be seen as the expression of a democratic sentiment: "you're the union" might be equivalent to "you're the supreme authority." In practice, though, the formulation of union strategy and policy is typically monopolized from at the top of the organization, and "the membership," who are mainly regarded as spoiled, apathetic, and ignorant, needs merely to legitimize these strategies and policies. In a mock dialogue with the union members among the Local PEL participants, this same union official explains:

> "Collectively, what do you think we ought to be doing about it? Here's some things that we would like to try, that we haven't necessarily got your cooperation in doing." [Local PEL is] beginning to refocus people and get them thinking back positive about the union and things that we should be doing.[44]

Or, in the words of another senior local union official:

> Knowledge is the key. I strive as Chairman of the Shop Committee to keep my membership as well aware of things that's going on . . . because the more knowledgeable they are, the more they understand what we're going through, and I think the more they'll support us because of it. So, I support the educational process.[45]

These local union officials express a common interpretation of Local PEL: it serves to motivate the membership to actively support their leaders' policies by throwing responsibility, if not actual power, back upon the rank and file's shoulders.

The second function of Local PEL is to contain and limit the meaning of participation to within acceptable institutional channels. Local union officials describe PEL as a type of consciousness raising program, but they clearly have a vested interest in exactly what type of consciousness is ultimately created. A mainstream Local 599 official explains, for example, the International Union's fear of mobilizing the entire UAW rank and file:

> Some people are afraid to organize that number of people because an organization that big you can't lead. You sort of channel it into a direction and hope like hell they keep going there. You can't lead it. It just takes over and has a consciousness of itself. It just goes.[46]

This same official then explains why it is important to control the rank and file on the shop floor as well:

> I can go in and stir up my membership on any issue. I've got the ability; don't know how I got it. I can create bullshit on the floor.
>
> But if you can't get the members back to where they should be—you know, you've got to come back at some point—if I can't do that, then why put them out there [on strike] to begin with?[47]

Because they fear the uncontrollable mobilization of their membership, local union officials closely monitor the content and presentation of the Local PEL curriculum.

Two aspects of the Local PEL program are especially highly valued by the leadership: the "reality" that is presented, and the UAW's necessarily subordinate position with respect to this reality. As one local union official remarked: "The people that put on these programs are educating the members to reality, as far as I'm concerned." For this official, this reality should contain the following characterization of the UAW:

> The UAW is doing its best, in my opinion, with what it has to work with. They can no longer be a militant group of people, like we used to, because [then] we could threaten to strike to keep the work here because we didn't have any competition. We have competition now. We must realize that.[48]

Or, in the words of another local union official:

> [Local PEL's] a good program in that it opens the eyes of the people as to exactly what is happening and the position that we're in—which is a losing position, and nobody's trying to sugar-coat the fact.[49]

This same official then explains the function of presenting reality in this way:

> By doing that, people then become concerned, and when you get people concerned they start looking to people for solutions. And hopefully, and so far, they're turning inward to the union.[50]

This hoped-for and encouraged "turning inward to the union" not only reinforces the mainstream leadership's authority, but it is also meant to undercut the NDM's more militant appeals.

Local union officials appear to be equally concerned with the instructors they hire. One official notes: "the program itself, of course, is only as good as the professors and instructors that we have in it."[51] Recognizing the need to control these instructors, another official describes how the local union leadership views and deals with this group:

> PEL's consciousness raising, and we're going to continue to monitor that and make changes in that.
>
>   We asked two instructors not to come back because they refused to deal with some of the issues that we wanted them to: the union and politics; why be involved; why should you vote; why should we be

ashamed when only 10 percent of the people vote that can vote; why is it dangerous; that kind of stuff.

He didn't want to talk about it, so he didn't talk about it. Well, he doesn't work with us anymore. I believe in academic freedom, but we're the customer. We bought something here.[52]

From the perspective of these local union officials, Local PEL needs to be "monitored," and this includes demanding that their hired "third party" help act at the behest of the local union officials.

The conflict between the NDM and the mainstream local UAW leadership raises many questions about the meaning of Local PEL as it is actually put into practice. In this case, the interests of the local union leadership, whether identified with the NDM or not, clearly plays an important role in shaping the presentation and content of the program. But there are other interest groups involved at the local level as well. In addition to the volunteer participants, who, if nothing else, see Local PEL as a paid week off from their regular work, Local PEL's paid instructors and the paid company and union "coordinators" also have a stake in the program. In one highly successful Flint-area Local PEL program, the company and union coordinators have developed a close working relationship with a regular group of instructors. The dynamic at this Local PEL program sheds further light upon the actual organization and presentation of Local PEL.

In the words of the UAW coordinator: "all of it is fun; it's all fun."[53] These coordinators enjoy their work, particularly their relaxed relationship with both the participants and instructors. They also take pleasure in and are stimulated by the content of the program itself. Indeed, these coordinators contribute, as all are expected to do, to the program's content as part of their responsibilities, by acting as a discussant for the group's daily round of newspaper analysis, for example. As the union coordinator notes:

> I like PEL because it deals with current events. It's not always pleasant. A lot of the information perhaps I wouldn't like to hear so pointedly, but that's the way the PEL program gives it. Current events is something that keeps me interested.[54]

The company coordinator, who likes "helping people," emphasizes the relaxing aspects of PEL as an "off-site" program:

> I think it's getting both hourly and salaried workers together in an environment that is not conducive to the workplace. And I think it's a place where you can freely express yourself, and let your guard down without feeling like you're going to be criticized.
>
> If you're a manager or a supervisor, do away with your tie for that week.[55]

From both company and union perspectives, Local PEL's purpose is to further jointness and to motivate the participants to become actively involved in their workplace and society. Again, in the words of the company coordinator:

> [PEL] changes your perspective after you find out why things are the way they are. The importance of working together; I think that's really stressed in this PEL program: it's all about people working together to bring about harmony—jointness, rather—among the people.[56]

And, in the words of the union coordinator, the purpose of PEL is all about "awareness, to build a greater awareness."

As viewed from the perspective of the company coordinator, this leads to the program participants to form the following conclusions:

> I think the competition is one thing that people really remember, and maybe that helps them understand why GM preaches "buy what you build."[57]

And, from the perspective of the union coordinator:

> It gives the people on the floor a chance to search their souls. We have a number of people . . . that own foreign cars and think nothing of it. If they choose to stay couch potatoes, then they choose to do that.[58]

These Local PEL coordinators have never had a disciplinary problem with their instructors, all of whom jointly work together to coordinate the practical details of the program, and who share mutual respect and friendly relations. But, from the perspective of the local instructors, there is more motivating their participation than merely the handsome paychecks and comradaire that is involved (although neither of these should be discounted). Local PEL instructors also have political interests, and in this they are surely no different than the National PEL instructors.[59]

A highly regarded and well-seasoned Local PEL instructor from outside the Flint area informally stated that his own political goals were to: "(a) humiliate management, and (b) undermine the notion of free enterprise." Participant observation suggests that these types of political sentiments are not uncommon among Local PEL instructors, particularly those whose academic fields include the social sciences and various forms of labor studies. These same Local PEL instructors are suspicious of instructors who are drawn from business colleges and departments of management or labor and industrial relations, because it is assumed that such instructors may express political sentiments that are common within their fields: sentiments, that is, contrary to those suggested in the above quotation.

Substantively, the left-leaning instructors tend to pursue developmental and comparative analytical strategies that reflect their political values and interests. For example, they emphasize the dehumanizing qualities of scientific management and explain its American origin in the work of Frederick W. Taylor. This developmental focus suggests the contemporary possibility of (and *responsibility* for) choosing alternative historical directions. These instructors also tend to describe the "Japanese Model" of political-economic organization in unflattering terms as authoritarian and exploitative, which is then juxtaposed to the positively evaluated social-democratic "Swedish Model," emphasizing Sweden's extraordinary unionization rates, the unusual historical success of the Social Democratic Party, and the development of Sweden's infamously lavish welfare state provisions, this, in combination with this country's export-led economic successes and relatively high standard of living. Whereas the Local PEL Instructor's Manual focuses on Japan as *the* new competitor and exemplary comparative model, these instructors offer what they consider as a viable democratic and egalitarian alternative.

Furthermore, participant observation also suggests that Local PEL instructors are self-conscious about their political goals, even to the point of paying a great deal of attention to their presentation of self. It is not unusual, for example, for these instructors to manage their appearance, style, and tone of presentation with hope of effecting a bond between themselves and union participants in particular. This includes a certain amount of self-flagellation as intellectuals and experts and some "just-plain-folks" propaganda. In the Flint area, jokes are made about the film *Roger & Me*, which many local auto workers and residents found insulting and biased. In addition to serving as a useful ice breaker, these types of jokes and self-mockery also clear the ground for the instructors' own political agenda.

Overall, the Local PEL instructors go to significant lengths to be entertaining as well as politically challenging. This latter factor is lost on some Local PEL coordinators, who, partly because their own review and analysis of participants' program evaluations demonstrates to them that participants are not aware of any significant political bias in the presentations, and partly because of the trust they have in their instructors, deny that partisan "politics" plays any role in the Local PEL program.

At the ground level, then, Local PEL's supposedly "realistic, unemotional look at the current situation" is in actuality shaped by the interests and perspectives of those who directly engage with the material and the program's participants. Behind its comfortable "off-site" facade lie very serious political questions and very powerful political interests (a situation that should come as no surprise given the actors and resources brought to bear). This point is illustrated by the fact that Flint's main economic planning agency includes the advocacy of Local PEL as one of its central goals for the economic development of Flint and Genesee County (see chapter 7).

The Local Paid Educational Leave Program is in many ways unique, in many ways symbolic of our nation's current efforts to address the process of dependent deindustrialization, and, thus, in many ways a political football. It is unclear how many of Local PEL's participants understand this, or even care to understand this.

LOCAL PEL IDEOLOGY

A Local PEL coordinator at one point remarked, "I would like to see them expand more on the history," while this coordinator's union partner suggested that "if a person has any inkling of a liking for education—be it history or current events—the program sells itself, it actually sells itself."[60] Although it was not their intention, this juxtaposition of perspectives suggests the tension that exists within deeper temporal structure of Local PEL ideology. While there is a longing for something that is missing, there is also recognition that, in Local PEL, history and history making are for sale. This is often called the "buy-in." Local PEL's buy-in mentality is achieved through adopting a strategic awareness of history that destroys historical precedent and future possibilities in the power vacuum of the ever present. Local PEL is a "school of reality" that provides no escape from the that-which-exists, and, as such, it reflects a tacit acknowledgment of its own powerlessness. Local PEL's temporal structure is "antihistorical," then, insofar as it forgets unrealized historical possibilities and rejects any sort of utopianism.

Four specific features of Local PEL demonstrate this flattened temporality. Local PEL collapses the past into the present, first, through a revisionist and, second, an evolutionist reading of history. These strategies suggest a type of normalized and mature present, the appropriate stuff of strategic planning. Two additional strategies collapse the future into the present. As strategic planning is dedicated to "managing change" in order to preserve the status quo as a going concern in the future, the future must be conceived as the present under altered, though controlled conditions. Furthermore, imaginative, aesthetic visions of the future are replaced by comparative model selection, where the future is effectively rendered as the present Other: not as a potentially "democratic society," for example, but in terms of the Swedish or the Japanese Model. These orientations are examined in turn.

Given the criticisms of jointness that stem from the rank and file's sour memory of Quality of Work Life, Local PEL cleverly justifies itself by adopting a low profile as just another instance of mutually beneficial cooperation in a long line of joint company/union programs. Local PEL is merely the second phase of the joint process. For example, the history of class conflict is analyzed exclusively within the boundaries of labor relations. That the participants in Flint's Great Sit-Down Strike believed themselves to be enmeshed in class conflict is not part of the Local PEL syllabus. This strike is only mentioned in passing as one of many equally important strikes. The history of the American labor movement is also portrayed as merely an analytical piece of the auto industry's historical puzzle. Market structure, industry structure, process technology, organizational culture, corporate structure, and so on, are instead the significant factors in this history. The labor movement appears only in terms of the structure of union organization and labor relations in various periods of the *industry's* history. This is a prelude to the discussion of *contemporary* union structure and labor relations, wherein, not surprisingly, "the basic goals of the labor movement *within* the system are identified."[61] Those radical, revolutionary aspects of the America labor movement that resisted the system, in other words, simply do not have a place in Local PEL's revisionist historiography.

Jointness, however, *is* a part of PEL's version of history, playing a conspicuous role in the history of auto industry labor relations. Although the program curriculum lists jointness (including PEL) as distinctively marking the current period of labor relations, it also suggests that the concept of jointness really had its origins in the advent of collective bargaining itself. For example, Local PEL's educational material includes a selection from John Barnard's 1983 book *Walter Reuther and the Rise of the Auto Workers*, entitled "Bargaining Landmarks." This reading glorifies the collective bargaining gains won by the UAW under Reuther's leadership, which helps to stress that working within the system pays off.[62] We learn that "Reuther never opposed new technology"; that he and GM chairman Charles E. Wilson had a "genuine mutual respect"; that, in effect, as "Reuther masterfully played the bargaining game," "the UAW functioned superbly as a bread-and-butter union."[63] But, as even Barnard notes, "The gains of the auto workers were, of course, predicated on a prosperous industry and a union monopoly of the labor that went into American consumers' cars—conditions that, by and large, prevailed during Reuther's lifetime."[64] The "Labor Relations" section of the curriculum develops this theme.

The Local PEL curriculum suggests—indeed, it assumes—that Serrin's "civilized relations" between company and union are here to stay, regardless of whether the industry is or is not "prosperous." There is no discussion of anything else, nor, given the civilized atmosphere that prevails at a Local PEL program, does there need to be. What has changed are the "conditions" that Barnard argues were the basis for Reuther's collective bargaining success. As the Local PEL manual states:

> We have seen this week that the traditional industrial relations system . . . developed in the period of US economic dominance and steady growth. Environmental factors were relatively stable. Today, as we have seen, this is no longer true.
>
> The result is that the existing formal structures and institutions of the traditional industrial relations system have increasing difficulty

in dealing with current conditions. There is increasing pressure for change.

Currently, the main direction of this pressure is toward some kind of cooperation between labor and management. This is not really surprising. It is frequently the case during a crisis that the parties involved move to establish a closer working relationship.[65]

By extension, the existence of Local PEL is "not really surprising" either. Local PEL participants should understand that the establishment of a "closer working relationship" is "frequently the case during a crisis." As one Local 599 official stated:

> Jointness? To me, it's been around for years. When you get two people setting down at the bargaining table, that's jointness. Because if they didn't have the company, you wouldn't need an [union] organization.[66]

Such selective historical memory reduces history's friction against the present. If Local PEL is merely an extension of union/management precedent, or merely an unsurprising, common reaction to "crisis," then the underlying implications of this joint program—all joint programs—need not be thematized and considered. The history of a militant, radical, and revolutionary social movement is thus systematically forgotten.

Local PEL also casts history in an evolutionary form so that prior historical content is portrayed as inherently regressive or immature. While this version of history is included in the PEL manual, it also finds a home among PEL's mainstream union supporters. It is, in fact, suggested by the existence of Local PEL itself.

The PEL manual's discussion of "New Patterns in Industrial Relations Systems" includes a description of this evolutionary consciousness inasmuch as it discusses the combined "growing maturity of the parties," the "force of necessity," and "the evolution of society," that have changed the "fundamental relationship between labor and management."[67] While this type of perspective is offered only as one among other possible interpretive frameworks, it appears to aptly characterize the dominant view among union officials who support Local PEL. Consider this sampling of remarks from mainstream Local 599 officials. The first says:

> I think the company's gotten very liberal.
>
> I used to be kind of a real hot tempered guy, you know, that's how I got into it. Well it just ain't that easy sometimes. You gotta work through 'em. So I work through people.[68]

Or, as a second official says:

> If the company doesn't make money, we don't have any jobs.
>
> You can be as hardcore as you want, you can be as radical as you want, but the bottom line is: if they're not selling cars, we're not going to work.[69]

Or, as a third official says:

> I'm comfortable with kicking their ass; that's my background.
>
> But also, we have to change just like society has changed. [*Are you saying that the union has to help manage the company?*] They certainly do.
>
> You can disagree and take a good union stand and still work with [the corporation]. That's leadership. You got to work within the system.
>
> The big picture is you have to adjust with the times. You can never go back.
>
> We're having to adjust to a more modern, skilled way of doing things.
>
> I think any group that advocates militancy as far as striking, shutdowns, walkouts, national strikes, things of that nature—[which] would, in a lot of cases, hurt the majority of the membership—is not looking at the best interest of the membership.[70]

This perspective is most strongly expressed by a fourth official. As a person who had been actively involved in the 1960s Anti-War Movement, who at one time considered himself a communist, and who is still regarded as a savvy political thinker by fellow political allies, this union leader now regards himself as having "matured." Consider a selection of his remarks:

> I have fantasies, you know: "let's get guns and do shit." Horseshit. That's fantasy. Yeah, I know who the enemy is, but I can't shoot them all. And the members aren't ready, nor do they want to.
>
> The most recent thing now is that we ought to scrap the two-party system and form a Worker's Party. [mockingly] Well, hallelujah, hallelujah: isn't that a revelation? Isn't that new stuff?
>
> I used to be a fellow-traveler. We started a third party: Citizen's Party. We had our party, and we all sort of leaned toward that and went to that.
>
> A lot of the people you see in the New Directions literature are out of that [Citizen's Party] movement, and I've crossed paths with them in my maturation process that I've gone through.

I'm not ashamed of that. I did some crazy things in the past. You
do that stuff when you're growing up, and I'm not ashamed of it. And
I'd probably do 'em again under the same circumstances. I'm in the
state police "red files," I know that. So what?

I believe in what I do . . . with my people. Is that paternalistic?
Yeah, maybe it is.[71]

All of these officials support Local PEL. Their tendency is to view themselves as
having matured with the changes in their union's relationship with the corporation. The "more modern, skilled way of doing things" includes working
through, not against, the corporation. The collective bargaining framework
provides the temporal boundaries of their "organizational imagination." As a
fifth Local 599 official says:

We have to deal with what's been negotiated for us for three years, we
have to look ahead to what we want to change and do differently for
the next three years, because that's the length of time of our contract.[72]

For this union official, the "contract" sets the parameters for historical thought.

The mainstream UAW's emphasis on jointness and collective bargaining
creates a normalized and mature "present," which jibes with Local PEL's presentation of history. Together, revisionism and evolutionism counter attempts
to redeem history as a force that would de-center the status quo. That Local PEL
students learn this history while in the midst of participating in the civilized
atmosphere of an educational joint program further encourages adaptation to
this type of historical consciousness. While Local PEL centers history's power
to suggest an alternative present, its strategic planning perspective captures
future possibilities within the structure of current power relations. If the present
represents nothing more than a mature form of the past, then the future can
represent nothing more than a continuation of this maturation process. One
of Local PEL's central foci, for example, is to encourage union rank-and-file participation in the formulation of "business strategy." (The corporation's own
management employees do not have to be encouraged to do this; they may simply be ordered to do so.) This proposed participation by union members takes
various forms. Union members are encouraged to exercise their right to vote
in union and governmental elections, attend union meetings, and participate
in joint programs. More generally, they are encouraged to a acquire an "understanding" of "the business." Local PEL is in part an effort to encourage union
members to see themselves and their future from the company's perspective.

When it comes to articulating the corporation's and union's joint direction—that is, when asked what the "ends" of their joint activities are—Local
PEL simply points to the corporation's and union's respective mission state-

ments. The ends of the joint process are thus the maintenance of corporate profits and union membership, the company's and union's respective bottom lines. The only remaining issues for discussion and decision are those that concern the means to achieve these preformulated goals. Local PEL provides an education in such techniques.

Even local union officials, when they are asked what the "direction" of their own International union leadership is, profess ignorance. A mainstream Local 599 official stated:

> I couldn't speak for them—I really couldn't—to say what their direction is.[73]

Or, in the words of a second Local 599 official:

> I may like to know their strategy, and then I can make a decision on it, Okay? I don't know what the strategy is.[74]

Indeed, these leaders generally have no vision of the future except that the future will include a struggle to maintain the present. For example, when asked to respond to a "negative futurist" statement, one mainstream union leader gave what he called an "honest answer":

> Certainly some things have to be given consideration for the future or a lot of that could come true. Our immediate future here, and the things that happen to us, probably make that secondary in nature to what we're dealing with, which is the loss of jobs of our members here, the immediate security for them and their families.
>
> Where once we as organized labor had a leadership role in both the public eye and internal[ly in the industry], I think now it's more a survival role.[75]

Such "it's more a survival role" realism is easily transformed into acquiescence. Another leader, who is apparently concerned about the possibility of future ecological disaster, reacted this way:

> A lot of our problems are related to improving our social comfort: how we exist, whether it be by automobiles versus the horse, you know? Or anything else similar to that: the air conditioning and the gases that it puts off rather than the old fans.
>
> I guess I could make the statement that, "well, I'll be alright 'cause I've only got maybe 50 more years max, you know? Probably 30 more, so I won't have to worry about that."

We're our worst enemy there. Shoot, the automation and the technology and the improvements to better our lives is basically killing us.

As far as the future itself, many times I think that it would've been much better if we went back to that horse 'n buggy, more of an easy way of living.

I don't know of anything we can do about it, personally.

But the big picture is you have to adjust with the times. You can never go back. Like we were talking about earlier—how the society is destroying us, the environment—but you can't go back. Nobody lets you go back.

I'll keep my car; don't give me that horseback. When I go home tonight, I want my air conditioner on.[76]

Utopian thinking is as absent in Local PEL as in these remarks. This is not surprising, given that the PEL educational process is based in strategic planning, and given that mainstream union officials no longer see themselves as part of a change-oriented labor movement. While it is recognized that the future is imperiled by unprecedented challenges, this is not enough to displace their overriding interest in maintaining the status quo.

The second strategy employed to flatten future-oriented thought concerns the conceptualization of alternative societal models. If imitation is the highest form of flattery, then the Japanese and Swedish socioeconomic strategies are much flattered by Local PEL. It is true, of course, that both of these nations have enjoyed economic success in the "newly integrated world economy": they are successful new competitors. Local PEL's attitude toward these models is comparable to a savvy reality broker offering a client the chance to play a type of futures market. Local PEL's participants are encouraged to bet on winners with proven track records. The problem is that this type of reified model-selection thinking, strictly applied, falsely reduces future possibilities to "current conditions."

Even those Local PEL instructors who, in sympathy with the position of the unionized workers, stress the unattractive features of the Japanese model in favor of the social-democratic virtues of the Swedish model, participate just the same in limiting the imagination of their students. One instructor, for example, described history to his Local PEL class as a battle between two opposing forces: the democratic and antidemocratic. But in this presentation, as in Local PEL's syllabus generally, the meaning of "democracy" is assumed, or, if not wholly assumed, then is effectively operationalized in terms of its realization in a specific society such as Sweden. It is as though "democracy" meant economic rights manifested through the power of trade union federations, established workers' parties, and a well-developed welfare state pursuing technologically progressive economic planning and equitable redistribution of income and resources. This is *all* that the concept of democracy would refer to: a robust welfare state. Whether or not Swedish society is a realistic or even attractive alternative for American society is here moot. More important is the point that Local PEL's "consciousness raising" is thus more aptly described as a "consciousness razing," for Local PEL implicitly demands of its participants that they make a commitment to the present—that, in effect, they concentrate on what is right in front of their noses: their own jobs, the bottom line, new competitors, pending legislation, and so forth. This, in fact, is what the "buy-in" is about.

Local PEL's antihistorical dimension is an important facet of its overall cynical structure. This is not to suggest that Local PEL's participants, instructors, coordinators, supporters, or any individuals at all connected with this program, suffer themselves, *as individuals*, from an idiosyncratic form of cynicism. What it means is that the program's selective and evolutionary rendering of history, and its antiutopian and instrumental presentation of the future, together form a discernable tendency to limit and discipline the scope of the human imagination and potential joint action. This tendency is built into the structure of the program. Even when leftist academics seek to quietly undo Local PEL's ideological constraints from within, they are contained by the program's overwhelming form: after all, to disregard or even openly criticize its official constraints would simply earn them a pink-slip.

Underscoring the Local PEL program's cynical *structure* does not, however, cancel the significance of its psychological impact. Local PEL ideology nurtures and implies a cynical consciousness. Witness, for example, what, after Gottfried Benn, Sloterdijk calls the "formulation of the century for cynicism": "To be dumb and have a job, that's happiness."[77] Consider, also, Sloterdijk's crucial description of cynical consciousness, keeping in mind the structure of the Local PEL program:

> The pressures to survive and the desire to assert oneself have humbled enlightened consciousness. It is ill from the compulsion to accept existing conditions which it doubts, to accommodate itself to them and finally even to conduct their business.
>
> In order to survive, one has to attend the school of reality. Certainly. Those who mean well call it growing up, and there is some truth to that. But that is not all of it. Always a bit unsettled and irritable, the collaborating consciousness looks around for its lost naivete, to which there is no return, since the attainment of consciousness is irreversible.
>
> Being "stupid" and trusting are no longer options, and innocence cannot be regained. Unhappy consciousness clings to the belief in the sheer weight of things, to which it is bound by its instinct for self-preservation. In for a penny, in for a pound.[78]

In its structure and meaning, the UAW/GM Local Paid Educational Leave Program is a cynical "school of reality." Local PEL represents a collaborator's solace in the "sheer weight of things." "In for a penny, in for a pound," is it not evident that UAW participation in this jointly orchestrated program is driven by its "compulsion to accept existing conditions that it doubts, to accommodate itself to them and finally even to conduct [General Motors'] business"? "Those who mean well call it growing up, and there is some truth to that." But what choice does the union have? "Being 'stupid' and trusting are no longer options, and innocence cannot be regained."

The structural condition of cynicism naturally affects the individuals who act in its context. The cynical "self" is "borderline melancholic," a type of self that is ultimately premised upon self-conscious hopelessness.[79] This is not an uncommon type. As Sloterdijk stresses: "Today the cynic appears as a mass figure, an average social character in the elevated superstructure."[80] Everyone directly involved in Local PEL understands this. They tacitly know that, in the larger scheme of things, they are effectively powerless, and that, in their immediate situation, they are quite comfortable.

This interpretation is suggested by the various roles played by Local PEL's participants. The union rank and file understand why they are called the "rank and file," or, even less picturesquely, the "membership." It is quite understandable why they would want a paid week off from work, and why they would feel comfortable being instructed in reality, for they are used to obeying, not wielding, authority; they are experienced participants in "programs." GM's middle- to lower-management employees are not part of a democratic organization—not even on paper—and their participation as students in Local PEL as in their participation in the company's "business strategy" is thus more a detail to their job description than anything else. Their occasional hesitation to participate in Local PEL has more to do with the fact that *their* regular workload, unlike their unionized counterparts, will still be waiting for them after their week-long educational commitment is over. Like most who serve in appointed union positions, a UAW Local PEL coordinator's work is typically (and understandably) more satisfying than work on the shop floor. The Local PEL coordinator's responsibilities are creative and interesting; it is, as they say, "positive" work. Theirs is not an appreciably different situation from the one in which elected local union officials find themselves, except that elected officials must please an electorate, whereas appointed officials need only to please their appointers. Coordinating a Local PEL is an attractive union job. The company's Local PEL coordinators also enjoy the "positive" feel of the program, speaking only of gingerly taking their students out of their "comfort zone." Local PEL instructors, besides supplementing their incomes, also supplement their typically routine lives cloistered within the university's walls. Perhaps they feel that through PEL they can "make a difference" in society.

But Local PEL *is* a "comfort zone," and not a departure therefrom. Local PEL is supposed to ready one for reconciliation to "current conditions," as in Sloterdijk's portrait of the cynical self:

> Psychologically, the contemporary cynic can be understood as a borderline melancholic; he is able to keep his depressive symptoms under control and remains more or less able to work. Indeed, the ability of the cynic to work is decisive in modern cynicism: in spite of everything, after all, especially that.
>
> Society's key positions have long since belonged to a diffuse cynicism of boards, parliaments, committees, company leadership, editorial offices, practices, faculties, law and newspaper offices. A certain elegant bitterness colors its activities.
>
> For cynics are not dumb, and every now and then they certainly see the nothingness to which everything leads. Their spiritual makeup has become elastic enough to make the constant doubt about their own pursuits part of their quest for survival.
>
> They know what they do, but they do it because, in the short run, the objective situation and the instinct for self-preservation speak the same language and tell them it must be so. Others would do it anyway, perhaps worse.
>
> The new integrated cynicism thus even feels itself, understandably, both as victim and as sacrificer. Behind the conscientiously hard facade of collaboration there is a mass of vulnerable unhappiness and the need to cry.
>
> Here is something of the mourning for a "lost innocence," for the better knowledge against which all one's actions and labors strive.
>
> In the new cynicism, we see a detached negativity that scarcely allows itself any hope, at most a little irony and self-pity.[81]

Local PEL offers an inviting environment for this cynical psychological type, so characterized. With "irony and self-pity," there is a mourning for the "lost innocence" of the labor movement that has been dashed both by the "objective situation and the instinct for self-preservation." As one union official remarked, "we're in a survival role now," which he regarded as a "mature" self-conception. Interestingly, on the first day of Local PEL's week-long course, students are introduced to the program's "norms," one of which is that "war stories" are to be kept to a minimum. The phrase "war stories" refers to the bitter tales of deceit and injustice that many of PEL's participants store within themselves. These are to be "kept to a minimum," of course, because everyone already knows that *they* are both "victim and sacrificer"; everyone already knows that they have made "concessions," but these have never been constant enough in number to stem the tide against them. Local PEL nevertheless teaches its participants that further "collaboration" is the answer. Indeed, Local PEL *is* further collaboration: it is a "positive" environment.

The union leaders who advocate and support Local PEL are not, as it were, "dumb." They know that they are in, as one official says, a "losing position," and "every now and then," when put on the spot, they "see the nothingness to which everything leads." This perspective is integrated into their "quest for survival": "there's no going back," says the local union leader who wants his "air conditioning" humming during his ride home from the union hall. And they keep working; after all, this is their raison d'etre. As one UAW official speculated when confronted with several examples of GM's having broken prior agreements with the UAW:

> That doesn't mean that we should just throw in the towel. We're not going to do that.
>
> Sometimes I wonder if General Motors' purpose here was for us to throw in the towel, and they could just say: "Well, hell, the union wouldn't do nothing for us, so we're just gonna shut all the plants down." Then we give 'em an excuse.[82]

Most local union officials see their main job as "getting work" for the membership. They must cajole the corporation; never "give 'em an excuse" to "shut all the plants down." This is what leadership means in today's union. As a Local 599 official remarked, when GM puts new equipment in a factory, they only "bolt it to the floor," they don't "cement it," suggesting the immense threat that capital mobility implies for local union leaders.[83] This same official says: "someone has to do it; someone has to take the bull by the horn and lead," as though closely following Sloterdijk's gloss on the cynical rationalization: "others would do it anyway, perhaps worse." This official may have put it best: "you got to work within the system. Umm-hum, yeah."

For Sloterdijk, the converse of Benn's cynical formulation "reveals its full content: to be intelligent and to perform one's work in spite of it, that is unhappy consciousness in its modernized form. . . ."[84] As we have seen, this second-generation joint program seeks to mold intelligent workers, albeit workers whose "awareness" is limited to a form of organizational consciousness. Workers should familiarize themselves with their "environments"—by reading the business section of their newspaper, for example—and then participate in these environments. In one Local PEL program, workers are given sample letters written to elected political representatives, which they are to use for guidance should they ever choose to participate in the political system. Local PEL even suggests that the new intelligent worker is not only more productive, but is also more "happy" than ever before. While team work, cooperation, mutual trust—jointness—make for a more productive worker, Local PEL suggests that it is great "fun" learning how to survive. One Local PEL coordinator believed that the program was reducing acrimonious feelings among workers and managers in the factory: there is a "better working relationship," and people tend to "do a better job," this person thought.[85] Yet, when this same GM Local PEL coordinator was confronted with a "negative futuristic" statement, her sentiments changed dramatically:

> We need to bring about change, that's for sure. One of the biggest problems is that the wealth is in the hands of a few, and then you have all the other people out there, and they're out there with very little.
>
> We're not dealing with devastation there [in Local PEL], or anything.
>
> Those who have the wealth have to be willing to give some of it out to help people. It's going to have to be a *total* change. Otherwise, we're going to bury ourselves.[86]

Does this turnabout—*it's going to have to be a total change; otherwise we're going to bury ourselves*—suggest that Local PEL's intelligent worker is actually a discreet "borderline melancholic?"

The "Message of Welcome and Program Overview" from the UAW's Donald F. Ephlin and GM's Alfred S. Warren, which prefaces the original Local PEL "Administrator's Guide," suggests that "the information you will receive in this program will . . . provide you with an opportunity to make a difference in creating your future."[87] Given GM's plans to eliminate one of ten of its white-collar and one of six of its blue-collar employees by 1995, lower-level officials in both the union and the corporation might be forgiven should they wonder: What future? Without "total change," how can they allow themselves "hope"? The answer, of course, is that they must keep working, for they have little choice but to continue to play along. As one mainstream union official said of himself and his colleagues: "We've got to be schizophrenic in our role. We have to be," suggesting Orwellian doublethink as a required occupational skill.[88]

Local PEL's conceptualization of social structure suggests why its participants feel as though they must participate in a reality that encourages a cynical schizophrenia. Local PEL teaches its participants to see the UAW and GM as bureaucratic organizations. It then offers, as we have seen, a "total systems view" of an increasingly interdependent world qua the UAW's and GM's "environment." In such a tableau, the relations of capitalist dependency are writ large, very large. Not only is the individual a cog in two great and interrelated bureaucratic machines, but these complex organizations themselves lead only a small existence in an ever more perilous "environment," itself filled with dangerous "new competitors." Local PEL renders these competing business organizations as machinelike as the larger "new global economic order." The individual is taught that they must participate in their own, vulnerable organization, and, in this way, in the larger global system, so that they and their organizations, whose fates are wed, may together survive.

But what power does an individual have to act in such an expansive and seemingly autonomous void as "the new global economic order"? Can a week spent at Local PEL be sufficiently empowering? The Local PEL manual explains:

> It is hoped that this local PEL will enable all GM employees to partic-
> ipate in the information sharing and joint decision making that is the
> prerequisite for reshaping the U.S. auto industry in today's competi-
> tive and rapidly changing environment.[89]

Participants are so "enabled" because they are initiated into the strategic plan-ning's "approach and outlook." The Local PEL participant is to envision their place in the world by telescoping backwards from the most abstract or global structural relationships to the most immediate or local situations: from the new global economic environment to one's industry, company, factory, and department. The closer the focus comes to the shop floor, the more potential empowerment is ceded to the individual. Local PEL deems such a perspective "realistic."

Important structural boundaries for action are thus defined. The new glo-bal economic environment may be altered—for example, through new trade laws—but for an individual to effect this type of change, he or she must partic-ipant in the appropriate lobbying group within the American legislative pro-cess. This may mean following the provided template when writing a letter to a senator, or voting this senator out of office should she or he prove unrespon-sive. The structure of the U.S. auto industry may also be changed—for exam-ple, by "buying what you build"—just as the structure of the union may be altered by attending union meetings, participating in demonstrations and ral-lies, and supporting the new system of labor relations. Local PEL participants are encouraged to act as conscientious voters, consumers, and union members. They are encouraged, in a sense, to act in mass society so that their organiza-tions may claim mass support. This is a crucial part of the strategic planning process: managing change by managing legitimacy and motivation.

The individual's workplace is naturally the most convenient venue for their direct participation. In this regard, Local PEL gives considerable emphasis to the "team concept" of work organization and the "living document" approach to contract arbitration. The phrase "team concept" means simply that work is jointly organized by workers *themselves*, who, in effect, discipline themselves to meet management's predetermined standards of production. This notion also goes by the name "employee involvement," and other similar monikers. Team concept typically means that workers receive a greater measure of autonomy in their work and are offered new opportunities. They may, for instance, choose to rotate from one job to another within the team framework, thus learning new skills and expanding their responsibilities. The team concept style of work organization also lessens the need for lower-level management's disciplinary function, thus blurring the roles of supervisor and supervised worker. Many Local PEL participants already work in "teams." The "living document" interpretation of a labor contract is a bit different. It simply means that a labor contract is to be viewed as open for constant revision in the face of changing conditions. Inasmuch as both of these policies attack the formality of rigid bureaucratic structures in favor of the informality of flexible cooperative relationships, they suggest possible avenues for local action.[90] Still, in contrast to the vast dimensions of the global "environment," Local PEL's version of employee involvement seems ordinary and unremarkable.

Yet Local PEL's conceptualization of social structure also has an emotional underbelly, which occasionally pierces the homilies concerning workaday participation in this or that bureaucratic context. Here one finds the fleeting images of predator and prey, life and death survival. In an intensive forty-hour program, such emotional undertones become paramount for the participants. The individual union member and company employee is called upon, for "survival's" sake, to engage in "cutthroat" competition on a global scale. There is an uneasiness. Catch phrases typically serve as convenient rationalizations for the tension generated by a Local PEL education. A remark commonly heard from UAW members and GM employees is: "we're going global now." Although this statement appears to announce a bold adventure, it is said with trepidation. After all, no one at Local PEL chose to "go global."

When C. Wright Mills conducted his study of America's labor leaders in 1948, they were sitting in the catbird seat as never before.[91] By virtue of their command over large, expanding, and strategically placed organizations, America's postwar union leaders were indeed new men of power. Yet these leaders were never fully accepted into America's power elite.[92] The labor movement that emerged from the war years became organized labor, whose leaders wanted to "move" no further than from one contract to the next. Aided by the prevailing reactionary climate that facilitated the jettisoning of socialists and communists from positions of union leadership and even from respectability, a defanged Big Labor settled into its "civilized relations" with Big Business. America's labor unions thus became junior partners in the strategic management of the nation's political economy, or, as one Local 599 leader put it, unions became "organizations within corporations."

Today, Flint's Local PEL program represents a cynical extension of this historical development inasmuch as it exemplifies the UAW's "reflexively buffered" strategy to adapt to the system that disempowers it, to protect only the immediate self-interest of its members, and to cut its losses with its past heritage in order to maintain the status quo in the short term. This strategic response is pursued with an enlightened sense of the fateful long-term consequences, which are already quite evident in Flint. With over 30,000 GM jobs gone already and more substantial cutbacks planned, the company appears to have abandoned its side of the partnership in the company/union town compact. The mainstream local union leadership knows that business as usual is over, but there is little that they can do. Even a public pronouncement of this kind, they fear, could give GM an additional "excuse" to leave more quickly. One UAW official may have captured their dilemma best:

> [GM] used to hide the exploitation of other workers for greed's sake. Shit, they're so damn proud of it now—that [they] got 50-cent-an-hour workers in Mexico—they're not even ashamed of it anymore! (more calmly) I don't know how you change that.[93]

NOTES

1. C. Wright Mills, *The New Men of Power: America's Labor Leaders* (New York: Harcourt, Brace and Company, 1948), p. 291.

2. Interview 8, July 10, 1991.

3. Interview 5, June 20, 1991.

4. Peter Sloterdijk, *The Critique of Cynical Reason* (Minneapolis: University of Minnesota Press, 1987), p. 6. This exact quotation is from Michael Eldred and Leslie A. Adelson's translation in "Cynicism—The Twilight of False Consciousness," in *New German Critique* 33 (Fall, 1984): pp. 190–206, 194, whereas Eldred's 1987 translation in *The Critique of Pure Cynicism* is, "In order to survive, one must be schooled in reality."

5. Harry Katz, *Shifting Gears: Changing Labor Relations in the U.S. Automobile Industry* (Cambridge: MIT Press, 1985). Also see Thomas A. Kochan, Harry C. Katz, and Robert B. MeKersie, *The Transformation of American Industrial Relations* (New York: Basic Books, 1986) and Harry Katz, "The Restructuring of Industrial Relations in the United States" (document source January 1991), the text of a presentation to the conference on "New Directions in Worker-Management Relations: Soviet and United States Perspectives," Moscow, USSR, June 2–8, 1991.

6. For a scholarly discussion of "jointness," which includes a discussion of the New Directions Movements' opposition to this policy, see Harry C. Katz, "The Restructuring of Industrial Relations in the United States."

7. Ronald Edsforth, *Class Conflict and Cultural Consensus* (New Brunswick: Rutgers University Press, 1987), p. 227. Also see Bryan D. Jones, Lynn W. Bachelor, with Carter Wilson, "Flint: Political Maneuvering and Buick City," in *The Sustaining Hand* (Lawrence: The University of Kansas Press, 1986), pp. 179–237; Mike Parker and Jane Slaughter, "Buick 81: Granddaddy Team Plant," in *Choosing Sides* (Boston: South End Press, 1988), pp. 192–195; "Local 599: 1937—20th. Anniversary—1957" (document source), the UAW Local 599 Collection, The Archives of Labor History and Urban

affairs, Walter P. Reuther Library at Wayne State University; and Interview 7, July 5, 1991.

8. Edsforth, p. 227.

9. Interview 12, August 1, 1991.

10. Ibid.

11. The phrase "third party" academics is used in the "Administrator's Guide" for Local PEL (document source), from the UAW-GM Human Resource Center (established in 1986) for use by Local PEL coordinators.

12. See "Administrator's Guide."

13. Data is here drawn from Gene Ridley, "Local P.E.L. Report," *Headlight,* 21 March 1991; Interview 11, July 25, 1991; Interview 12, August 1, 1991; and Interview 13, July 25, 1991 (where it is suggested that there are 80 programs nationally, with 37 new programs soon to be started). In fact, however, there are only 78 established Local PEL programs as of July 1995. My thanks to Howard Erikson of the UAW-GM Human Resource Center for kindly providing this up-to-date information.

14. Interview 11, July 25, 1991.

15. Local PEL "Instructor's Manual" (document source).

16. Ibid.

17. Ibid., p. 9–1 and p. 1–1.

18. Ibid., p. 1–1.

19. See C. Wright Mills, *The Sociological Imagination* (Oxford: Oxford University Press, 1959).

20. See "Local PEL Instructors Manual."

21. Note that the area of action for Local PEL participants is limited to what the official syllabus describes as "Group, Division/Staff, and Plant/Strategic Business Unit," which are distinct from the "Corporate" level, where decisions that "involve the overall shape and nature of the corporation" are decided. "Local PEL Instructor's Manual" (also termed in this study: "official syllabus"), pp. 9–7.

22. "Local PEL Instructors Manual," p. 9–6.

23. Herbert Marcuse, *One-Dimensional Man: Studies in the Ideology of Advanced Industrial Society* (Boston: Beacon Press, 1964), p. xi, fn. 1.

24. "Instructor's Manual."

25. Note that there is some variation from program to program. This description is based on participant observation and study of the official Local PEL syllabus.

26. "Instructor's Manual," p. 2–v.

27. Ibid., p. 3–v.

28. Ibid., p. 4–iii, 4–13.

29. This characterization is based on several participant-observation experiences, as well as on the many documents that were provided as part of this simulation. By all accounts, participants regularly enjoy this exercise.

30. "Instructor's Manual," p. 7–v, where these points are organized under the headings: "Nobody Knows"; "It's Going to Happen"; "You Can Have Influence."

31. "Instructor's Manual," p. 8–1.

32. Ibid., p. 8–2.

33. Ibid., p. 8–2f. Also see Kochan, Katz, and MeKersie.

34. "Instructor's Manual," pp. 8–11 and 8–12.

35. Ibid., p. 8–12.

36. Ibid., p. 8–2.

37. Interview 4a, May 28, 1991.

38. Interview 3, July 19, 1991.

39. Ibid.

40. These characterizations are drawn primarily from Interviews 3 and 4a, but also see, Dave Yettaw, "The President's Report," in *Headlight,* 7 March 1991, where he writes: "Management demanded that our Union Awareness classes be cancelled in favor of the ONE-week P.E.L. (Paid Education Leave). Why would Management want to pay you to be out of the plant for a week? Usually they penalize you for being out of the plant when being paid. DOES MANAGEMENT HAVE SOMETHING TO GAIN by this? YOU DECIDE . . . it is another joint company-union program. The P.E.L. program puts forth Management's arguments of why we must help Management achieve their goals and also justifying the job loss of hundreds of thousands of auto workers' jobs while the BIG THREE BUILD PLANTS IN MEXICO. Should the full program continue, I will be there on Union Pay, to discuss the issues with you. If Management does not object."

41. Interview 4a, May 28, 1991.

42. Interview 6, July 3, 1991 and Interview 7, July 5, 1991.

43. Interview 9, July 26, 1991.

44. Ibid.

45. Interview 5, June 20, 1991.

46. Interview 6, July 3, 1991.

47. Ibid.

48. Interview 5, June 20, 1991.

49. Interview 9, July 26, 1991.

50. Ibid.

51. Interview 5, June 20, 1991.

52. Interview 6, July 3, 1991.

53. Interview 11, July 25, 1991.

54. Ibid.

55. Interview 13, July 25, 1991.

56. Ibid.

57. Interview 13, July 25, 1991.

58. Interview 11, July 25, 1991.

59. This section is potentially disruptive to various parties involved in Flint area Local PELs. Information is derived from participant observation in the community as well as from specific Local PEL programs, but, because of the sensitive nature of the material, direct attributions are kept to a minimum.

60. Interview 13, July 25, 1991, and Interview 11, July 25, 1991.

61. "Instructor's Manual," pp. 2–8, 8–v (emphasis added).

62. See Ibid., p. 2–29 through 2–42. According to the UAW Region 1-C Education Director: "A lot of people don't understand that the joint process started in 1967. Walter Reuther put it on the table. Walter got killed in 1970, and Leonard Woodcock and [Irving] Bluestone took the ball." Interview 12, August 1, 1991.

63. "Instructor's Manual," especially pp. 2–41, 2–42.

64. Ibid., p. 2–42.

65. Ibid., p. 8–3.

66. Interview 7, July 5, 1991.

67. "Instructor's Manual," p. 8–1.

68. Interview 7, July 5, 1991.

69. Interview 12, August 1, 1991.

70. Interview 5, June 20, 1991.

71. Interview 6, July 3, 1991.

72. Interview 8, July 10, 1991.

73. Interview 8, July 10, 1991.

74. Interview 6, July 3, 1991.

75. Ibid.

76. Interview 5, June 20, 1991.

77. Sloterdijk, *Critique of Cynical Reason*, p. 7.

78. Sloterdijk, "Cynicism—The Twilight of False Consciousness," p. 194.

79. Ibid, p. 192.

80. Ibid., p. 191.

81. Ibid., pp. 192, 194.

82. Interview 12, August 1, 1991.

83. Interview 5, June 20, 1991.

84. Sloterdijk, "Cynicism—The Twilight of False Consciousness," p. 194.

85. Interview 13, July 25, 1991.

86. Ibid.

87. "Administrator's Guide."

88. Interview 6, July 3, 1991.

89. "Instructor's Manual," p. 1–1.

90. See Ibid., especially pp. 8–1 through 8–12.

91. Mills, *The New Men of Power.*

92. C. Wright Mills, *The Power Elite* (Oxford: Oxford University Press, 1956).

93. Interview 6, July 3, 1991.

Chapter 4

THEORETICAL
CONCLUSIONS
TO PART I

Critique is as much opposed to cliche as it is to positivist science. Where the former says, for example, that the more things change the more they stay the same, the latter proposes immutable social laws to explain why this must be so. In this, both approaches to the interpretation of social life suggest the immense power of the individual while ironically at the same moment erasing this power. When individuals believe that they can capture objective societal relations through common sense or science, the end product—*society*—is ceded both agency and objectivity. The individual is thereby denied both the power to change the structure of social life and the subjectivity capable of imagining otherwise. In other words, while *the world* may be understood and explained, little can be done about it; where thought is omnipotent, practice is pathetic.

In contrast, critique is situated, reflexive, and communicative; the sociological imagination is its self-consciousness. C. Wright Mills' triad of history, biography, and social structure (what he called "coordinate points"), form a constellation of the human imagination that is oriented to thinking the life of the individual back into the *history* and *society* that appear alien to the individual.[1] That these appear alien to the individual means also that the individual appears alien to herself or himself. Critique hopes to talk these potential suicide victims down from their self-objectivating ledges, so that they may participate in their own lives and so that they may make their own history. Critique also knows of itself that it is an historical phenomenon—a peculiarly modern one at that—for Reason lies behind its best efforts to see a humanity living at peace with itself. For Mills, this is the promise of sociology.

Critique therefore knows that its concepts work only as well as they mediate. As Ben Agger states: "intending community, critique hopes to overcome its isolation."[2] If they are to be true, then, sociological concepts such as class, work, and class consciousness must be analyzed immanently within public discourse: as historicized reflections upon lives that are lived by individuals, and not as the facts that in themselves determine these lives. Reified concepts are unreasonable and dangerous inasmuch as we practice what we preach.

That critique seeks to historicize reified concepts does not mean, however, that social structure is a production of the mind. Critique is self-conscious of its situatedness, and it is thereby empirically orientated, recognizing that humanity is always already embedded in historically rooted social and cultural relationships, and that these relationships are constitutive, if not, even in the last analysis, determinative, of what we are. In other words, as humanity is objectively bound to live and die on the Earth, and as there is no position "outside" of history, critique must be both materialist and immanent. As Theodor Adorno suggested, critique must "break out" of the "objective context of delusion," but this can only be done "from within."[3]

The foregoing analyses of the New Directions Movement, The Center for New Work, and the GM/UAW Local Paid Educational Leave program suggest that class, work, and class consciousness remain vital concepts in Flint. Because Flint is an extreme case—an exaggeration—of capitalist social relations, the local history of these concepts suggests not only their changing local meaning, but also their significance for American capitalist society as a whole.

The streets of Flint in 1936–37 were the scene of an American capitalist society at odds with itself. The issues were unusually clear. Sickened by forced labor, the people of Flint's industrial working class articulated their protest against capitalism's structured class relations by self-consciously throwing their bodies before its enforcers. Through their struggle, they modified the meaning of class, work, and class consciousness as they altered the structure of the capitalist system. After 1936–37, America remained a capitalist society, to be sure, but the relative power of capital was curtailed by labor unions and the welfare state.

In this period, the oppositional working class became, as organized labor, an integral part of the newly configured capitalist system. Labor's new struggle was to wrestle from contract negotiations a lifestyle of middle-class consumption. Concern for the sphere of production, and with this the meaning of work, was devalued in favor of concern for the sphere of consumption, and with this the meaning of leisure. Class consciousness now meant accepting this trade off: alienated work in exchange for second cars, cabins, boats, household conveniences, and a university education for the young. The American Dream.

This is Ronald Edsforth's thesis in *Class Conflict and Cultural Consensus: The Making of a Mass Consumer Society in Flint, Michigan*. As Edsforth points out:

> By 1957, weekly wages in the Vehicle City were 37 percent higher than the national average.
>
> Indeed, Flint seemed to present a model of labor-management harmony to the nation. In articles like *U.S. News and World Report*'s "Labor Peace: It's Wonderful" (July 1950), *Look*'s "All American City" (February 1954), and *Coronet*'s "Happiest Town in Michigan"

(June 1956), the national news media used Flint as an example of how the country had transcended the bitter, divisive class conflicts of the 1930s and early 1940s to enter a new era of consumer-oriented normalcy.[4]

During this period, Flint was the site of exaggerated capitalist abundance. But in order to remain the "Happiest Town in Michigan," Flint depended upon the business success of the General Motors Corporation and the bargaining power of the United Auto Workers. With deindustrialization, this situation changed dramatically: the media today is more apt to describe Flint, with equal nonchalance, as the *worst* city in America. Not surprisingly, with the decline of Flint as a prosperous industrial community, the meaning of class, work, and class consciousness has shifted once again.

The NDM seeks to revive the oppositional meaning of all three concepts. Just as the 1936–37 sit-downers struggled against the speed-up, so does the NDM now struggle against jointness, which they perceive as legitimizing a new form of management by stress. And, like their historical counterparts, whose sit-down strike kept GM from moving key dies from Flint's struck factories, New Directions challenges the corporation's right to move capital assets from country to country, challenging, in effect, a private interest's power to dispose of social assets. For the NDM, class consciousness means realizing that the old New Deal compromise is over, and that the struggle must again be joined.

Yet, in seeking to redeem the unmediated historical meaning of class, work, and class consciousness, the NDM runs the risk of falling into cliche. For example, the world of 1936–37 had not come to appreciate the threat that advanced capitalist-industrial society would pose to the Earth, whereas today, for the most part, it is understood that economic activity for profits' sake is causing irreversible damage to the ecological balance of life. The extinction of more than 100 *species* of plant and animal life every day is but one result. Because of capitalism's systematic tendency toward what Schumpeter famously termed "creative destruction," this process (in its many forms) can only end with the cessation of capitalism as an economic system. By resurrecting the idiom of the New Deal, however, the NDM commits itself to perpetual economic growth. As such, it cannot consider "growth" *as such* as an ecological problem. The NDM is a productivist movement.

For this reason, the NDM can never make alliance with those who Jürgen Habermas dubs the "critics of growth," for it is unprepared to, in effect, break out of our contemporary context from within.[5] As the NDM's Dave Yettaw reflected in response to this issue:

I knew that we were losing plant and animal species; I knew that. I didn't realize it was a hundred a day! I mean, if that keeps up, I don't think we have long left, a very long time left.

I think that goes to the fact—being Christian, I believe in Christ—it goes to the fact that Man will destroy himself, and his only savior is Christianity, or whatever the Koran believes, or the Buddhists, or whatever. It's devastating.

I think that's meant to be. Reading the Book of Revelations, it talks about the rivers will be unfit to drink, the fish will be unfit to eat—we're already there.[6]

Yettaw believes that "history repeats itself," but such a formulation cannot address the unprecedented, except, perhaps, in otherworldly terms. From a sociological perspective, this response suggests one way in which myth or cliche disempowers, at least in *this* world. It is not surprising that otherworldliness would develop in the midst of structured dependency.

The Center for New Work interprets class, work, and class consciousness quite differently. As much as it is possible, New Work ideology ignores capitalist social relationships, conceiving of Flint as a dinosaur of the fading *industrial* era. In the framework of industrial/postindustrial societal transformation, class is determined by one's relationship to knowledge and technology, and not by capitalist property relations, and the meaning of work is determined by its relation to the self, and not in relation to its commodified form on the capitalist labor market. Class consciousness is merely a hindrance to utopian thinking and potential self-actualization. In New Work's imaginative utopian thinking, the immanently oppositional meanings of all three concepts are erased from the top through a metanarrative of technosocial development, whose goal is to free humanity of its fear of change so that it may embrace its posited future as the realization of its dreams.

While critique also seeks emancipation, it opposes such a forward-looking mythos as much as it opposes a backward-looking myth: if an unmediated future is offered to the present, then is it not offered as fiat? New Work's articulation of Flint's dependent postindustrialization denies power to those who are already in a relatively powerless position. It may be true that the people of Flint are "so desperate that they are willing to listen to a philosopher," but, in a democratic society, philosophers are not free to be kings. Utopianism that is unmediated by historical experience disempowers humanity before its unrealized and indeterminate future. It instills fear and self-doubt even when this utopia's promises appear rosy. This is the case with all social science that reifies and thus dehumanizes history and humanity. Of course, critique does not shy away from utopian thought *as such*. Indeed, as Habermas suggests, "the collision of historical and utopian thought ignites the Zeitgeist."[7] But critique seeks to articulate this "collision" from within, and, in this, it knows that it is in for a struggle. In other words, New Work's win/win strategies may be utopian, but are not so in an emancipatory sense.

The GM/UAW Local Paid Educational Leave program offers its own interpretation of class, work, and class consciousness. These concepts, in fact, are interpreted as being identical to those current during Flint's postwar prosperity. In the present context, though, participation within the capitalist system offers none of the security and luxury that were forthcoming to organized labor in the previous period. As Local PEL suggests, the capitalist system itself has changed. This threatens the established institutionalized powers, which further requires an increasingly intensive integration of the individual into the system's dynamics.

The UAW membership is to see itself as a single competing fraction among the nation's and world's total working class, with Local PEL teaching the methods and sensibility of this new competition. The implementation of flexible manufacturing technologies has not only reduced the demand for industrial labor, it has turned the meaning of industrial work on its head. Local PEL teaches that brains and not brawn are the workers's chief asset. Given the (non)decision to participate in the changing system, class consciousness is replaced by an organizational consciousness that, through strategic planning, intends the management of this change for organizational self-interest. Local PEL teaches the lesson that survival requires adaptation to "objective" conditions, and, by corollary, that suicide will come with anything less. Local PEL is concerned with immediate gains in power and security, and this is recognized and accepted as reality.

Critique opposes this as a form of cynicism. From a strictly sociological perspective, it is expected that complex organizations will seek to reproduce themselves by controlling factors that are controllable, and by adapting to "environments" that are not controllable. But Local PEL presents itself as a free educational forum. When organizations' strategic interests are presented as education, the students' self-consciousness is colonized for purposes outside their control. An organizational imagination replaces a sociological imagination—not to mention worker solidarity—and with these it replaces transcendent values with strategic interests. The Local PEL curriculum limits and narrows the participant's understanding of societal relationships in order to encourage a studied acceptance of the status quo.

In contrast with New Directions and New Work ideology, then, Local PEL offers a present that is mediated by neither a potentially subversive past nor a potentially subversive future. Neither myth nor mythos, Local PEL casts a cynical eye toward both: it seeks to *manage change*. This consequence is achieved through the structure of strategic planning, where technical concepts reduce the meaning of education to little more than survival training. But critique cannot accept the reduction of Reason to Technique, for this, too, is a false reification.

In summary, critique must oppose New Directions' unmediated return of the repressed, New Work's great leap forward, and Local PEL's cynical response to dependent deindustrialization, for each in their own way, in their own particular style or form, collapse the tensions that are historically sedimented in the content of their own concepts. But merely opposing these ideological trends is not enough. Critique that itself wishes to avoid cynicism also seeks to empathetically reestablish what remains of a miscarried dialogue. Critique seeks to further mediate consciousness that is falsely reified, or, stated differently, critique seeks to further the realization of self-consciousness that is informed by an integrated understanding of history, biography, and social structure. In terms of the previous three chapters, this would involve public reflection upon the shared situation that confronts each separate response to Flint's economic and social decline.

When mythic redemption, utopian mythos, and cynical strategy resist consideration of each other's merits, or when, in other words, the form of each is privileged at the expense of distorting the content of their shared concerns, then what may seem obvious from without becomes fuzzy to those who operate within the confines of a particular or "local" consciousness. This study suggests that class, work, and class consciousness are concepts whose historical content is thrice distorted in Flint, and that, upon mediated reflection, these distortions are the product of what each response seeks to understand and address—that is, the structure of dependent deindustrialization and the possibilities for economic security. The first part of this study's overall thesis is thus: in the context of structured dependency within the global capitalist system, local dialogue is understandably "miscarried" inasmuch as specifically local responses to this situation are not sufficiently empowered to address, alter, or otherwise control the root causes of the community's economic and thus social decline. In a catch phrase: dependency distorts consciousness.

It is not that the "global capitalist system" is uncontrollable; this, too, is a reification. Clearly, though, the changing dynamics of this increasingly integrated and transnational system have altered the status of previously core regions such that they are presently more aptly conceived as peripheral regions within the core. Stated differently, private capital interests are increasingly unconstrained by community and nation-state control, and communities are thus increasingly situated within an unevenly developed global—as opposed to a regional or national—economic system. More and more, then, community livelihoods are dependent upon increasingly abstract, distanced, and, from a local position, uncontrollable global economic relationships. The temptation is to assume or accept this position as permanently unalterable; in effect, to think globally, act locally.

Local action, however, does not and cannot itself address global relationships. Just as individual solutions to social problems are doomed to failure and frustration, so too are local solutions to global problems destined to reify or otherwise block from consciousness the reality of contemporary social structure. Flint's local responses to its status as a dependent region within the core of the global capitalist system founder upon this self-deception. That this is also otherwise blocked from consciousness is the subject of the second half of this study, where each type of ideological response is traced to a parallel cultural manifestation.

NOTES

1. C. Wright Mills, *The Sociological Imagination* (Oxford: Oxford University Press, 1959), p. 143. For an elaboration on this theme, see Steven P. Dandaneau, "'Minimalist' Sociology versus 'Taking It Big,'" in *Current Perspectives in Social Theory*, vol. 14 (Greenwich, CN: JAI Press, 1994), pp. 213–239.

2. Ben Agger, *Fast Capitalism: A Critical Theory of Significance* (Urbana, IL: University of Illinois Press, 1989), p. 12.

3. Theodor W. Adorno, *Negative Dialectics* (New York: Continuum, 1973 [1966]), p. 406.

4. Ronald Edsforth, *Class Conflict and Cultural Consensus* (New Brunswick: Rutgers University Press, 1987), p. 218.

5. Jürgen Habermas, "The New Obscurity: The Crisis of the Welfare State and the Exhaustion of Utopian Energies," *Philosophy and Social Criticism* 11, no. 2 (Winter, 1986), pp. 1–18.

6. Interview 4a, May 28, 1991.

7. Habermas, p. 1.

PART II ~ *Culture*

As a "citadel" in America's rapidly expanding automobile industry, Flint was once at the center of modern American culture.[1] As Robert and Helen Lynd foresaw in their 1929 *Middletown* study, the mass production and mass consumption of automobiles would be largely responsible for the peculiar character of America's twentieth-century way of life.[2] What's good for General Motors is good for America? Prior to the Great Sit-Down Strike, however, Flint's industrial working class shared neither in the management and control of this industrial giant, nor widely in the much-desired fruits of automobile and related consumer production. Although they were at the center of America's immense industrial economy, Flint's auto workers remained a cultural underclass.

The form of the sit-down strike suggests the values that were at stake in this conflict. At one level, the strikers' passive occupation of the factories dramatized their desperate desire to have a say in the control of the their work. They were not interested in destroying or even in having this property for their own. In fact, the strikers self-consciously took great care of these facilities, which, in a sense, they were merely borrowing as a means of communicating their resolve.[3] By sitting down, Flint's auto workers were, in effect, standing up, not only in opposition to a corporation that treated them as little more than factors of production, but also in opposition to a wider culture that devalued their labor, and, indeed, their very lives. By occupying a place in the factory, they merely sought a place for their occupation in society. In cultural terms, then, Flint's victorious strikers achieved exactly what they wanted: recognition.

Marcuse would have been intrigued. By 1964, the year that his *One-Dimensional Man* was published, Flint's Depression-era experience with class conflict was largely forgotten.[4] As Marcuse had envisioned, the coordinated management of America's postwar economic *and* cultural systems created in Flint a nationally recognized integration of what Ronald Edsforth calls America's midcentury "culture of abundance" and its related and much-vaunted "cultural consensus." Once the site of the Great Sit-Down Strike, Flint had become the "Happiest Town in Michigan."[5]

Cultural engineering was certainly involved, particularly through the good offices of the C. S. Mott Foundation. During the postwar boom, Mott Foundation support helped to establish Flint's Cultural Center, which included an automotive and art museum, a performance arts and music center, and a library and planetarium. The Mott Foundation was also instrumental in creating and trumpeting Flint's internationally recognized community schools program, which made public schools available for neighborhood and community use, and offered lifelong educational opportunities to Flint's citizens. Numerous such experiments were carried out in the social laboratory that was Flint, in the hope that this city's successes would serve as a model for all of industrial society. But too much significance is easily given to these top-down efforts to make Flint a harmonious example of mass industrial culture. That the majority of Flint's once oppositional working class *themselves* desired what in effect was a civilized relationship with their own society is a cultural fact of equal if not greater importance in the explanation of Flint's postwar cultural consensus.

There was good reason for this desire. Flint not only enjoyed an above-average standard of living (relative to history's most materially abundant way of life), the city also lavished in a type of cultural centrality, reflected in the national media attention given its social engineering successes, the economic security emanating from the great brick factories that fortified the city, as well as the widespread practical realization of what at the time constituted the American Dream. That this cultural centrality depended upon the local presence of a single capitalist firm was understandably ignored in Flint's version of C. Wright Mills' "American Celebration."[6] If GM dependence meant economic abundance and cultural prestige, then Flint was grateful for it. Of course, Flint's once-extraordinary industrial base is now greatly diminished due to GM's decision to steadily curtail its Flint-based operations: to disinvest, in other words, from what is, in the corporations' evolving global perspective, little more than an old and decaying, high-wage, branch-plant city. The New Directions Movement, the Center for New Work, and the GM/UAW Local Paid Educational Leave program all have emerged in this context, as local responses to the shifts in Flint's class relationships.

But the question arises: What cultural responses have emerged as a result of Flint's dependent deindustrialization? Or, as Edsforth writes:

When it is healthy and expanding, advanced consumer-oriented capitalism may indeed create "a pattern of one-dimensional thought and
behavior," as Herbert Marcuse once explained.

But what happens when the flow of new products and pleasures
into working people's everyday lives slows down or stops altogether?
What happens when the system cannot deliver more goods and leisure time, when living standards decline instead of rise continuously?

If past events in Flint . . . are any indication, then new possibilities may open up.[7]

As the political-economic infrastructure has failed to deliver the proverbial
goods, Flint's local culture has become politicized by the reception of cultural
phenomena that encode divergent social values and competing self-interpreta-
tions, and which, in fact, as Edsforth predicted, suggest "new possibilities" for
Flint and America. These phenomena are a widely discussed film, an important
new building, and the articulation of a new vision for Flint's future development. This is not to suggest, however, that Flint's culture is today any less one
dimensional.

Adorno would have recognized this. The liberatory significance of these
cultural phenomena, such as it exists at all, lies more within themselves than in
their objective power to mobilize social change. For Adorno, the truth of a cultural object—be it in the form of art work, sign, or discourse—lies in its capacity to capture societal contradictions, which are, by definition, aesthetically
irresolvable. This is a *negative* power as what is mirrored is an *absence* of cultural consensus that in a one-dimensional society is reduced to a technical
achievement. In his introduction to a recent translation of Adorno's writings
on the notion of a culture industry, J. M. Bernstein echoes Adorno when he
suggests that

The more one-dimensional society becomes the more critique must
pay attention to the internal structure and relatively autonomous
logic of cultural objects.[8]

In the analysis of the "internal structure and relatively autonomous logic of cultural objects," negative dialectics offers a counterpoint to any straightforward
rendering of popular culture as a sphere of liberation. Culture critique instead
reveals the contradictions within cultural objects as well as between cultural
objects and the society that invests in them their contradictions. Particularly
insidious is the culture industry's administration and commodification of
ostensibly oppositional works, ensuring that their potential negation of the status quo will be safely contained within the limits of dominant, prevailing social
forms. This process is no more evident than in the controversy surrounding the
film *Roger & Me*, and thus we turn to the cultural politics of the silver screen.

NOTES

1. This description of Flint as a "citadel" is drawn from Frank Marquart, *An Auto Worker's Journal* (University Park, PA: Pennsylvania State University Press, 1975), p. 66, where Marquart quotes a 1934 letter from Joe Brown to Marquart that states, in part: "There will be more strikes in auto centers; some will be lost, some will be partially won, and all of them will be like dress rehearsals for the Big Drama to come—when the workers tackle the General Motors citadel in Flint."

2. The Lynds, for example, note this interview exchange: "'Why on earth do you need to study what's changing this country?' asked a lifelong resident and shrewd observer of the Middle West. 'I can tell you what's happening in just four letters: A-U-T-O!'" See Robert S. Lynd and Helen Merrell Lynd, *Middletown: A Study in Modern American Culture* (New York: Harcourt, Brace and Jovanovich, 1956 [1929]), p. 251.

3. See especially Henry Kraus, *The Many and the Few*, 2d ed. (Urbana, IL: University of Illinois, 1985 [1947]).

4. See Herbert Marcuse, *One-Dimensional Man: Studies in the Ideology of Advanced Industrial Society* (Boston: Beacon Press, 1964).

5. See Ronald Edsforth, *Class Conflict and Cultural Consensus* (New Brunswick, NJ: Rutgers University Press, 1987).

6. See C. Wright Mills, "On Knowledge and Power," in *Power, Politics, & People*, Irving Louis Horowitz, ed. (Oxford: Oxford University Press, 1979 [1963]), pp. 599–613, 603.

7. Edsforth, p. 226.

8. J. M. Bernstein, ed., *The Culture Industry: Selected Essays on Mass Culture* by Theodor W. Adorno (London: Routledge, 1991).

Chapter 5

THE SILVER SCREEN

Michael . . . you are at the center of popular culture. And it should be said that your play is no less than an allegory—it's a morality play. It does force America to look in the mirror, and ask itself, "Where are we going? What has happened to us? And whose responsibility is this?"

—Phil Donahue, *Donahue*[1]

As a tragicomic essay on the powerlessness of traditional American Boosterism in the face of true economic cataclysm, *Roger & Me* succeeds hilariously—and sometimes poignantly.

—Richard Schickel, *Time*[2]

I've heard it said that Michael Moore's muckraking documentary *Roger & Me* is scathing and Voltairean. I've read that Michael Moore is "a satirist of the Reagan period equal in talent to Mencken and (Sinclair) Lewis," and "an irrepressible new humorist in the tradition of Mark Twain and Artemus Ward." But the film I saw was shallow and facetious, a piece of gonzo demagoguery that made me feel cheap for laughing.

—Pauline Kael, *The New Yorker*[3]

In art an object is a man-made product containing elements of empirical reality while at the same time changing their constellation, which is a twofold process of dissolution and reconstruction. This sort of transformation alone, not some photographic procedure, gives reality its due.

—Theodor W. Adorno, *Aesthetic Theory*[4]

For a brief moment, Michael Moore's 1989 film *Roger & Me* propelled Flint's experience with dependent deindustrialization into the center of popular culture.[5] *Roger & Me* depicts Moore's ("Me") unsuccessful attempt to have then-GM chairman Roger Smith ("Roger") witness and thereby recognize the dele-

107

terious social impact that GM's plant closings were having on Moore's (and GM's) hometown of Flint. But the film's allegory transcends this strict plot line to suggest a direct relationship between the fate of similarly dependent communities and the structural inequalities inherent in America's capitalist economic system. Indeed, by addressing social conflict primarily through the on-camera reportage of Flint's citizens, *Roger & Me* literally represents a "miscarried conversation" about dependent deindustrialization. In what amounts to a contemporary ode to classical "cheekiness," *Roger & Me* is unadulterated enlightened dissent.[6]

Although *Roger & Me* initially received surprising critical acclaim (winning numerous film festival prizes, including top honors at Toronto and Vancouver), and has since become the all-time top-grossing documentary (earning over $25 million for Warner Brothers), rarely has it been treated as a serious cultural phenomenon, and certainly not as a film whose complicated self-referential tension requires examination in relation to the case of Flint.[7] Instead, the film's significance has been diminished and distorted by the tendency of its would-be dialogue partners to reduce its meaning to only one of its several dimensions. Only from the perspective of the film's multifaceted inner structure, however, can its oppositional content be dislodged from the societal mechanisms that would reinterpret it as more of the ever-same kitsch; only from this perspective can the (non)response that this film received be fully appreciated. Although commentators lauded *Roger & Me* by calling it the "most talked-about film of 1990," that what was talked about was a *film*, and not the causes, effects, and meaning of *dependent deindustrialization*, suggests none other than the culture industry as the ultimate victor in *Roger & Me*'s struggle to politicize popular culture.

ROGER & ME AND ITS RECEPTION IN FLINT

At first blush, *Roger & Me* appears a simple film. Its overarching historical and theoretical allegory is amenable to succinct recapitulation: Flint/America is dependent on GM/Big Business; GM/Big Business does well; times seem good in Flint/America; GM/Big Business leaves/deindustrialization; Flint/America suffer; enter Michael Moore, the young, left-leaning, organic intellectual with evident journalistic as well as comedic skills; Moore asks, as though naively, Why? The substance of the answer is neither original nor surprising: capitalism is not (and never was, and never was supposed to be) a *democratic* economic system, nor is it designed to care for (any specific) humans and their (specific) needs. *Roger & Me* points out that Flint is suffering from the practical consequences of this logic, and from the contradictions that it sends rippling throughout American culture and society. Much of this film, then, is a complaint: too much concentrated, unaccountable, capitalist power, and not enough jobs, income, security, continuity, autonomy; too many false promises in the past, and not enough open, free dialogue in the present; too much uneven economic development, prejudice, and blatant exploitation, and not enough caring, community, and cooperation. What's more, the film suggests that GM's withdrawal created a local power vacuum, into which flowed corruption, including political, moral, and physical decay. In addition, evidence is offered of a reality vacuum, filled not only by run-of-the-mill foolishness but also false consciousness, corporate propaganda, government boondoggle, and cynicism. In this, *Roger & Me* addresses the outstanding features of the rust-belt sector of American society and culture.

But several additional factors make this documentary unusual, and, in some ways, probably unique. Moore's sardonic and self-effacing narration is certainly unexpected. Indeed, as with TV's Roseanne, Moore's just-plain-folks *Roger & Me* persona provides cover for his film's decidedly left-of-center politics. Mass audiences apparently more readily accept the presentation of socialist perspectives when they can identify with the messenger on class, generational, and especially pop-cultural terms. This leaves *Roger & Me* strangely unthreatening *because* it is so safely populist. In addition, *Roger & Me* blurs established boundaries by using the Hollywood feature film to engage in this surprisingly serious political discourse. In this, it parallels Oliver Stone's *JFK* and Spike Lee's *Malcolm X*.[8] Moore's film is unique, however, in that it deals with real people, in real situations.

Thus, to facilitate the spread his political message as much as for the rights to his entertaining, creative effort, Moore accepted Warner Brothers' millions in exchange for its widespread promotion of the film. Originally a shoe-string budget, first-time-director flick meant primarily for marginal union and community audiences, *Roger & Me* now graced the nation's and world's silver screens. And for a brief shining moment, Michael Moore lived out his fifteen minutes of fame on dozens of talk shows, news programs, and other similar public forums, as this bottom-up response to Flint's and America's deindustrialization was catapulted into the star chamber of contemporary mass culture.[9]

Beyond the various twists and turns in the film's mass reception, it is also crucial to consider *Roger & Me*'s inner multifaceted complexity, the specific dimensions of which are suggested by the strikingly divergent characterizations that the film originally inspired in critics and interpreters. *Roger & Me* was variously dubbed a tragicomedy, mockumentary, documentary, and morality play, although each characterization actually emphasizes only one of the film's several dimensions: tragicomedy denotes the structural tension between tragic and comic themes within the film itself; mockumentary highlights the muckraking political intentions of its creator and on-screen narrator; the term documentary refers to the film's intention to address nonfictional, sociohistorical content via journalistic interviews and social analysis rather than fictional characters and scripts; and morality play suggests the film's invitation to its audience to identify with its characters and participate in their situations inasmuch as the film mirrors the audience's own moral dilemmas. As it turns out, this four-pronged schema highlights the standard aspects of any art work: the work itself (the film qua tragicomedy); author (Moore as muckraker); referent (the documentation of Flint and America's deindustrialization); and audience (the American Citizen, who is asked, in effect, if what is good for General Motors is really so good for America). Indeed, these separate dimensions are also each related to a specific theoretical focus in the film, concerning, respectively, popular culture, social power, the logic of capitalism, and the moral foundation for an economic system in a democratic society.[10] Even though the following analysis suggests the primacy of the film's moral dimension—that is, the film's relationship to its audience as advanced through its moralistic critique of capitalism—each dimension exists in the film in complicated tension with the other, and, by way of a brief, orienting introduction to the film's content, each is explicated in turn.

First, consider *Roger & Me* as a *Waiting for Godot*-like tragicomedy. That *Roger & Me* indulges in both tragic and comic themes is evident, for example, in the film's specific reporting on American culture in an age of economic decline. Indeed, as the creative product of a self-styled organic intellectual of the TV generation, *Roger & Me* depicts numerous sacred and profane symbols from popular culture as they humorously interpenetrate, only to finally explode against Flint's (America's) increasingly barren social landscape. *Roger & Me* accomplishes this tragicomic cultural critique via the method of ironic juxtaposition, where comic scenes are immediately undercut by sequences depicting related—although not necessarily *directly* related—human tragedies. While the film contains dozens of such juxtapositions, note, by way of example, the contours and implications of just three.

Roger & Me opens with Michael Moore's self-effacing personal introduction, in which he emphasizes his roots in Flint and his naive faith in the purported cultural consensus of his youth. By reversing home-movie footage, for example, the thirty-five-year-old Moore facetiously implies that his off-beat adult politics is somehow rooted in the fact that he was a "strange child," as evidenced by his having "crawled backwards until the age of two."[11] Moore also notes his youthful admiration for the greatness of Flint's midcentury industrial infrastructure, and suggests that the extent of his longstanding social concern is revealed in his having memorized President Kennedy's inaugural address at the tender age of six. Moore's off-camera recollection of his childhood and childlike belief that only three people in the whole wide world worked for GM—Pat Boone, Dinah Shore, and, as Moore's sentimental voiceover reveals, "my dad"—along with his many similar "Leave It to Beaver"-like remembrances of popular culture circa the Great American Celebration, together suggest the identification of Moore's personal and family biography with his youthful pride in an industrial Flint and a powerful America. But, just as the reference to Kennedy evokes the memory of the President's eventual fate, the innocence of Moore's socioautobiography is quickly shot through with tragic content.

Although newsreel footage of Flint's 1958 hometown parade in honor of GM's fiftieth birthday portrays the Flint of Moore's youth at the center of America's midcentury material abundance and cultural consensus, upon closer inspection, this consensus is revealed as built upon a series of tragic shams. For example, while *Roger & Me* depicts the parade as featuring a smiling GM chairman Harlow Curtiss waving at racist and sexist pop-culture images ("Sergeant Garcia and the swordsman named Zorro," "the radiant Miss America," the dancing all-black "Elks Junior Drill Team" and the all-white "Mr. and Mrs. America"), Moore narrates that "everyday was a great day" just as the newsreel voiceover enthusiastically intones "it's a great day alright," as if naively affirming Moore's sardonic statement.

In contrast to this fast-paced, 1950s glitzy, "it's a great day alright" newsreel backdrop, Moore recalls his Uncle Laverne's participation in the forty-four days of Flint's 1936–37 Great Sit-Down Strike. The sit-down quality of the strike implies a slower time: a time of stubborn, real, face-to-face sociopolitical conflict; a political age; a time of momentous decision; a time when, as Moore states, "the eyes of the world were on Flint." But scenes of the victorious strikers parading out of the plants are immediately undercut with a poststrike GM film that states the paternalistic, soulful corporation's wish that all its employees "prosper," "even those who at times cause trouble." Later in *Roger & Me*, Moore even spins the "big parade" on its head with his 1987 footage of a Flint parade in honor of the fiftieth anniversary of the Sit-Down Strike. As though in accordance with Marx's oft-quoted remark concerning the historical relationship between tragedy and farce, the 1958 parade footage depicts the tragedy of a materially abundant cultural consensus built on open racist and sexist oppression and a tenuous class compromise, whereas the 1987 parade conjures thoughts simply of bread and circuses.

A second revealing instance of *Roger & Me*'s tragicomedy involves Ben Hamper, the Flint autoworker who Moore placed on the cover of *Mother Jones*, and who is now the author of his own best-selling (and equally tragicomic) book entitled *Rivethead: Tales from the Assembly Line*.[12] In *Roger & Me*, Hamper turns up "shooting hoops at the local mental health clinic" after learning that he would be laid off from his GM factory job for the fifth time in five years. Hamper suffered what he describes as a "panic attack," poignantly noting his tearful attempt to cheer himself by singing along with the naive and wishful pop-lyrics of The Beach Boys' "Wouldn't It Be Nice?" For recent generations these are familiar lyrics: "maybe if we wish and hope and pray it might come true . . . we could be happy, we could be married . . . oh, wouldn't it be nice." As they play over sobering scenes depicting seemingly endless rows of Flint's boarded-up businesses and homes, as well as news reports describing the

County's decision to reduce the rate of garbage collections because of budget cutbacks, subsequently leading to Flint's rat population surpassing its human population, audiences typically react with shock and nervous laughter. The depiction of Flint's devastation and decay are tragically at odds with the song's innocent (simple boy-girl) longing for a better life. Indeed, the simultaneity of their presentation decenters the facticity of Flint's slums and bankrupt lives, rendering them the end product of failed politics and dashed dreams. In other words, the song's wishfulness for that which does not exist renders that which does plainly tragic.

Early in the film, industrial, blue-collar Flint is directly contrasted with the contemporary culture of the upwardly mobile young urban professionals (suggested by the image if perhaps not the reality of San Francisco's coffee houses and dessert shops). Evidently, *Roger & Me*'s subsequent depiction of Hamper's and Flint's breakdown is meant not only to reveal the immediate results of deindustrialization in Flint but also to undercut optimistic portrayals of American culture that focus selectively on prospering areas and particular class experiences. In the end, these scenes seem to plaintively question contemporary American culture: Why are the simple wishes, hopes, and prayers for happiness expressed for so many in popular music so often irreconcilable with the political-economic realities of capitalist society? Moore depicts Flint as a city that goes from the mass production of automobiles, not to the postindustrial Yuppiedom of San Franscico, but, as a later scene reveals, to the mass production of *lint rollers*. *Roger & Me* simply queries as to the meaning and human consequences of such social change.

The third example of *Roger & Me*'s tragicomedy centers around the film's basic premise: "My mission was a simple one [Moore tells his audience]: to convince Roger Smith to spend a day with me in Flint, and meet some of the people who were losing their jobs." Moore pursues "the chairman" over three years and through countless situations, with Moore's tongue (and presumably the audience's as well) planted firmly in cheek. Moore's quixotic quest to meet the aloof Chairman Smith continues late into the film, that is, until Moore and his film crew somehow gain entrance to Smith's annual Christmas message, broadcast from GM's Detroit headquarters to its facilities worldwide. With a squeaky-clean choir's singing of "Santa Claus is Coming to Town" fading in and out as background ("you better watch out, you better not shout"), Moore switches between, on the one hand, Smith's awkwardly delivered, apparently insincere pro forma address, and, on the other hand, previously filmed scenes of Flint citizens being evicted from their homes on Christmas Eve. Addressing the theme of Christmas as a "*total* experience," Smith ironically quotes from Charles Dickens, who is credited with the sentiments that Christmas symbolizes the "dignity and worth of each human being" and is a time when people "open their hearts freely." As Smith is reading these lines, Moore reveals to the audience scenes of Flint families placing their Christmas trees, presents, and other belongings on the curbs in front of their former homes. One women angrily shouts obsceni-ties at her children, who apparently serve as scapegoats for the absentee land-lord whose Scroogelike impatience for $150 she deems responsible for her fam-ily's embarrassing and distressing Christmas Eve eviction.

After the speech, Moore finally manages to directly confront Smith, telling him of the evictions occurring in Flint. After Smith denies any knowledge or responsibility, Moore then states, "they used to work for General Motors, now they don't work there anymore." Smith replies, "Well, I'm sorry." Moore: "could you come up to Flint?" Smith: "I *cannot* come to Flint, I'm sorry" (and abruptly turns away). Back in Flint for the last time, Moore's camera moves through the downtown area as The Singing Dogs bark the tune of "Jingle Bells." Switching to the site of the Great Sit-Down Strike—Flint's Fisher One factory, mostly demolished but still flying an American flag—Moore's last words are then heard with the hallowed chorus ("Hallelujah, Rejoice, Rejoice, Rejoice") of a Christian psalm in the background:

Well, I failed to bring Roger to Flint. As we neared the end of the twentieth century, the rich were richer, the poor poorer, and people everywhere now had a lot less lint, thanks to the lint rollers made in my hometown. It was truly the dawn of a new era.

The credits roll to "Wouldn't It Be Nice," followed by Pat Boone singing "I'm Proud to be an American."

Given these examples, the question arises: Is *Roger & Me*'s tragicomic struc-ture merely the product of a creative editing that splices comic scenes next to tragic scenes to form an artificial editorial point-counterpoint, or does the film's representation of popular culture accurately reflect the union of tragic and comic elements within cultural symbols themselves? The former interpretation emphasizes the film's technical structure, while the latter perspective examines the tension between what the film says and what, in effect, it is talking about. For his own part, Michael Moore explains his creative intentions this way:

I knew that I wanted humor to be a dominant factor in *Roger & Me,* but it was scary because I thought some people would be really upset about me making a comedy about the unemployment capital of America. But that's what absurdist humor is all about, I guess. Keep-ing your sense of humor is how you cope with depressing times.[13]

The author's therapeutic intentions notwithstanding, the film itself suggests a somewhat different answer.

Roger & Me resists an exclusively technical reading because it self-critically examines and internalizes the contradictory dimensionality of its various the-

matized symbols. For example, the powerful cultural significance of Christmas
is first raised in Smith's surprising public expression of appreciation for Charles
Dickens. Parallel to Dickens' tale of the miserly Scrooge's mystical realization
of the "true meaning of Christmas," *Roger & Me* suggests Christmas' immanent
(Christian) meaning by playing a hymn's call for redemption over the barren
view of a once-vibrant industrial community. This meaning is in direct contrast to Smith's wooden, obligatory Christmas homilies. *Roger & Me*, however,
also recognizes and pokes fun at Christmas' commercial aspects, deploying for
this purpose The Singing Dogs' kitschy version of "Jingle Bells." In addition, the
film offers a darkly ironic interpretation of the faintly authoritarian lyrics of
"Santa Claus is Coming to Town," suggesting that "you better watch out" or you
will be evicted on Christmas Eve. That racial segregation and inequality are
interwoven throughout these scenes—in the contrast, for example, between
the predominantly white and affluent gathering at GM's Detroit headquarters
and the predominantly nonwhite residents of Flint's Christmas Eve curb-
sides—reveals yet another tragicomic dimension of the American experience
of "White Christmas."

Clearly, *Roger & Me* is not itself responsible for Christmas' many contradictory symbolic dimensions, regardless of its author's intention to produce
"absurdist humor." Instead, inasmuch as the filmmaker is in control of the
film's content at all, *Roger & Me*'s cinematic juxtapositions merely intensify
already existing cultural contradictions by drastically reducing the experiential
time/space that typically separates, in this case, opposing significations among
Christmas' "total experience." Between transcendent Christian values and capitalist commercialism, in other words, profane and sacred meanings of "Christmas" waver under the tragicomic tension of their own internal contradiction.
The "big parade" and "home movies," and other examples from the film, such
as "dream jobs" and the "American Dream," all contain such internal tensions.
Regardless of its author's intention, then, *Roger & Me*'s tragicomic structure is
in touch with the immanent cultural meaning(s) of internally self-contradic-
tory symbols, which, in the linearity of language and film, appear as hyphen-
ated splices of lived experience. Moore's film *is a Waiting For Godot*-like tragicomedy.

Next, consider *Roger & Me* alternatively as a mockumentary. This neolo-
gistic variation on the concept of documentary highlights the significance of
Moore's halfheartedly veiled political agenda by implicitly contrasting it to an
ideal of unbiased, disinterested, value-free reporting. After all, Moore is not
only the "me" of *Roger & Me*, he is also its writer, producer, and director. Not a
one-man show, perhaps, but *Roger & Me* is nevertheless chiefly Moore's creative product. And who is this author, this Michael Moore?

Moore was a known political activist long before *Roger & Me*. In 1972, just
at the age of eighteen, Moore won election to his suburban Flint school board,
making him one of the nation's first eighteen year olds elected to public office

after the ratification of the 26th Amendment. Four years later, he founded his own alternative newspaper, the *Flint Voice*, which later became the *Michigan Voice*. Over the next ten years, Harry Chapin's annual benefit concerts for these publications became a mainstay of local Flint culture, as did the *Voice* itself. From these precocious beginnings, Moore then went on to enjoy a national reputation as a young mover and shaker within the world of the so-called alternative press. In 1985, Moore became a regular commentator on National Public Radio's "All Things Considered" program, and, in 1986, he served briefly as editor of *Mother Jones* magazine.[14] Thus, by 1987, the year he began filming *Roger & Me*, Moore was already a public figure with an impressive journalist and activist resume.

While *Roger & Me* itself (and, moreover, the 1992 *Pets or Meat?*) openly reveals Moore's left-leaning activist biography, many critics nevertheless deem that *Roger & Me* is best understood as primarily ill-concealed propaganda for Moore's political agenda. *Time*'s Richard Schickel calls Moore a "demagogue," emphasizing that his *Roger & Me* is not "simply recording reality but imposing on it a fictional design that proves the predetermined point he wants to make," while *The New Yorker*'s Pauline Kael pursues an ad hominem attack in tersely writing Moore off as a "big, shambling joker in windbreaker and baseball cap" whose film is "humanly very offensive."[15] (GM's public relations experts so appreciated this perspective that they circulated Kael's review with others of similar tone as part of their "truth packet" response to the film.[16])

Roger & Me's mocking dimension *is* surely important, yet far more complicated than such simple reductive criticisms imply. This is illustrated in *Roger & Me*'s implicit theory of social power, which follows a logic that is irreducible to the mere expression of its creator's political sympathies. For example, in presenting himself as a naive, lowly citizen seeking an audience with Chairman Smith, Moore adopts the persona of the proverbial "average Joe" in order to use *personal accessibility* as a metaphor for *public accountability*. That is, Moore's plain-folks ("windbreaker and baseball cap") foil enables him to illustrate the power that corporate figures have to escape interpersonal dialogue, including any face-to-face test of their sincerity. Instead of direct public accountability, then, *Roger & Me* illustrates how powerful figures (mainly Roger Smith, but also other GM, UAW, and local, state, and national government officials) use spokespeople (underlings, surrogates, lobbyists, damage-control experts, security guards, etc.) to buffer their contact with the public. Unfortunately for their bosses, though, these spokespeople make mistakes, commit faux pas, and occasionally appear ridiculous. Were it not for Moore's camera, these gaffs would evaporate into particular, fragmented, dissolving memories, where bygones are typically treated as such. *Roger & Me*'s active intervention into the flow of history, however, captures these ideological gems in a repeatable, reproducible electronic universe, making public scrutiny possible and subsequent public outrage and demand for accountability that much more likely.

In this vein, Moore's film clearly attempts to make a mockery of the on-camera statements made by the elites' middle-level minions. This is accomplished, importantly, only insofar as these spokespeople and public relations artists mock themselves in blatant attempts to mislead, distort, or otherwise publicly dissemble. *Roger & Me* contains dozens of examples of this dimension. These include scenes that hang on the often audacious perspectives forthcoming from still proud former GM-celebrity spokespeople (Anita Bryant and Pat Boone) as well as scenes that focus on those unpaid celebrities of the status quo who apparently have recognized vested interests (the middle- to upper-class guests at Flint's "Great Gatsby" and "Jailhouse Rock" parties and representatives of Flint's country club set, etc.). These and similar scenes of seemingly endless and shameless fabrication, aloof insensitivity, and class-based naivete are undoubtedly some of the most memorable in the film. For present purposes, though, *Roger & Me* as mockumentary is illustrated but by only two scenes that focus on Moore's main target: General Motors.

Roger & Me's first instance of official GM dissembling comes as a company spokesperson announces "the first major plant closing" in Flint, a statement that he immediately follows with

> let me rephrase that [in a deadpan tone, apparently hoping to deflect attention from his error]. This is not a plant closing, it's the loss of one product line.

Why does this spokesperson catch himself and remember to carefully differentiate between a "plant closing" and "the loss of one product line"? Perhaps "plant closing" too clearly suggests a specific entity that could be held responsible for permanently closing a culturally significant workplace, a workplace, moreover, that workers have not only depended on for their livelihoods but have also come to identify with over decades of work experience. "The loss of one product line" is presumably preferable inasmuch as it obscures any source of decision making or responsibility. Indeed, the carefully chosen phrase "one product line" even obscures the existence of an integrated workplace at all, let alone, as we shall see, its "loss."

Of course, the main ideological work of this "loss of one product line" phrase is simply to substitute for the emotionally charged image of a "plant closing." Even though this term is now used in even rather dry, scholarly literature, for the public, "plant closing" still suggests the specter of community abandonment, permanent job loss, and regional economic catastrophe. The "loss of one product line," however, is an unalarming technical phrase that buffers such politically divisive associations because it suggests that only one aspect of the current production work has been lost. In addition, the notion of *loss* (as opposed to *closing*) reverses the vector of responsibility from capital (which would "close" a plant) to organized labor and the community, which might, perhaps by some short-sighted, selfish, antibusiness act, make continued business impossible. After all, how could GM "lose" its own "product line"?

Several years later, after numerous run-ins with GM security guards, public relations representatives, and even a close call with Roger Smith at a GM stockholder's meeting, *Roger & Me* draws to a close with a scene that depicts Moore outside the closing of Flint's historic Fisher One factory.[17] Wishing to interview workers through the factory's ground-floor windows during the last hour of its operation, Moore is quickly accosted by a GM spokesperson, one Mrs. McGee, who patronizingly informs Moore that he is not only trespassing on private property but is also invading the worker's emotional space. In her words:

> It's a very sad time, and it's a very private, personal time. A very private, emotional, family time, and we would not let outsiders in the plant.

Looking over Moore's head and abruptly changing her tone, she curtly summons a security guard standing nearby: "Jerry, this guy, out!" Later, Moore once again begs for the opportunity to speak with the workers, although now expressing his willingness to settle with talking with Mrs. McGee. After first agreeing, McGee then quickly changes her mind, having apparently remembered an important detail from her instructions as an official GM spokesperson:

McGEE: You're a private interest, and no I won't speak to you.

MOORE: We happen to be citizens of this community here; that's not a private interest.

McGEE: We're all citizens of the community. Jerry?

Moore's attempt to establish direct communication between average workers and their company hierarchy is thus coldly rebuffed. Indeed, this scene's barren winter background underscores the feeling of hopelessness and rejection.

There are several telling ironies to this vignette. Note, for example, that the GM spokesperson explains to Moore that the employees he wants to interview are "working right now," although the factory is in the last hour of its operation. Moore is then told that this last hour constitutes a "personal, family time," not a working time. The viewer is also implicitly reminded of the first GM spokesperson who described a previous plant closing as merely the "loss of one product line"—not an event seemingly worthy of a company-sponsored mourning process. Of course, McGee's on-camera condescension toward Moore is evident in her immediate switch from "family time" rhetoric to "this guy, out" authoritarianism. Moreover, Moore is refused an interview because he "doesn't represent anyone" and is thus a "private interest," while the viewer is left wondering whether it is really GM that is the private interest, particularly given its evident lack of concern for the status of a "citizen of the community." That these ironies are immediately apprehensible to even the most casual viewer provides the popular basis for Moore's implicit mockery of GM's open contempt for honest and straightforward relations with Flint and similar American communities. That numerous such scenes populate this mocking dimension of *Roger & Me* suggests an apparently endless supply of managed, ideological speech in capitalist-democratic society. Indeed, this fact leads us back to the critics.

Recall that Kael describes Moore as "a big, shambling joker in a windbreaker and baseball cap," to which she adds that he is "glib" in his "puckish sanity," and that his "picture is like the work of a slick ad exec."[18] In her view, Moore's attempt to "persuade Roger Smith to come to Flint and see the human results of his policies" is both a "mock mission" and a convenient excuse to mock others.[19] For his part, Schickel adds the insight that "far from being a hick, Moore is an experienced professional journalist who knows perfectly well that getting in to see the chairman of anything without an appointment is virtually impossible."[20] In this regard, both critics reduce *Roger & Me* to the latter half of the film's couplet title, ignoring the fact that Moore's on-camera persona is but a foil for the film's intended focus on the symbolic meaning of "Roger."

In contrast to Kael's and Schickel's criticisms, *Roger & Me* as mockumentary follows a critical theory of power relations and is not therefore simply an exercise in personal vendetta. Moore's "mock mission" can be discounted only if it is assumed a priori that public dialogue concerning the human impact of deindustrialization is *not* in any way limited and distorted by unequal power relations, or that the distorting effect of unequal power relations is a phenomena unworthy of exploration and critique. While Moore *did* try to make an appointment (on camera) to see Roger Smith, only the most naive would believe that such a face-to-face meeting was ever a possibility, especially for a person like Moore who is a recognized critic of GM. Indeed, it is worth reemphasizing that the entire film is a *result* of this suppressed conversation—a product of "miscarried dialogue," as it were. Whether Moore's persona is best described as a "shambling joker," a "slick ad exec," or even, as Schickel intones, "a sort of Rust-Belt Garrison Keillor," is beside the point.[21] Who would believe that a GM CEO would join *anyone* for a face-to-face meeting with Flint's laid-off auto workers? The film suggests a far more significant point when it depicts Roger Smith's power to long avoid such encounters. It is important to note in this regard that Smith not only refused Moore an interview, he also rejected Moore's invitations to view the film together, which Smith claims never to have watched.

Next, consider *Roger & Me* in the form in which it first gained recognition, that is, as a documentary. As noted, *Roger & Me* received numerous prestigious film festival prizes in this category. In fact, so highly regarded was the film as a documentary that initially many critics widely assumed that *Roger & Me* had a lock on the Best Documentary Oscar. However, *Roger & Me*'s only acclaim on Academy Award night came from the street outside of the Hollywood ceremony, where homeless people and their organized representatives presented

Moore with their first annual "People's Award." According to *Variety*, "protesters chanted '*Roger & Me* Is Reality'" and "held up placards bearing such slogans as (GM) 'Stop Killing Our Families for Profit.'"[22] While Moore told this gathering that "this is a lot nicer award (than the Oscar)," he had little choice in the matter.[23] Despite the early spate of rave reviews, *Roger & Me* failed to receive even an Academy Award nomination, as by this time the film's status as a documentary had been thrown into doubt by repeated criticisms of its accuracy. Moore explained from the outset that he wanted to avoid what he called "the public television syndrome" by not making a "Dying Steeltown documentary with all the cliches about how horrible it is to be unemployed," but this creativity was eventually turned against the film.[24]

Most of *Roger & Me*'s critics in this category raise what amount to chronological issues, criticizing the film for its edited sequencing, which on occasion does not parallel the historical flow of events. That Moore includes events in the film that did not occur during the two and one-half years of actual filming is also identified as a source of distortion. Minor points of fact have also been criticized. For example, Pauline Kael, who summarizes these criticisms, is especially concerned that the film's scenes depicting Ronald Reagan's 1980 visit to Flint imply that Reagan was president when, in fact, he was only a presidential *candidate*.[25]

The more significant empirically oriented criticisms, however, suggest that Moore's main focus on the impact and response to Flint's (and America's) deindustrialization is significantly distorted, thereby making *Roger & Me*, as in the pithy title of David Bensman's widely read and reprinted *New York Times* editorial, "Narrow, Simplistic, Wrong."[26] Certainly *Roger & Me* does in fact propound an identifiable conceptual approach to capitalism, seeking to explicate Flint's dependency status as well as theorizing the forces that encourage deindustrialization. Having thus delved into the world of social science, *Roger & Me* opens itself to empirical criticism. Since Bensman is an academic expert on deindustrialization,[27] it is worth considering the details of his specific quarrel with *Roger & Me*.

Bensman's article begins:

Many people were outraged that Michael Moore's documentary *Roger & Me* was shut out in the Academy Award nominations. I can't understand why. The film mocks American culture brilliantly, but forfeits any claim to distinction by manipulating its audience to believe that General Motors abandoned Flint, Mich., in the pursuit of profits.

In reality, General Motors poured billions of dollars into its domestic plants, including Flint's, in the 80s. In fact, it embarked on the largest industrial modernization drive in the history of the world. The company bought thousands of robot welders, computer-con-

trolled machine tools, sophisticated computer systems and auto-
mated paint shops.

Because of this modernization effort, 50,000 GM employees still
work in Flint, in the new Buick City complex (sic). Some of the highest quality cars made by Big Three auto makers are manufactured
there.

Moore conveniently ignores GM's efforts so he can convey his
sense that American society has turned its back on the working
class. . . . The story of Flint's ruination is much more complicated
than Mr. Moore's explanation of GM's arrogance and indifference to
the working class.[28]

According to Bensman, then, *Roger & Me* "forfeits any claim to distinction"
because it fails (as a documentary) to adequately detail the complete story of
"Flint's ruination," especially with regard to the actions of General Motors.

Seeking to substantiate his criticism of *Roger & Me*'s "simplicity" (as well
as qualifying his overriding apology for GM), Bensman immediately offers
three criticisms of the giant automaker. First, he concedes that "there was bun-
gling," as "much of GM's massive investment was wasted because the company's attempts to find quick, technological fixes simply threw money at problems."[29] Bensman has already suggested, however, that Flint should be grateful
for the 50,000 remaining GM jobs that such "quick technological fixes" pre-
served. Second, Bensman notes that GM suffers from "bureaucratic paralysis."
However, it is not clear why or even how *Roger & Me* might have examined the
internal workings of GM when, as Bensman's third point concedes, GM is also
characterized by "corporate authoritarianism."[30] Bensman notes further that
"public policy played a role" in GM's decline. As he writes, "high consumer
interest rates and the elimination of tax advantages on consumer debt and sales
tax certainly do not encourage consumers to buy cars," although it is unclear
how *Roger & Me* might have addressed such specific issues without overly tax-
ing *its* audience's interest. "Had Mr. Moore considered these factors," Bensman
suggests, "his analysis of the auto industry would have been more politically
useful," yet "Mr. Moore . . . appears unwilling to provide such inspiration."[31]

Bensman's brief but condensed statement also defends Flint's working
people from what he calls their wrongful depiction as "pathetic . . . victims," as
they have, according to Bensman, "organized food banks, church service societies and unemployed movements," "run for political office, lobbied their leg-
islators—often with success—to gain trade adjustment assistance and
improvements in unemployment coverage," as well as "gone back to school,
learned new skills, [and] started new careers."[32] These criticisms raise additional empirical claims against *Roger & Me*'s voracity as a documentary.

What, then, *is Roger & Me*'s empirical standing as a documentary film? Perhaps, better: What is *Roger & Me* seeking to document?; What is this film talk-

ing about? It is important to stress initially that no critic questions whether or not Flint *has* experienced "ruination" as a result of its loss of high-wage jobs, which, because of GM's dominating presence in Flint, is clearly traceable to this single corporation's capital investment decisions. Rather, as highlighted by Bensman's charges, empirical criticisms center on *Roger & Me*'s implicit *explanation* for these events: Is the film's depiction of capitalism and its theory of deindustrialization sufficiently broad, sophisticated, right? *Roger & Me*'s implicit answers direct attention to the film's central empirical claim that many Americans are experiencing deindustrialization as a social crisis of severe proportions, while little attention is publicly given to their plight.

Following this thematic impulse, *Roger & Me* pays dubious credit to GM's Smith by wryly imputing to him the following deindustrialization strategy. As Moore narrates:

> Roger Smith . . . appeared to have a brilliant plan. First, close eleven factories in the U.S., then open eleven in Mexico, where you pay the workers 70 cents an hour.
>
> Then use the money you saved by building cars in Mexico to take over other companies, preferably high-tech firms and weapons manufacturers.
>
> Next, tell the union you're broke, and they *happily* agree to give back a couple billion dollars in wage cuts.
>
> You then take that money from the workers and eliminate their jobs by building more foreign factories. Roger Smith was a true genius.

This "theory" focuses attention on the irrelevance of social values (human needs, honesty, loyalty to employees and communities) and the lack of public accountability (concern for the long-term national interest) in the short-term, bureaucratic calculus of capitalist profit-maximization strategies. While globalization trends, the uneven international division of labor, union weakness, the military-industrial complex, and so on, are invoked, *Roger & Me*'s explanation for deindustrialization is thus concerned more with what is *absent* in the capitalist system than with the specific structural causes for capital flight and the technological displacement of industrial jobs. *Roger & Me* does not address the factors that increase productivity, the impact on the auto industry of new production technologies and increased foreign competition, changes in financial markets encouraged by deregulation, nor any related issues that are, nonetheless, understandably relevant from GM's perspective. Rather, *Roger & Me* views GM (and by implication all of capitalist society) from the perspective of workers and communities, willingly ceding to GM management the responsibility for the corporation's future viability.

This concern for the social rights of workers and for the communities dependent upon the viability of giant, transnational corporate enterprises is explained in later segments of the film that explore GM's rationale for its investment decisions. This rationale is depicted through Moore's running conversations with Tom Kay, a Flint-based GM lobbyist. The substance of these mini-philosophical debates reveals *Roger & Me*'s general theory of capitalist society.

KAY: General Motors wouldn't be doing anybody any service if it goes bankrupt. It has to do what it has to do to stay competitive in today's economic climate.

MOORE: Even if that means eliminating 18,000 jobs?

KAY: Even if it means eliminating 20,000 jobs.

MOORE: Or 30,000?

KAY: Whatever.

MOORE: How about all the jobs here in Flint?

KAY: It could feasibly happen.

Later, Kay continues his explanation of capitalism:

KAY: I don't understand, though, your connection that by saying "because General Motors was born here it owes more to this community." I don't agree with that.

MOORE: Why not?

KAY: Because I just don't agree with it.

MOORE: But why?

KAY: I believe [GM] is a corporation that is in business to make a profit, and it does what it has to do to make a profit. That's the nature of corporations or companies. It's why people take their own money and invest it in a business, so that they can make money. It isn't so they can honor their hometown.

Finally, in the film's closing credits, Kay says to Moore:

> Well, if you're espousing a philosophy, which apparently you are, that the corporation owes employees cradle-to-the-grave security, I don't think that can be accomplished under a free enterprise system.

After Kay finishes this statement, it is indicated that he too has been laid off. More tragicomedy. More mocking.

These segments document that GM, by its own account, recognizes no obligation to Flint or to any community or group of employees (regardless of its past willingness to participate in parades in its honor), because, in a free-enterprise capitalist economic system, its only concern is and should be to max-imize profits regardless of the social cost this might entail. *Roger & Me* recog-nizes that this is the case, and, in fact, the film depicts numerous empirical instances of this process at work.

Yet, *Roger & Me* still criticizes the transcendence of the capital accumula-tion process by appealing to the degree of imbalance between the additional monetary benefits that an already profitable corporation receives from its dein-dustrialization strategy and the extreme social costs that this process produces. A moral dimension is thus injected into the otherwise amoral logic of perpetual profit maximization. *Roger & Me* suggests that corporate downsizing strategies are justified only as a last resort in an effort to maintain solvency, not as a strat-egy designed to increase already existent profits. There is, of course, no legal basis for *Roger & Me*'s critical perspective: it is strictly a moral claim rooted in the film's documentation of the social costs of GM's decisions.

Given this self-understanding, it is odd that Kael would state:

> Whatever the reasons for the GM shutdowns, the company had a moral and financial responsibility to join with government agencies and the United Automobile Workers in arranging for the laid-off workers to reenter the labor force. Moore doesn't get into this—at least, not directly.[33]

Kael's statement that "the company had a moral and financial responsibility" is incorrect, as GM had (and has) no legal, moral, or financial responsibilities for its laid-off workers or abandoned communities (other than via the joint pro-grams that the UAW negotiates for its own members), nor, as has been noted, does GM voluntarily recognize a moral or financial responsibility, nor does it officially recognize its connection to those indirectly dependent upon the com-pany's local payroll. Besides Kay's remarks, we need only to refer to *Roger & Me*'s first plant-closing scene in which a GM spokesperson stresses "there is nothing out there for them [the newly unemployed workers] to depend upon for the future." *Roger & Me* recognizes the truth in this, but argues, nonetheless, that the company *should* have honored a moral and financial responsibility. Contrary to Kael's claim, then, *Roger & Me does* "get into this," and quite directly.

But how does *Roger & Me*'s economics square with Bensman's critique? In general, Bensman apparently misreads the empirical focus of the film: it is not a documentary presentation of the auto industry as seen from GM's perspec-tive. The logic of the film's (albeit limited) explanation for deindustrializing processes is grounded in the lives of Flint's working people and the larger com-munity, and thus its "narrow" focus. That *Roger & Me* (as an entertaining fea-ture film) offers a relatively simple explanation for deindustrialization should go without saying, but nothing that *is* stated in the film fails to jibe with empirical data. Bensman suggests, though, that *Roger & Me*'s economic theories are too simple because the "audience comes away feeling the company deserves every bit of red ink on its balance book," as though his concern is that the audience will forget their dependency on GM and similar corporations. But there is nothing in *Roger & Me* that suggests that its purpose is to encourage or applaud GM's bankruptcy when, in fact, the film's moral point hinges upon the company's wealth and power in juxtaposition to Flint's and GM employees' lack thereof. It is unclear, furthermore, whether Bensman believes that *Roger & Me* is empirically *or* morally "wrong," although he implies that it is both. This is especially true of his claim that the film portrays Flint's working class as "pathetic," while "the truth is that these working people have not let themselves be destroyed." This is simply an inexplicable interpretation of the film itself, for *Roger & Me* includes several scenes of Flint's working people struggling against GM's decisions; resisting, that is, the best they can. It is also clear that Moore himself is sympathetic to these struggles, although his intention is mainly to participate and intervene in them, and not, as Bensman does, to view them solely from the outside. Lastly, while the film does criticize organized labor, its criticisms are clearly pointed at the UAW's mainstream leadership and not at its rank-and-file membership.

On the other hand, there is a certain ironic truth to Bensman's view that *Roger & Me* portrays Flint and its people as "victims." In effect, the film responds: Given Flint's "ruination," is it not in fact a victim? Bensman further states that Moore "wants us to laugh with him at those who believe that companies like GM are good for America," and that Moore "plays on our moral and cultural superiority to the rich corporation that destroyed the beloved working-class community of the past." Indeed, but this moral and cultural "superiority" derives from *Moore's* community—from his Uncle Laverne's struggles through to today's cinematic version of a sit-down strike—in which the amoral structure and dynamic of capitalism is questioned by average citizens in very plain and human terms. The final irony is Bensman's charge that *Roger & Me* depicts Flint's working people as "politically ineffective," while his own editorial was circulated by GM in its coordinated effort to undercut the sting of *Roger & Me*'s political appeal.

Despite the questionable validity of these specific criticisms, *Roger & Me* nevertheless deserves the critical scrutiny that "documentary" efforts necessarily invite, for, inasmuch as it is a work of politically committed art, *Roger & Me* addresses legitimately debatable sociohistorical material. And, as an art work, there is no question that the film draws many checks on the bank of poetic license, telling small lies in its effort to capture big truths (in an entertaining and humorous fashion no less). Thus, perhaps the more appropriate question would be: Is *Roger & Me* true *enough*? Given the film's interest in sketching only a basic rationale for deindustrialization as the background for its central focus on the cultural silence regarding the legitimacy of the capitalist system, the preceding analysis suggests that *Roger & Me*'s empirical dimension is, contrary to Bensman's view, focused, simple, correct. It could be said with Adorno that, while the film dissolves the complexity of political-economic systems into a landscape of cultural analysis, its poetic reconstitution of the two nevertheless gives "reality its due."[34] In the end, *Roger & Me* was not nominated for an Academy Award in the documentary category, nor in any other, as its reflexive play with the harrowing fact/value distinction ultimately left it far too epistemologically controversial for Hollywood's guardians of the silver screen.

Of course, *Roger & Me* was never intended for "the critics" anyway. As noted, this was Michael Moore's first film, produced with money in part raised from bingo games and yard sales, and originally conceived only for union audiences, dissident groups, and communities suffering the ill-effects of deindustrialization. Moore's original hope was that *Roger & Me* would serve as a type of political catalyst that would, in his words, encourage "people to do something," "even if it's just to talk to their neighbor about the situation."[35] Only *Roger & Me*'s unexpected success on the film festival circuit pushed it toward its eventual national and international distribution. Now that *Roger & Me* occupies shelf space in most American video stores, the question is whether or not it has achieved anything other than a career for its creator and a sort of sublime fame for his hometown. What *have* people thought and done in response to this film? Consider, then, *Roger & Me* as "morality play."

There is no question that *Roger & Me* was formed for audience appeal. Comparing the film's combination of humor and social commentary with that of Charlie Chaplin's "The Little Dictator" and "Modern Times," Moore explained his intention to make a popular film:

> We don't go to art house movies in Flint. Where do we go? We go to *Lethal Weapon, Pee-wee's Big Adventure, Batman.* I wanted *Roger & Me* to play more like *Pee-wee's Big Adventure* than *Hotel Terminus.*[36]

In addition to making the film palatable to a mass audience, *Roger & Me* also clearly intended specific types of audience response. As noted, Moore wanted his audience to "do something," "even if it's just to talk to their neighbor about the situation." However, Moore also hoped that his film would convey a "lesson." While he feels that it is "too late for Flint," Moore believes that "it's not too late for the rest of the country."[37] As he explains:

> If the rest of the country can learn a lesson from Flint, it's best to learn it quick, because what's happening in Flint is coming to your hometown.
>
> As long as decisions that drastically affect people's lives can be casually made without any sort of government control, they're going

to do it. They're going to go wherever they can to make the biggest buck. It's not enough just to be able to elect politicians. There should also be democracy in the workplace and democracy in the economy. And I'd like to see that happen in my lifetime.[38]

In other words, Moore intended that *Roger & Me* would not only describe the menacing impact of deindustrialization, but that it would also make a moral appeal for the rightness of what has come to be called "economic democracy" (read socialism), much as Chaplin, for example, did in his work. Moore hoped that his audiences would be entertained as well as morally aroused, and that, as a result, they would become politically mobilized.

Prior to its national commercial release, Moore suggested that "the response to the film has really cut across social and economic lines" because, "thankfully, intellectuals and working-class audiences both know what the film is talking about."[39] But these enthusiastic film festival audiences—from New York to Telluride—were hardly representative of mass audiences. In order to assess the film's mass reception, it is necessary to listen to a more representative audience. In fact, it might be hypothesized that the most significant audience would be Flint residents themselves, for it is their experience that provides the film with its moral as well as empirical basis, and it is this community's fate that *Roger & Me* offers as a mirror for the entire country.

Predictably, Flint did become a site of intensive discussion of the film. Some of this was provoked by Moore's request that Warner Brothers premiere the film there, free of charge, for thousands of Flint residents. The *Roger & Me* "world premiere" became the industry's largest-ever, on-location opening night. This event was packaged with television interview call-in programs featuring Michael Moore and Flint mayor Matthew Collier, and it attracted national and international coverage. This avalanche of media attention spurred community-wide debates that rippled through university classrooms, union halls, and public and private spaces large and small.[40]

ENTER PHIL

But the most popular forum for community debate over *Roger & Me* appeared in late January of 1990. Phil Donahue, the daytime television icon who pioneered the issue-oriented, audience-participation talk show, brought his program to Flint for a double-segment interview with Michael Moore.[41] Of the approximately 2,000 Flint-area residents who packed the city's largest auditorium for the much-anticipated chance to participate in the national broadcasts, 144 received the opportunity to speak their minds.[42] The frenzied theatrical atmosphere of these programs provides a convenient case study in Flint's circus reception of the film.[43] In fact, a close examination of these interactions reveals *Roger & Me*'s ultimate moral/political quandary.

At one point in the *Donahue* program, its host tells the Flint audience and his television viewers that, in his view, *Roger & Me* forced the country to "look in the mirror, and ask itself, 'Where are we going? What has happened to us? And whose responsibility is this?'"[44] If these questions are used to arrange the 146 televised audience statements as "answers" or responses to the film itself, content analysis suggests that approximately two-thirds of the total statements implicitly respond to the question of "whose responsibility is this?" whereas the remaining one-third are divided between thoughts on the city's and country's future (question 1) and the nature of their current condition (question 2).[45] Close attention to the quality and content of these remarks reveals the contours to Flint's popular reception of the film.

Where are we going? or, as one audience member asks:

> I'd like to know, after this hour is over with, after the hype of *Roger & Me* has quieted down, what is all this going to amount to, and what good is it going to do? Somewhere along the line, some power people are going to have to care. And how are we going to make them care?[46]

Recognizing the fleeting nature of media "hype" and the intransigence of "power people," this audience member essentially rearticulates Donahue's first question. Highlighting the question's significance, another audience member suggests: "If Flint falls, America will fall,"[47] while two others state: "A lot of people don't realize, the bottom-line solution to the problem of job loss in Flint is political,"[48] and "Why don't we . . . go against the government?"[49] Three additional audience members express their general feelings that "We have to do something,"[50] "We need to start pulling together,"[51] and we need to "get busy getting ourselves together, and prepare for action."[52] While these comments are vague and insubstantial, they stand out as articulate and coherent when compared to the other statements that fall into this category.

The following responses, for example, emphasize the community's perceived dependence on corporate investment decisions:

> Flint, Michigan, today would like to ask big industry all over the world: "Come to Flint, please."[53]

> Wake up, America. We're going towards international government, but we have national greed. Let's keep it here in the United States.[54]

> I'd like to say, I love America. I love Michigan, and I love Flint, Michigan. Keep my job here in Flint, Michigan.[55]

In begging "big industry" for their livelihoods, Flint residents assume that they are powerless to do much else. For these Flint residents, Donahue's "Where are we going?" is not considered a practical question, that is, a question within their power to answer or address.

Other responses in this first category typically appeal to the powers of positive thinking or divinity, even though both of these "solutions" are explicitly criticized in *Roger & Me*:

> I just think—everyone here, in Flint, Michigan, you work for GM—I don't mean to sound religious, but everybody just pray about it. Because the Lord up above can bring us through all things.[56]

> What we need to do is pick a positive thing, and all take all this energy that everybody's fighting about, and put it towards one thing—the city of Flint. Pick a positive goal, and go for it.[57]

> Let me tell the world that the people of Flint are still working, and they're going to work and make this town back where it used to be. Believe it![58]

Here, "Where are we going?" depends upon the efficacy prayer and the intensity of personal belief in positive goals, even if such goals entail nothing more than achieving what "used to be."

Lastly, the community's articulation of its self-image exposes an area of controversy. Some audience members express confidence in the city's future, while others disagree, sometimes quite strongly. Consider this typical exchange of viewpoints:

> I am a GM worker. I've been laid off, and I have suffered the consequences of having inhuman practices in the plant, as well as on the streets. Our schools are going as a result of the raping of our tax system. Our police forces—everything we need in this town is dying because of what GM is doing to this town. We appreciate you. We love you, Michael, for making this film and telling our story![59]

> That's not true! That's not true. I just reeducated myself, and I think this town's doing great. We've come back up on our feet, and Genesee County is one of the greatest places in the world to live in—to raise your family.[60]

> Phil, this town is not coming back on its feet. The reality is, what he did, he put Flint on the map for everybody in the world to see the dis-

graceful kinds of things that's happened to the people in this town. He did it. I'm glad he did it. We're going to support you. And we're going to get *20/20* here. We want *Primetime*, NBC, ABC—you've got to bring them here! Bring them to Flint![61]

While some agree with the film's suggestion that Flint's future is "bleak," others call it "one of the greatest places in the world."

Summarizing the above, approximately one of six statements (23 of 146) implicitly address Phil Donahue's question concerning Flint's and America's future. While these statements generally lack substance and coherence, their implicit content suggests that the response of Flint's residents to the question "Where are we going?" is scattered between calls for the salves of solidarity, corporate favor, faith, and media attention. Of course, these responses also imply an answer to the second of Donahue's questions: "What has happened to us?" Parallel to the first ratio, roughly one in six audience statements directly address this question (25 of 146), with nineteen of these specifically articulating a conception of Flint's social conditions. However, the content of these statements reveals a significant division among them.

On the one hand, only a third of these remarks can be said to support the film, and, of these, less than half reflect a theoretical understanding of deindustrialization. For example, one statement mentions the term "outsourcing," which refers to the subcontracting of production to non-UAW facilities: "We have a problem here with—they keep outsourcing jobs to Mexico and places like that, where they're only making 80 cents an hour."[62] The second statement notes the possibly deleterious impact of international concentration in the auto industry: "General Motors, Ford, and Chrysler are so diversified in their foreign auto companies, that they're their own foreign competition. And we're losing our jobs due to that."[63] The third statement refers to experience with covert corporate downsizing and community exploitation. This is a comparatively articulate statement, and ironic in that this person is not a Flint resident:

I am not from Flint, but I'm from a town about 40 miles to the south of here, Pontiac, who (sic) has been devastated by GM also. It goes back to 1982. And this movie brings attention to whether or not the integrity of General Motors is any good.

GM told us in 1982, at the height of the Japanese invasion, "Give us concessions. Do a better job. Work harder. Take a little less pay. And we'll have equality of sacrifice." That has not happened. Communities are being pitted against one another. Tax abatement concessions continue to rise, and there has been no equality of sacrifice from the top of this organization in General Motors.

They have reduced people at the lower level of management, but the main sacrifice has come from the workers.[64]

The remaining pro-*Roger & Me* statements in this category refer to the impact of deindustrialization on Flint. One audience member states simply that the film shows "what Flint really is,"[65] and another suggests that people "should not want to come to Flint and live right now" because of the city's poor living conditions.[66] A third audience member states that the film is "overdramatized, but it'll let everybody know that it can happen to them, not just here."[67] Two additional statements note the relationship between GM unemployment and other social problems, namely divorce and small business failure.[68]

Although some audience members tended to sympathize with the film's implicit approach to the question "What has happened to us?" two-thirds were critical of the film's depiction of Flint. One subset of these statements proclaims, in effect, That did not happened to me! Consider these several examples:

> I'd like to know how come in the movie—I know it's bringing attention to Flint, and these are—everybody here is on an equal base—everybody in Flint is good people. You put dumb people out. Where are the middle-class people? Where are the lower-class people in your movie?[69]

> I'd like to know why you filmed the Oak Park urban renewal area and implied in the film that it was the unemployed, laid-off, displaced people?[70]

> I was just wondering, for whatever reason possessed you to make this movie—whether it was good or bad—because I'm not old enough. I don't understand all this. But I was just wondering why you would show—I don't know if I can name streets, but you showed the slummiest areas. And—yeah, I mean—and then, you know, you can tell from the people that have gone from riches in the shop to having nothing, then from the people that have been slums all their lives. And that's what that was. That wasn't people that had anything, and then went back to nothing.[71]

> I think your example in your movie of the evicted people was in poor taste. You didn't show, like, an average, hard-working General Motors family that was losing their home. You made it look as though it was a very poor, low-class type of people that were renting. And General Motors people that work hard are buying their homes.[72]

In these typical statements, Flint audience members refuse to identify with their fellow Flint residents depicted in the film. Criticizing *Roger & Me* for failing to show the struggles of smart, middle-class, hard-working, home-owning, former or current GM employees, implies that these audience members not only identify themselves thusly, but also differentiate themselves from others upon these criteria. It would appear, in some cases, that the classic distinction between a deserving versus an undeserving poor underlies and motivates these efforts to differentiate among levels of community stratification.

A second subset of statements criticize the film for ignoring various particular developments, social groups, or lifestyles. Several apparently affluent suburbanites even suggest that the film's depiction of Flint has influenced them to further avoid and remain ignorant of what is happening in some sectors of the city. For example:

> I got news for you Roger [sic], I live in Owosso. And I've shopped in Flint all of my life. But if I'd have seen your movie, I would have been afraid to come to Flint.[73]

> I'll have you know that I live in Owosso, also. And I shopped in Flint many times before I went and saw that movie. Had I seen that movie first, I'd never shopped in Flint, I'll tell you.[74]

> Michael, I've got a question for you. You showed a lot of clips of the closing of Flint [Fisher Body] 1, and when it fell down. Why didn't you show any when they built up the Great Lakes Technology Centre?[75]

> The largest employer has been forgotten—that is the small business-man that employs approximately 60 percent of the work force of the state of Michigan. The small businesses receive nothing. Just SOL. Ask me, because I'm a businesswomen across from the closed Fisher plant. I do feel that we can pick ourselves up by our bootstraps. I've reinvested. And, hopefully, we'll attract new trade from the new Great Lakes Technical [sic] Center.[76]

> I thought the movie was good, but I don't think you showed enough positive images, like the Bobby Crim Road Race, which brings a lot of people into Flint all over the world [sic].[77]

If nothing else, these responses suggest little community-wide agreement on "What is happening to us?" Not only are few interested in addressing this question in theoretical terms, there is also little consensus concerning who "us" is. Whereas those who identify with the characterizations in the film typically say, "that's what Flint is" or "thank you for telling our story," those who do not identify with the film's portrayals respond either by challenging the depiction with anomalous cases or by accepting it while also rejecting their identification with the city as a whole. Considering the seventeen representative examples cited above, the clear trend is toward a community response decidedly uncomfortable with the film as a cultural "mirror."

Yet, the above considerations aside, the Flint *Donahue* programs were implicitly dominated by the question: "Whose responsibility is this?" Approximately two of three audience statements (95 of 146) indicate that some institution or individual should be blamed for Flint's experience with dependent deindustrialization, or, on the other side of the coin, are intended to exonerate and defend one or another institution or individual from blame. Before drawing conclusions about the nature of Flint's reception of *Roger & Me*, it is necessary to consider its most crucial dimension.

Of these ninety-five comments and questions, five criticize the UAW in some form (with two defenses), two cast blame on so-called big shots, and one simply blames "the government."[78] Predictably, the main targets for the audience's attacks were General Motors (29), Michael Moore (14), and Flint citizens and/or workers themselves (12), with each of these entities defended eleven, eleven, and seven times, respectively. This quantitative representation, however, does not reflect the extreme levels of animosity, incoherence, and self-blame contained in most of these responses, nor the intense quality of the bitterness and resentment directed at Moore from his hometown crowd.

Note, first, the criticisms directed toward GM. Although invited to do so, GM did not dispatch an official spokesperson to the *Donahue* programs. Indeed, GM sought to undercut the programs by discouraging its dealers from advertising during them, stating in a letter to the *Donahue* producers, "We are not interested in doing anything that might help promote a film that is inaccurate and totally unfair to the city of Flint, its people, and the thousands of dedicated GM employees working there."[79] Yet, GM did have an unofficial spokesperson in the audience. After informing Phil Donahue that her husband heads GM's Flint Automotive Division, this audience member states:

> I'd like to say that we really need—I mean, we can use Roger to blame all we want. He's a name that everybody knows. But I think you and all the people in America that buy foreign cars are to blame. And don't you—[audience agitation] Excuse me, I'm not done! And don't you for a minute think that those guys at the top don't give up a lot and don't work their rears off to do what they're doing for General Motors. Don't you think it! Don't you think it![80]

During the second program segment, this same women (who was the only audience member to speak twice), continued her defense:

I think there's always employment security worries for everyone that works. And I'll tell you one thing, the families of these people who still work in the upper ranks are always worried about, "Gee, is he going to come home for dinner, tonight?"[81]

To this, a majority of the audience exclaimed "Awwwww!" in a growl of disbelief and mock sympathy, representing the only occasion when the audience appeared in general agreement.[82] Swipes at this most unofficial representative of GM's upper management (e.g., "Well, I just want to say I think it's pretty comical that the one lady's worried about her husband coming home for dinner, when most of us here are worried about putting a dinner on the table"[83]) continued throughout both programs.

More pointed criticism of GM generally reflected such themes from *Roger & Me* as the corporation's abandonment of Flint, its perceived betrayal of its 1908 hometown, and GM management's perceived indifference toward laid-off workers:

For years, General Motors has been stripmining the pockets of the American people through their tax dodge—loopholes and dodges. It's a fact that General Motors is making a profit right now. They have for several years. They acquired Hughes Aircraft, they have not brought any of that manufacturing back to this town, nor do they intend to. General Motors does know that it's not going to be building cars in the very near future. It's too bad that a lot of people here in this town are going to suffer because of it.[84]

I'd just like to know, you know, a corporation that has told us time and time again, "Cooperate with us. Give us your support. We're all in this together"—you know, they have no loyalty to us, according to the film. The GM representative for Flint said he has no loyalty. GM doesn't owe Flint anything. Well, how can they expect loyalty from us as workers for their corporation? They don't want to give us any loyalty back![85]

I think Roger Smith said what he thought of General Motors employees at the end of the movie, which was he didn't want to come to Flint.[86]

In contrast, the pro-GM responses tend to lack focus and content:

I'm a thirty-five-year-old employee at an hourly rate at General Motors. Raised two children, bought a home, been treated fairly. And I thank the Lord for this country and for this job.[87]

I would like to say that, after all, General Motors hasn't been all bad. There's some good in General Motors. And, Phil, I would like to say, it's good seeing you![88]

I closed down the truck plant, and GM sent me to school. And now I'm a designer for General Motors. I work for modern engineering, but I design cars now. And it's—thank you, General Motors, for paying for that school.[89]

I'm a General Motors retiree. And thank God for General Motors.[90]

Indeed, only the programs' first audience member comment and Moore's quick response to it actually reflect the substance of the film's internal debate over the proper role of corporations in society:

AUDIENCE MEMBER 1: General Motors is in business to make a profit. Every company in the United States is in business to make a profit. They are not in business to keep Flint employed.[91]

MOORE: They're citizens of this country. Let me tell you something. They're citizens of this country, and they're part of this community. They don't operate separate from everybody else. They have a responsibility to the people here that built them into the world's largest corporation.[92]

This series of audience responses suggests Flint's internally conflicted view of GM. Some see GM as the hand that has always fed them, while others react to having been slapped. Yet, Flint's particular ambivalence toward Michael Moore is even more pronounced and emotionally charged. Many of the most hostile and resentful comments are directed, not at GM, but toward Flint's boy-made-good. Moore is attacked for his monetary gain from the film (Warner Brothers paid him approximately $2 million for the rights to a film that cost approximately $250,000 to produce), but also for his purported belittling and abandoning of Flint as well as his purported disloyalty, opportunism, and even racism:

Are you giving any of the money that you made to Flint?[93]

I'd like to know, Mr. Moore keeps talking about the money that General Motors makes, and I don't believe he answered this young girl's question. You purport to be a supporter of Flint, and yet you made a mockery in the film of a couple of fundraisers that put more than

$75,000 back into this community. What are you going to put back into this community?[94]

I have a question for you. How many cars of the last five years that you've purchased have been American made?[95]

You know, the only real positive thing that's come out of this movie, Mike—I guess, outside of that which has gone into your pocket—is that it's unified this city, because this is a damn good place. And if you didn't show it, you should have![96]

I find it sad that you think University of Michigan–Flint is *just* a college. It has one of the finest physical science and theater departments in the Midwest, and the nation.[97]

Michael, recently I did some research on your paper that you have published in the past. And I was wondering, when did you have a sudden change of heart, and concern for the working people? There was a cartoon in there about the shop rats. I thought you made fun of the labor workers. When did you have a sudden change of heart about the people in this town?[98]

And I understand that, like, you have—you're making a movie about pro-Palestinian, and you're very anti-Semitic. Well, then, how come half your cast is Jewish? I mean, half the credits are Jewish?[99]

At one point, Donahue (himself evidently sympathetic towards Moore and the film) is overwhelmed by the audience's eager willingness to impeach Moore's integrity:

May I ask Michael Moore—Michael, how do you feel about the general tone and what has transpired here, yesterday and on our program today? I mean, how do you feel personally? Are you surprised by this reception? Did you know it would be like this? What's going on here?[100]

Moore responds:

Oh, no. I'm not surprised at all. I mean, I think, first of all, the majority of the people in this town know how rough it's been, because they've lived through it. And they're very grateful that you're here, so that their story can be told. There are those, Phil—there are those, though, who are doing quite well. And you can travel through neighborhoods in this city and see how well they're doing, while the rest of the people here are struggling to survive. I'm not surprised that the Junior League, or the Mayor's Office, or the UAW leadership, or the GM executives are upset at this film. They should be upset. I want them to be upset.[101]

Although eleven statements can be generously interpreted as favorable toward Moore, they are typically incoherent or insubstantial:

I'd just like to say, I think you did a good thing. And I think it's going to help us out. And I heard someone over there say, "No one's going to come to Flint"—Phil came to Flint.[102]

I would just like to say that Michael Moore did not embarrass Flint, Michigan. What embarrassed Flint, Michigan, was the unemployment and the crime in this town.[103]

I just say that we need a lot more Michael Moores.[104]

Michael Moore, you really have brought attention to Flint. And I want to know, did you pray about this and have God behind you, or what?[105]

One pro-Moore statement that stands out comes from a black member of the audience who supports Moore's self-conscious attempt to address Flint's racial divisions:

I'd just like to say that I'm tired of those Hollywood fern bar types trying to condemn Mike, and not give him an Academy Award, claiming inaccuracies. The way they've been misportraying black folks for four generations, and Mike portrayed us so accurately in a few minutes, it's just, you know, unconscionable. Good luck, Mike.[106]

Overall, though, as Donahue's bewilderment suggests, much of this program's sound and fury came in these numerous attacks against Moore. While General Motors is often defended in Flint on personal and even emotional terms, Michael Moore (qua self-appointed Flint spokesperson and social critic) is often similarly impeached. This should not be surprising, as Moore intends to criticize various groups and institutions: "I want them to be upset," he says.

Perhaps, though, the most poignant moments in this "morality play" involve the many instances of the audience's (community's) own snarling self-blame and infighting. This last subset of implicit audience responses to the question "Whose responsibility is this?" is illustrated in these statements:

I want to know why, when there were so many layoffs and everything, and the colleges around here geared up—they hired more teachers, more administration—why didn't you go back to school and get a better job than what you had before? You blame yourself![107]

I'd like to say to the people that keep complaining about Flint—blood is thicker than water. If you don't like Flint, go back where you came from.[108]

You have a lot of GM workers complaining. But you still have a lot of GM workers driving foreign cars.[109]

I'm a middle-class small business owner. And I deal with GM workers all day long. And I believe that 75 percent of GM workers got what they deserve. They've brought a lot of this on themselves. I think 25 percent of the people are honest, hard workers. But the general amount of GM workers put in an honest three hours work out of eight. They get a buddy or foreman to clock them out if it's a nice day. And you can walk in the plant and see TVs going, and newspapers everywhere. I mean, if you're going to cry over losing the job, why not try putting in an honest day's work. And that's why automobiles cost $20,000 today.[110]

My husband stood up [and made a statement previously]. He worked for GM for two years. He got laid off. He went out to a $4 job. He's got two kids to support. He found a job. You guys, you can find it, it's out there.[111]

The President of the United States does not even have job security. Why do you guys want it?[112]

There's quite a few of them sitting out there right now that have made careers out of welfare. McDonald's may not be a lot, but it's something.[113]

I know that my family doesn't work for GM. And I think if my family can get jobs without GM, everybody else here that doesn't have a job can, too.[114]

These statements suggest that it is average individuals and GM workers alike who should shoulder the blame for Flint's deindustrialization. They say, in effect: If you haven't returned for more education, "blame yourself"; If you don't like Flint, "go back where you came from"; If you drive a foreign car, you are a traitor or suicidal; If you want economic security, you want more than you can ask for; If you are a GM union employee, there is a 75 percent chance that you are dishonest and shiftless, and so "deserve" unemployment; If you can't support a family of four with a minimum wage job, such as those at McDonald's, then you are unmotivated; and because non-GM jobs do in fact exist, everyone who wants one can find a job.

In the face of this emotionally charged onslaught—supported in Flint by a common and well-entrenched resentment toward UAW employees for their above-average wages and the relative power they can draw upon in their places of work—only a few audience members rose in their own defense:

I'd just like to say that we don't make the kind of money that people think we do for putting up with all that junk in there [i.e., the factories].[115]

Well, I'm tired of hearing—of blaming everyone for buying foreign cars. Are there any foreign companies left that the Big Three don't own?[116]

I just want to say, I work for Chevrolet Truck. And a lot of us are good workers. We work every day. And we do not go to the bar and drink.[117]

We deserve everything we get, because we fought for it, we have organized for it, and we would advise other workers who are being exploited to get out and organize and fight for their jobs. And we want to tell Reverend Robert Schuller to take his message of positive thinking to Consumers' Power [Company], and see if they'll accept that for our utility bill.[118]

People are saying that they should have went to college. What about the people that were less fortunate, and couldn't go to college—that didn't have the money?[119]

To the gentleman that said to get an education, and then you can do things—my son, he got a master's degree two years ago, and he's been trying to get in General Motors and hasn't got there yet.[120]

Apropos of this struggle among audience members to assign blame (even to one another) for the city's economic and social decline, Phil Donahue observed late in the second program segment:

You know, Marx and Engels, if I might put it this way, would not be surprised that the workers are fighting with each other. This is what they predicted capitalism would do. Does this embarrass us? And how do we speak to this monumental philosophical question, at a time when America uncertainly moves into the twenty-first century?[121]

While Moore tried to answer this question at the moment it was posed, none of the dozens of Flint citizens participating in these *Donahue* programs, nor the many thousands more participating in the community-wide conversation over *Roger & Me*, ever effectively spoke to this "monumental philosophical question." Instead, as suggested by the *Donahue* audience, Flint's response to *Roger & Me* was and continues to be largely dominated by childish "moral" concerns: Is Michael Moore good or bad?; Is *Roger & Me* good or bad?; Am I good or bad? What explains this reception?

Moore originally hoped that audiences would "leave the theatre with some spirit in them, some life, some sense of humanity, and hopefully, some anger," and that, as noted, they would "do something, even if it's just talk with their neighbors" about "democracy in the workplace and democracy in the economy." He reasoned, "I think getting people depressed only paralyzes them."[122] Yet, the film's emphasis on questioning the *moral* basis of the *capitalist system* and its *class structure*—as exemplified in its focus on "Roger" and other "spokespeople"—is nothing if not paralyzing. *Roger & Me*'s particular brand of moral entrepreneurship drives self-reflection on individual responsibility to the forefront of the film's reception, thereby, ironically, deflecting attention away from the constraining structural elements of the system itself in favor of attention on those who are, as it were, caught in its gears. This is particularly true in Flint, where, simply by virtue of membership and participation in the community's way of life, individuals can automatically fall under suspicion for their complicity with the film's subject matter. In Flint, it is easy to see why the generalized question "Whose responsibility is this?" is so often understood as "Who *among* us is to blame?"

Many of Flint's residents are apparently less confident than Moore in their own irreproachability, tending instead to suffer doubt and self-blame. This is understandable insofar as most have directly or indirectly participated all their lives in a day-to-day, taken-for-granted dependency on GM (capitalism). In contrast to Moore's biography, for example, few of Flint's residents can appeal to such substantial entrepreneurial achievements; few have been as independent, creative, and productive, let alone the fearless editor of their "own muck-raking newspaper." As the *Donahue* programs suggest, the questioning of such evidently vulnerable (powerless, dependent, occasionally hysterical) individuals' moral responsibility on the basis of whether they accept or deny the legitimacy of the structural process of deindustrialization (which they have no control over)—as reflected through whether they accept or reject *Roger & Me*'s "truth" (which is as easy as forming an opinion on a "movie")—drives a wedge between them that is similar to the divisions created by blaming individuals for any social problem. *Roger & Me* individualizes moral blame for social problems, and, inasmuch as both *Roger & Me* and its audience conflate moral identity and class position, this self-blame gnaws at every audience member who can afford to buy a ticket. In this regard, *Roger & Me* impugns everyone who has played along as well as (even after *Roger & Me*, even after having looked into this mirror) everyone who continues to play along in *the system*: all are ipso facto the bearers of false consciousness.

The paralyzing dynamic set in motion by *Roger & Me*'s moralism is further underscored by the following field research experience. In October of 1990, at the height of his renewed, post-*Roger & Me* local celebrity, Michael Moore addressed the students of a University of Michigan–Flint course dedicated to the sociological study of "social problems."[123] As part of their course work, the students had watched *Roger & Me* as well as read in their assigned textbook Moore's reprinted article "General Motors and Flint, Michigan."[124] A revealing moment in Moore's visit to the classroom came when, after the student audience had subjected Moore to personal criticism similar to that forthcoming from the *Donahue* audience, and, after several students had articulated their dismissive and unsympathetic feelings toward people who were unemployed and poor, a somewhat bewildered and angry Moore retorted, "Doesn't anybody go to church anymore!?"[125] While this and similar interactions clearly revealed that the most vocal students' prior sociological studies had no discernable effect upon their evidently well-entrenched prejudices, Moore's outburst and continued questioning of these students' moral development thereafter also suggests the centrality of a moral discourse for *Roger & Me*'s writer, producer, director, and on-screen narrator.

Indeed, like the students of this class, Flint as a whole was effectively *forced* to look in the *Roger & Me* mirror. Due to the film's search for corporate accountability in a clear language of moral responsibility, the community reacted defensively and evasively for essentially self-interested, though understandable, reasons. Even if a viewer is not directly challenged by the film's mockery of capitalism, identification with Flint's way of life is potentially enough to draw an individual under the pointing figure of moral accusation. This is true for non-Flint residents as well, that is, inasmuch as Moore is correct in his observation that "Flint is the epitome of the industrial revolution, the American dream."[126]

But is it not contradictory to depict the power of cultural manipulation while also criticizing individuals for succumbing to this manipulation? Is it, in fact, legitimate for Moore to impugn the morality of his fellow hometown citizens merely because he has apparently escaped its parochial company-town culture? The tendency of the people of Flint to deflect blame onto one another, and to redirect it toward Michael Moore especially, in part reflects a resistance to *Roger & Me*'s unexpected although unavoidable, and thus resented, moral judgements. Ironically, then, in this dimension, *Roger & Me* adds the fear of being judged complicitous with deindustrialization to deindustrialization's already tragic and paralyzing effects. Perhaps this reception represents an unfortunate unintended consequence, although it must be recalled that Moore believes it may well be "too late" for Flint anyway. *Roger & Me*'s "lesson" for non-Flint viewers is, after all, a negative one: be wary because, in Moore's haunting words, "what's happening in Flint is coming to your hometown."[127]

Overall, then, *Roger & Me* combines the structure of tragicomedy, mockumentary, documentary, and morality play. Working immanently from within the internal contradictions of popular cultural symbols, the film explores the tensions between the idea of cultural consensus and the society that undermines its possibility. *Roger & Me* depicts systematically distorted dialogue by mocking rationalizations for these cultural contradictions. In documenting the causes and effects of deindustrialization, the film tells a tale of concentrated economic power and social inequalities. In combination, each of these facets points toward the film's primary intent to spur public debate over the moral standing of contemporary American capitalist society, although, in Flint especially, the film's punchline simply hits too close to home.

COMPARING *ROGER & ME* AND NEW DIRECTIONS MOVEMENT IDEOLOGY

Recognizing the mythic quality of Flint's midcentury cultural consensus as well as the exceptional nature of its culture of abundance, *Roger & Me* nevertheless seeks to exploit this particular history for all the symbolic value that it is worth. In *Roger & Me*, in other words, Flint's industrial history is heroic, literally larger than life. Indeed, given the film's appeal for social change, this history represents a generalized and ironic paradise lost, the stuff of childhood memory and childlike wishes that adults are supposed to have learned to repress. *Roger & Me* acts as a guardian of these historically repressed cultural memories but also attempts to turn the pop-cultural manipulations of the past on their head by taking their promises today at face value. Instead of the political gravity of New Directions' "unfinished American revolution," then, *Roger & Me*'s historicist ideology is centered upon an immanent critique of the midcentury pop-cultural version of the "American Dream."

The film presents at the outset a stylized version of Flint's industrial history. Noting that Flint was the birthplace of the "world's largest industrial corporation," Moore says,

> There were more auto factories and auto workers here than in any other city on Earth.
> We built Cadillacs, Buicks, Fisher bodies, GM trucks, Chevrolets, and AC sparkplugs.

We enjoyed a prosperity that working people around the world had never seen before.

Then the manly chorus of a GM theme song ("Teamwork, teamwork, the nation's secret is teamwork") swells as a joyous and overflowing crowd is shown intermingling with a marching band during a downtown Flint parade. Having noted the city's relationship with GM and the automobile industry, the film then shows Flint as the home of an equally heroic working-class militancy:

> My Uncle Laverne was in something called the Great Flint Sit-Down Strike. Just hours before the year's end in 1936, he and thousands of other GM workers took over the Flint factories and barricaded themselves inside, refusing to budge for forty-four days.
>
> The National Guard was called out, and the eyes of the world were on Flint. On February 11, 1937, GM gave in, and the UAW was born.

File footage follows, depicting a GM spokesperson crediting the "ingenuity, imagination, hard work, and dedication" of GM's work force with helping to build and sustain "America's industrial leadership in the world."

In just the film's opening sequences, then, Flint's industrial history is presented five times in world-historical terms: GM is the "world's largest industrial corporation"; Flint had more auto factories and workers than any "city on Earth"; Flint's working people enjoyed a prosperity "the world had never seen before"; during the sit-down strike, "the eyes of the world were on Flint"; and Flint sustained "America's industrial leadership in the world." The film might have also noted that the UAW is America's largest industrial union, but the general point is clear: Flint can lay claim to an industrial history of heroic and world-historical significance.

But Flint's posited greatness does not end there. The film's autobiographical depiction of Flint's industrial history helps carry this theme to the present. Born in 1954 during the heyday of Flint's economic boom, Moore recalls that the culture of his youth was filled with celebrities and parades. Flint's established economic centrality lent it a high degree of cultural recognition, as the city was envisioned as a symbol of harmonious capitalist-industrial society. For Flint, with its class conflict behind it and its class compromise still uncompromised, it was a "great day alright." But Moore's own coming of age parallels Flint's industrial decline. By 1989, at the age of thirty-five, Moore shows that the achievements and pride that were once Flint's claim to fame had become little more than memories of a past era. Did Moore and his fellow baby boomers experience the expected rise in their standard of living that his family and their society had promised? The film in effect asks, What has become of the "promise of the future" that GM chairman Harlow Curtiss, in the 1958 parade in honor of GM, assured Flint was theirs?

As noted above, the presentation of this specific 1958 parade shows that America's so-called cultural consensus has always been, at least in part, a sham. Rooted in what might be called Moore's "60s" political sensibilities, the film depicts the easy and accepted racism and sexism that was then part and parcel of America's "Leave It to Beaver" form of cultural hegemony. The "teamwork" that supposedly stood behind the nation's immense industrial power was, in reality, patched together on separate and unequal terms. Nor was this oppression and inequality and its ideological justification strictly the product of naivete: the integration of Flint's working class into a rapidly expanding popular culture (dominated by consumerist values) militated against the ideological basis of Flint's quickly forgotten militant labor movement.

Moore shows that, when GM chose to break its "promises" in the 1970s and 1980s, these same cultural symbols that were so prominent in touting the symbiotic relationship between Flint and GM in the 1950s were again trotted out to quash any thought of a return to the militancy of old. For example, *Roger & Me* depicts Anita Bryant, the former spokesperson for AC Spark Plug, offering to the people of Flint the message that "every day is a new day," a quasiprotestant slogan that, if repeated enough and eventually internalized, severs historical consciousness into daily, bitesize fragments. Bryant continues:

> I read something interesting. Margaret Thatcher, she says, "Cheer up America." She says, "America, You live in a great country, you're a free country, you've got a great President, and not everything is perfect, but cheer up, because you live in a free America."
>
> So, we live in a free society. Today is a new day. It's an opportunity to do something with yourself. If nothing else, thank God for the sunshine and for the fact that you're not starving to death, and go out and do *something* with your hands.

The camera continues to hold on Ms. Bryant while she looks quizzically at her own hands, finally saying with a bit of frustration: "I don't know." Another similarly pious former GM spokesperson, Pat Boone, makes several prominent appearances in *Roger & Me*. His nostalgic "Mr. Chevrolet" reminiscing turns Flint's history into a foggy (and soggy) memory of the good ole days. If there is any doubt about his ideological role, Boone dispels it in this interaction with Moore:

BOONE: Flint is Bedrock America.

MOORE: Who's to blame for what's happened here in Flint?

BOONE: I don't think it's *anybody's* fault. In a free society—in a capitalistic-democratic society—things just *do* change. There's shifts and trends. I'm sure General Motors doesn't have any desire to either close down a plant or put people out of work.

Boone goes on to celebrate Amway Corporation as an opportune vehicle by which laid-off auto workers can "earn dollars."

Roger & Me also suggests that Flint's heroic historical narrative has been conveniently forgotten by precisely those whose leadership could revitalize this history into a living memory of consequence. At the 1987 parade in honor of the Great Sit-Down Strike, Moore asks UAW President Owen Bieber and then-Michigan Governor James Blanchard if, in their view, Flint is in need of another sit-down strike. Bieber is shown having difficulty remembering the year of his union's founding strike, much less articulating its cultural meaning, while Blanchard, whose New Deal Democratic Party predecessor, Frank Murphy, significantly aided the 1936–37 sit-down strikers, gives this view of the potential relevance of a contemporary sit-down strike: "I don't think it would do any good. That's the problem." In these scenes, *Roger & Me* depicts disconnection from, and skepticism toward, the significance of Flint's heroic working-class past.

Yet, is there a historical promise lying forgotten between this cultural manipulation and social amnesia? Recall Moore's closing statement, which implicitly raises a set of related questions: ". . . the rich were getting richer, the poor poorer, and people everywhere now had a lot less lint thanks to the lint rollers made in my hometown. It was truly the dawn of a new era." Promised a culture of abundance, only to receive greater class divisions? The home of automobile production, now the world's leading producers of lint rollers? Is this the American Dream? Is this what the end of the millennium has in store? In a sense, then, *Roger & Me* invokes Flint's heroic industrial past and mythic cultural history in the hope of shamming American society into political action. The film ironically ends with Pat Boone singing "I Am Proud to be an American," including the ridiculously patriotic lyrics, "I am proud to be an American, part of this great democracy; where our equal rights are for everyone, thanks to justice and liberty."

Compared with the New Directions Movement's "unfinished American Revolution" and its implicit notion of a progressive extension of democratic political rights, *Roger & Me*'s self-consciously ironic evocation of history appeals to its audience's collective recollection of a time when such promises were supposed to have been already realized. In this regard, history is shown in need of redemption today: it's *still* unfinished. At the end of the *Donahue* programs, Moore described America's once upwardly mobile working class as living now through a "modern-day 'Grapes of Wrath,'" implying that they should once again rise in dissent much as their forbears, and Moore's forbears, did in response to the Great Depression.[128] By portraying the betrayal of current events against the larger-than-life achievements and dreams of past generations, *Roger & Me* suggests that the realization of the so-called American Dream is something that requires as much social struggle today as it did in the non-mythic past. For the now culturally marginal Flint, at least, this appears the only hope.

Interestingly, Michael Moore's on-screen persona resembles Bugs Bunny more than it does Red Emma. Described by Vincent Canby in *The New York Times* as a "folksy crackerbarrel Marxist,"[129] Moore substitutes personal verve and wit and his version of seat-of-the-pants midwestern common sense for political slogans spoken in the highbrow jargon of social theory. Inasmuch as the audience comes to identify with *Roger & Me*'s call for social struggle, it is *not* because of the film's sophisticated, or even "slick," political rhetoric.

As we have seen, in addition to its historical narrative, *Roger & Me* also plies a moral theme. Against the barren industrial backdrop that is Flint in its economic decline, the film not only portrays Flint's individual citizens as powerless and ineffectual in their isolated efforts just to get by, but it also portrays Moore himself as an average person who is rebuffed and ultimately defeated in his simple wish to bring Roger Smith to Flint. While former autoworkers try to regain their mental health by singing along to "Wouldn't It Be Nice?" Moore finds that his childhood faith in the goodness of America is simply out of sync with the cold realities of capitalist society. Moore's autobiographical disillusionment is thus presented as the basis for a palatable form of mass dissent. For those who find American political philosophy and labor history abstruse and exacting topics, *Roger & Me*'s fast-paced, *Pee Wee's Big Adventure* narrative offers dozens of pop-cultural symbols to grab hold of: some comic and some tragic, but all accessible to an audience reared on "Loony Tunes." This is the ideological significance of the film's autobiographical structure. Both as the film's on-screen "star" and off-screen narrator, Moore's reflective but just-folks locution confronts a society whose hierarchical authority prefers jargon and silence over plain talk. As Moore confronts the phalanx of spokespersons and public relations staff, he offers to the audience the opportunity to identify with struggles for social recognition everywhere. And, as Moore recalls his childhood pride in his family, community, and country, even the sophisticated, jaded viewer, whose political sympathies discount the importance of these "conservative" institutions, is nevertheless often easily swept into an identification based upon a remembrance of their own simple childhood wishes and dreams. "Wouldn't It Be Nice?" is *Roger & Me*'s theme song; it is not uncommon for audience members to weep while this song provides a counterpoint of innocent yearning to Flint's dilapidated social and physical infrastructure.

Indeed, staying true to his film's ironic structure, Moore regularly undercuts his own witty "What's up Doc?" approach. While Bugs Bunny always figures a way to pull the rug from underneath his arrogant and condescending Elmer Fuddlike opponents, Moore's mission ends in failure precisely because he never really gets the chance to directly pose his questions or to match his wits

with "Roger." As Moore tells his audience in a somber scene near the film's conclusion: "After three years of trying to bring Roger to Flint . . . I failed." Having
sacrificed three years of his life in a simple quest to speak with Roger Smith—
and instead running headlong into the brick wall of GM spokespeople, two of
whom at one point in the film literally turn their backs to his appeals—Moore
evokes a nearly Christian empathy for martyrdom, for self-sacrifice even in the
face of overwhelming forces. In this, *Roger & Me*'s narrator acts as a type of
transference object. Whereas the audience may initially identify with his pluck,
the ultimate failure of his mission transfers the audience's identification to
those, like Moore, whose individual initiatives lack the power to effect social
change.

In this regard, note once again David Bensman's relatively common criticism of the film. Bensman concludes his "Narrow, Simplistic, Wrong" critique
by stating:

> Only Michael Moore and his film crew seem to have any spunk, any
> persistence, any desire to understand what's happening and to call
> GM to account. At least the title is perfect: *Roger & Me*.[130]

Besides the point that the film does include scenes of Flint's citizens resisting
their situation in various ways, it is more important to consider the possibility
that *Roger & Me* intends to redirect the question of political action back onto
its audience. For example, in his own sophisticated reading of the film, Tony
Russo suggests that:

> In the last analysis, no work of art or social analysis can do for people
> what they must do for themselves. Nor can Marx, Lenin, or Michael
> Moore do it.[131]

By depicting the futility (not the transformative power) of individual spunk in
the face of social systems, *Roger & Me* suggests that solidaristic social action
remains the only viable source of power available to otherwise isolated citizens
and marginalized communities.

Similar in this way to the New Directions Movement's remembrance and
identification with past models of self, *Roger & Me*'s autobiographical structure
invites its audience to identify with the naive but as yet unrealized values of
both their childhood and the society of their youth. The film's irony derives
from its appeal to these values and promises (as though written in fat and col-
orful crayon letters) through the profane medium of popular culture, whereas
the NDM appeals to its own sacred history in an unfolding American labor
movement. Yet, both responses to Flint's dependent deindustrialization are
committed to self-sacrifice in their respective projects of redemption, although

the ultimate hopelessness of *Roger & Me*'s Flint more strongly echoes Walter Benjamin's injunction that "It is only for the sake of those without hope that hope is given to us."[132] In the end, the film asks its audience to change the empirical conditions that, in listening to the film's story, cause them to feel morally repelled by their own society. *Roger & Me* captures the absence of individual autonomy, power, and hope but, in doing so, preserves them in their negativity as potentially transformative values.

Of course, there is much that *Roger & Me* doesn't say: program and policy recommendations, for example, are certainly not its strong suit. But the film nevertheless presents its own (albeit stylized) version of American society, intimating its allegiance to an identifiable political viewpoint that, Moore, outside of the film, has been more than willing to discuss. Recall his statement to Phil Donahue:

> We live in an economic system in this country that's unfair, and it's unjust, and it's not democratic. And until it's more democratic, we're going to have a difficult time making sure that everybody gets an equal slice of the pie. And I think we need more democracy in the economy, and we need it in the workplace.[133]

This statement is obviously critical of American capitalist society's inherent tendency to produce inequalities in wealth and power. *Roger & Me* appeals to democratic values by linking the notion of economic equality to political equality.

On the other hand, the characterization of Moore as a Marxist, even a "crackerbarrel Marxist," is a misnomer, for this film does not call for a revolutionary restructuring of American capitalist society. Moore states, for example:

> As long as decisions that drastically affect people's lives can be casually made without any sort of government control, they're going to do it. [Corporations are] going to go wherever they can to make the biggest buck.[134]

This statement indicates that the desired direction of political change is to reestablish "government control" over the private sphere of capitalist investment and production, not to undermine the private property basis of capitalist society as such. Indeed, a review of *Roger & Me*'s content reveals that the film has the same allegiance to the model of New Deal liberalism as found in the New Directions Movement, although, as with other aspects of the film's ideology, *Roger & Me* adds a few twists.

With regard to America's power structure, for example, the film subtly portrays a type of hegemonic "power elite" formed by the executives of giant corporations (e.g., GM/Roger Smith), federal-level political authorities (e.g., Reagan), and the military establishment.[135] In the early scenes that delineate Roger Smith's deindustrialization strategy, Smith is pictured sitting at the front of a large room filled with uniformed military leaders while Moore describes GM's diversification into "high-tech firms, particularly weapons manufacturers." Furthermore, as stated during the *Donahue* program and as implied in the film's lampooning of Ronald Reagan, Moore is a quintessential critic of the infamous Reaganomics because he considers this tendency toward the *deregulation* of capitalist production to be largely responsible for allowing private business to pursue profits regardless of social costs. Moore rejects, for example, a *Donahue* audience member's suggestion that the UAW and GM should unite their forces against the "government" by responding "the government is on the side of General Motors." As Moore states: "After ten years of Reagan and Bush, it's not 'morning in America' for all of us."[136]

As we have seen, however, the film also criticizes the weakness of America's traditional sources of political opposition. Via the representations of UAW President Owen Bieber and Democratic Michigan Governor James Blanchard, as well as through Moore's criticism of the editorial policy of *Mother Jones*—which Moore claims fired him from his job as editor for his having refused to support an investigative story on herbal tea over a story on Flint's laid-off autoworkers[137]—*Roger & Me* attacks the loyal establishment political opposition for its having abandoned advocacy for the public interest over and against unfettered capitalism. Much like the NDM, then, *Roger & Me* appeals to the people to mobilize their political will against any form of staid, bureaucratized political involvement.

But *Roger & Me* is not wholly focused on economic problems. The film also addresses the issues of racism, sexism, and homophobia, these sometimes in relation to depictions of economic inequalities, but not exclusively so. The film ironically juxtaposes, for example, the manager of Flint's Star Theatre, who displays exaggerated effeminate characteristics that some might associate with a stereotypical image of gay men in "showbiz," with Anita Bryant, the well-known strident Christian fundamentalist antigay activist. Bryant's stated belief that America is a "free society" is also thus ironically juxtaposed to her public intolerance of homosexuality. Perhaps even more so than the New Directions Movement's appeal for a widely based "social movement," *Roger & Me* addresses itself to many forms of inequality not directly attributable to the structure of capitalist society.

Although *Roger & Me* neither states any firm political allegiance nor directly appeals to New Deal ideology, the film's larger-than-life edification of Flint's industrial past and its debt to working-class militancy nevertheless provide enough clues to adduce these sympathies. But more than merely a latter-day New Deal social democratic, Moore and his film also express distinctly New Left sensibilities by articulating the significance of noneconomic forms of exploitation and inequality, and by freely experimenting in the realm of consciousness raising. During the *Donahue* telecasts, Moore states with a certain amount of pride and vindication that, having supported Reagan, "by the middle part of the [1980s], the people of Flint had realized the lie. And in 1988, in the Michigan primary in Flint, the city voted 9 to 1 for Jesse Jackson. And the county, which is 82 percent white, voted 4 to 1 for Jesse Jackson."[138] Whereas the New Directions Movement is understandably focused on economic issues, *Roger & Me* represents what might be called Flint's version of a Rainbow Coalition response to dependent deindustrialization.

Complex in form and ironic in content, then, America's "most talked about film of 1990" not only brings attention to Flint's particular experience with deindustrialization, it also addresses the universal concerns represented in its implicit enlightenment self-consciousness. In seeking a free and open discourse concerning the relationship between economic power and social justice, *Roger & Me* embodies a faith in the power of speech. What if Michael Moore and Roger Smith had toured Flint hand in hand, speaking with unemployed auto workers and surveying the community-wide impact of massive unemployment? What sorts of validity claims might have been raised? How could Smith have justified his corporation's private gain in a face-to-face confrontation with what in Flint are its all too evident and human social costs? That these questions never had the opportunity to be asked represents the motive force behind the film itself: *Roger & Me* is a form of "miscarried conversation," hijacking the medium of a documentary/feature film as the "other means" by which to force the challenge of the better argument.

But as the *Donahue* audience reception suggests, the film's intention to spur public debate ultimately failed. Flint remains only slightly less culturally marginal and definitely no less economically dependent six years after the film's appearance. The fleeting media attention that so vexed one *Donahue* audience member has indeed moved on to countless more sensational issues.[139] Neither did *Roger & Me*'s release spur a discernable national debate on industrial policy, as many had initially and optimistically hoped the film would eventuate. Undermined by its moralistic focus, the film's reception provoked no meaningful political action, nor even much substantive public discourse, ironically, not even in Flint itself.[140] Instead, the film's reception in the popular media, in the economic and political sphere, and in Hollywood, all suggest that the film's cultural significance has been ignored or suppressed by its easy assimilation into the very commerce of popular culture that *Roger & Me* hoped to turn on its head.

Moore has stated:

It's one of those strange ironies that fits with the rest of the film, that the largest media conglomerate in the world [Warner Communications] is distributing an anticorporate film simply because they think

they're going to make a lot of money. Didn't Lenin say that the capitalists will sell you the rope to hang them with?[141]

In this case, though, Lenin's rope is just as easily ignored, or better, transmuted
into an off-beat entertainment commodity, in fact, one that carries with it the
suspicion of empirical inaccuracies and the stigma of left-of-center propaganda. Warner Brothers states in its press release that "Moore tells a funny and
honest story of the many winding roads leading to the American Dream,"[142] as
though the film were not more accurately described as a story of the many
human lives whose "winding roads" have *not* lead to the American Dream! Perhaps the film's final irony is that, much as in its own depiction of the frailty of
frustrated individual and isolated community responses to a globally structured political-economic process, *Roger & Me* may itself be fated to dwell
silently in the belly of the whale called "mass culture."

NOTES

1. Phil Donahue, *Donahue*, "On Location in Flint, Michigan: Filmmaker Michael
Moore, 'Roger & Me'—Part I," Show 0129–90, 29 January 1990, *Journal Graphics, Inc.*,
Transcript 2870, p. 11.

2. Richard Schickel, "Imposing on Reality," *Time*, 8 January 1990, p. 77.

3. Pauline Kael, "The Current Cinema," *The New Yorker*, 8 January 1990, pp. 90–
93.

4. Theodor W. Adorno, *Aesthetic Theory* (New York: Routledge & Kegan Paul,
Inc., 1986 [1970]), p. 366.

5. *Roger & Me*, A Film by Michael Moore, is a 1989 Dog Eat Dog Production,
released by Warner Brothers, Inc., 1989.

6. For a discussion of "cheekiness," see Peter Sloterdijk, *Critique of Cynical Reason*
(Minneapolis: University of Minnesota Press, 1987), especially chapter 5, pp. 101–133.

7. See *Roger & Me: Production Information*, Warner Brothers, Inc., 22 November
1989 (document source); John Marchese, "Me: The Continuing Adventures of Michael
Moore," in *Esquire* (January, 1993), pp. 44–47); Elizabeth Kolbert, "The 'Me' of 'Roger
and Me' Is Trying Network TV," in *New York Times*, 10 May 1993, sec. B, p. 3; Richard
Corliss, "How the Winner Lost," in *Time*, 27 February 1995, p. 66. Note that *Roger &
Me*'s production cost approximately $250,000, and was paid for, in part, by bingo games
and rummage sales. Warner Brothers paid approximately $3 million for distribution
rights. Note also the exceptional analysis by Tony Russo, "Roger & Me: A Review Essay,"
in *Rethinking Marxism* 3 (1990), pp. 164–173. Michael Moore himself has commented
upon *Roger & Me* most extensively and revealingly in his 1992 addendum entitled *Pets
or Meat?: The Return to Flint*, a short film produced for and aired by The Public Broad-
casting Systems' "Point of View" (P.O.V.) program.

8. *JFK, Malcolm X,* and perhaps also Tim Robbins' *Bob Roberts,* join Moore's *Roger & Me* as America's most celebrated and controversial 1990s leftist-oriented feature films. *JFK* and *Malcolm X* are especially similar in their historically grounded and openly political self-consciousness. The latter two films appeal directly to their audience to engage in specific political actions. However, only *Roger & Me* depicts empirical and historical situations and is largely based on interviews with laypeople. That is, among these films, only *Roger & Me* has been called a documentary.

Validity claims are easily blurred in an era of info-tainment, info-mercials, and, as they have been dubbed, reality-based cop shows. Whether this genre blurring is a unique contemporary phenomena, and whether and to what extent *right-wing*-oriented politics has previously found a home in feature films (*The Green Berets?*), are here left open questions. See Richard Bernstein, "'Roger and Me': Documentary? Satire? Or Both," *New York Times,* 1 February 1990, Sec. C, p. 20; Suzanne Moore, "On the side of the man in the street," in *New Statesman & Society* 3, no. 48 (27 April 1990), p. 48.

9. For information on *Roger & Me*'s production and distribution, and on Michael Moore, see: "'*Roger & Me*': Production Information"; "Moore—to the Point," *The Flint Journal,* 3 September 1989, Sec. G, pp. 1, 4; "Maker of Documentary That Attacks G.M. Alienates His Allies," *New York Times,* 19 January 1990, Sec. C, p. 12; "Independents' day coming in movies," *The Flint Journal,* 6 October 1989, Sec. B, p. 8; "Disturbing hit: 'Excellent' film on Flint unsettles viewers," *The Flint Journal,* 11 September 1989, Sec. C, p. 1. For a convenient summary of the extensive media attention lavished on *Roger & Me* as a result of its national (and international) release, see Michael Moore's 1992 *Pets or Meat?: The Return to Flint.* For present purposes, though, note that Moore made guest appearances on such programs as *The Tonight Show, Late Night with David Letterman,* and *Donahue,* and that Flint was featured on programs such as *The Today Show, Prime Time Live,* and later, on ABC's *World New Tonight* and CBS's *Evening News.*

10. This schema is borrowed from M. H. Abrams, *The Mirror and the Lamp: Romantic Theory and the Critical Tradition* (Oxford: Oxford University Press, 1971 [1953]), especially pp. 3–26, where Abrams explicates "mimetic," "pragmatic," "expressive," and "objective" approaches to art criticism. The points concerning *Roger & Me*'s theories of popular culture, social power, and the systemic and social aspects of capitalism, are discussed and substantiated immediately below.

11. All quotations from the film are the product of the author's selective transcription.

12. Ben Hamper, *Rivethead: Tales From the Assembly Line* (New York: Warner Books, 1991). This book is prefaced by Moore. Hamper also appears in Moore's *Pets or Meat?* Moore was the editor of *Mother Jones* at the time when Hamper made his appearance on its cover.

13. "'*Roger & Me*': Production Information."

14. Data is drawn from a review of Moore's *Flint Voice* and later *Michigan Voice,* publications held at the Genesee Historical Collections Center at the University of Michigan–Flint, Flint, Michigan. Note also that Moore has published articles in *The Columbia Review of Journalism, The Nation,* and *In These Times.* This information is

largely drawn from "'Roger & Me': Production Information." Since turning *Roger & Me* over to Warner Brothers, Moore has been active in the 1992 Brown for President campaign, established a foundation to support independent filmmakers, produced his 1992 *Pets or Meat?* addendum to *Roger & Me*, and completed both a season of "TV Nation," an NBC television series, as well as his next feature film, tentatively entitled "Canadian Bacon." See "The 'Me' of 'Roger and Me' Is Trying Network TV," and "Me: The Continuing Adventures of Michael Moore."

15. Schickel, p. 77; Kael, p. 91, 92.

16. See "Maker of Documentary That Attacks G.M. Alienates His Allies." Note that the UAW's public relations experts used Kael's review for the same purposes as GM, as they opposed *Roger & Me*'s portrayal of UAW President Owen Bieber.

17. Note that this scene was actually filmed at the beginning of the *Roger & Me* project.

18. Kael, pp. 91, 92.

19. Ibid., p. 91.

20. Schickel, p. 77.

21. Ibid.

22. "Moore receives hero's welcome from homeless," in *Variety*, 28 March 1990 (document source); "'Roger' shutout sparks protest in Hollywood," in *Variety* 338, no. 14 (21 February 1990), p. 340.

23. Ibid.

24. "'*Roger & Me*': Production Information," p. 6.

25. See Kael, p. 92.

26. David Bensman, "'Roger & Me': Narrow, Simplistic, Wrong," *New York Times*, 2 March 1990, Sec. A, p. 28.

27. See David Bensman and Roberta Lynch, "The Revitalization of 'Sunset' Industries: The Case of Steel," in *The Reshaping of America: Social Consequences of The Changing Economy*, D. Stanley Eitzen and Maxine Bacca Zinn, eds. (Englewood Cliffs, NJ: Prentice-Hall, 1989), pp. 398–404. This excerpt from *Rusted Dreams: Hard Time in a Steel Community* (New York: McGraw-Hill, 1987) is ironically included in a volume that also features Michael Moore's "General Motors and Flint, Michigan," pp. 329–333, originally "In Flint, Tough Times Last," *The Nation*, 6 June 1987, pp. 753–756.

28. Bensman, *"Roger & Me": Narrow, Simplistic, Wrong.*

29. Ibid.

30. Ibid.

31. Ibid.

32. Ibid.

33. Kael, p. 92.

34. See Adorno, *Aesthetic Theory*.

35. "*Roger & Me*': Production Information," p. 7.

36. Ibid.

37. Ibid., p. 8.

38. Ibid.

39. Ibid.

40. This information is largely based on taped local TV broadcasts in my possession.

41. Information for this section is taken primarily from both the taped *Donahue* segments in question, which are in the author's possession, as well as from official Multimedia Entertainment, Inc. transcripts: "On Location in Flint, Michigan: Filmmaker Michael Moore, "Roger & Me"—Part I, Show 0129–90, 29 January 1990, Transcript 2870, and "On Location in Flint, Michigan: Filmmaker Michael Moore, "Roger & Me"—Part II, Show 0130–90, 30 January 1990, Transcript 2871. In the following citations, Show 0129–90 is referred to as *Donahue*, "part I," and Show 0130–90 is referred to as *Donahue*, "part II." Note that both program segments were taped for broadcast on 29 January 1990 at Flint's Whiting Auditorium. In addition to these sources, informal conversation with audience participants has also been used in an effort to confirm interpretations.

42. These figures are based on a content analysis of the program telecasts and transcripts. Note that two additional local citizens entered the telecasts as "callers."

43. Note that this data is used for the obvious reason that it provides the opportunity to document, with transcripts and video recordings, Flint's popular response to the film. This author has not noted in over two years of fieldwork in the community any group or type of response that is not represented in these transcripts. Importantly, the field work data in question includes the presentation of this film to over 400 area university and college students in classroom situations, where the author was able to note responses to the film, both immediately during and after its viewing, as well as through over 400 essay responses. What's more, this field work also includes having Michael Moore address one of the author's classes at the University of Michigan–Flint. While younger people and suburban residents are typically over-represented in these student groups, the author's experience includes groups characterized by an over-representation of auto workers (as one course was conducted on-site at a local GM site), and groups with substantial adult, city-resident composition. This is not to claim, however, that this "data" is perfectly representative of Flint's overall response. Yet, to date, no survey research has been conducted to ascertain Flint's attitudes about the film. Thus, this data is the best available and may be used as the basis for cautious, if not definitive, interpretation.

44. *Donahue*, part I, p. 11.

45. These figures are based on a content analysis of the program transcripts, cross-checked with visual and audible clues as to the speaker's intention, which are derived from a study of the video-taped segments. These figures are intended to better approx-

imate and describe the content of the program. The implications drawn below are confirmed, in part, by reflexive descriptions in the transcripts themselves, as well as by informal discussion with audience members.

46. 24th Audience Member, *Donahue*, part I, p. 10.

47. 100th Audience Member, *Donahue*, part II, p. 15.

48. 19th Audience Member, *Donahue*, part II, p. 4.

49. 76th Audience Member, *Donahue*, part II, p. 12.

50. 20th Audience Member, *Donahue*, part II, p. 5.

51. 27th Audience Member, *Donahue*, part II, pp. 5–6.

52. 88th Audience Member, *Donahue*, part II, pp. 14–15.

53. 8th Audience Member, *Donahue*, part I, p. 5.

54. 53rd Audience Member, *Donahue*, part II, p. 9.

55. 54th Audience Member, *Donahue*, part II, p. 9.

56. 79th Audience Member, *Donahue*, part II, p. 13.

57. 81st Audience Member, *Donahue*, part II, p. 13.

58. 89th Audience Member, *Donahue*, part II, p. 15.

59. 21st Audience Member, *Donahue*, part I, p. 10.

60. 22nd Audience Member, *Donahue*, part I, p. 10.

61. 23rd Audience Member, *Donahue*, part I, p. 10.

62. 4th Audience Member, *Donahue*, part I, p. 3.

63. 23rd Audience Member, *Donahue*, part II, p. 5.

64. 84th Audience Member, *Donahue*, part II, p. 14.

65. 51st Audience Member, *Donahue*, part II, p. 9.

66. 57th Audience Member, *Donahue*, part II, p. 9.

67. 22nd Audience Member, *Donahue*, part II, p. 5.

68. See 87th Audience Member, *Donahue*, part II, p. 14, and 63rd Audience Member, *Donahue*, part II, p. 10.

69. 10th Audience Member, *Donahue*, part I, p. 6.

70. 12th Audience Member, *Donahue*, part I, p. 7.

71. 40th Audience Member, *Donahue*, part II, p. 8.

72. 10th Audience Member, *Donahue*, part II, p. 3.

73. 16th Audience Member, *Donahue*, part II, p. 4.

74. 17th Audience Member, *Donahue*, part II, p. 4.

75. 9th Audience Member, *Donahue*, part II, p. 3.

76. 30th Audience Member, *Donahue*, part I, p. 12.

77. 11th Audience Member, *Donahue*, part II, p. 3.

78. See, for criticism of the UAW, Audience Members 13 and 17 from part I, and 1, 2, and 26 from part II; for criticism of "big shots," see Audience Members 105 and 106, part II; for criticism of "government," see Audience Member 104, part II.

79. As stated by Phil Donahue, *Donahue*, part I, p. 9.

80. 18th Audience Member, *Donahue*, part I, pp. 9–10.

81. 33rd Audience Member, *Donahue*, part II, p. 7.

82. "Awwwww!" is a direct quotation from the official transcript. See *Donahue*, part II, p. 7.

83. 52nd Audience Member, *Donahue*, part II, p. 9.

84. 16th Audience Member, *Donahue*, part I, p. 8.

85. 19th Audience Member, *Donahue*, part I, p. 10.

86. 5th Audience Member, *Donahue*, part II, p. 2.

87. 56th Audience Member, *Donahue*, part II, p. 9.

88. 71st Audience Member, *Donahue*, part II, p. 11.

89. 74th Audience Member, *Donahue*, part II, p. 11.

90. 92nd Audience Member, *Donahue*, part II, p. 15.

91. 1st Audience Member, *Donahue*, part I, p. 3.

92. Michael Moore, *Donahue*, part I, p. 3.

93. 5th Audience Member, *Donahue*, part I, p. 3.

94. 8th Audience Member, *Donahue*, part I, p. 5.

95. 14th Audience Member, *Donahue*, part I, p. 7.

96. 8th Audience Member, *Donahue*, part II, pp. 2–3.

97. 24th Audience Member, *Donahue*, part II, p. 5.

98. 48th Audience Member, *Donahue*, part II, pp. 8–9.

99. 73rd Audience Member, *Donahue*, part II, p. 11.

100. Phil Donahue, *Donahue*, part II, p. 4.

101. Michael Moore, *Donahue*, part II, p. 4.

102. 31st Audience Member, *Donahue*, part II, p. 6.

103. 31st Audience Member, *Donahue*, part I, p. 14.

104. 3rd Audience Member, *Donahue*, part II, p. 2.

105. 77th Audience Member, *Donahue*, part II, p. 12.

106. 96th Audience Member, *Donahue*, part II, p. 15.

107. 26th Audience Member, *Donahue*, part I, p. 10.

108. 43rd Audience Member, *Donahue*, part II, p. 8.

109. 67th Audience Member, *Donahue*, part II, p. 10.

110. 1st caller, *Donahue*, part II, p. 13.

111. 90th Audience Member, *Donahue*, part II, p. 15.

112. 97th Audience Member, *Donahue*, part II, p. 15.

113. 98th Audience Member, *Donahue*, part II, p. 15.

114. 101st Audience Member, *Donahue*, part II, p. 15.

115. 4th Audience Member, *Donahue*, part II, p. 2.

116. 45th Audience Member, *Donahue*, part II, p. 8.

117. 50th Audience Member, *Donahue*, part II, p. 9.

118. 85th Audience Member, *Donahue*, part II, p. 14.

119. 33rd Audience Member, *Donahue*, part I, p. 14.

120. 69th Audience Member, *Donahue*, part II, p. 10.

121. Phil Donahue, *Donahue*, part II, p. 12.

122. "'*Roger & Me*': Production Information," pp. 6–8.

123. The author was the instructor for this course (Social Problems 180). This data is thus drawn from field notes. Note that UAW Local 599 President Dave Yettaw was also in attendance.

124. See Eitzen and Zinn.

125. Perhaps this reflects upon Moore's early interest in the church. Moore, for example, spent a year in Catholic seminary at the age of 14. Later, he became an Eagle Scout. See "Moore to the point."

126. Ibid.

127. "'*Roger & Me*': Production Information," p. 8.

128. Michael Moore, *Donahue*, part II, p. 16.

129. See "Independents' day coming in movies."

130. Bensman, "Narrow, Simplistic, Wrong."

131. Russo, p. 173.

132. As quoted in Herbert Marcuse, *One-Dimensional Man* (Boston: Beacon Press, 1964), p. 257.

133. Michael Moore, *Donahue*, part II, p. 12.

134. "*Roger & Me*: Production Information," p. 8.

135. The reference to a "power elite" is from C. Wright Mills, *The Power Elite* (Oxford: Oxford University Press, 1956).

136. Michael Moore, *Donahue*, part II, pp. 12, 16.

137. According to Warner Brothers, the actual issue concerned Moore's refusal "to run an article attacking the Sandinista government of Nicaragua." See "*Roger & Me*: Production Information," p. 3.

138. Michael Moore, *Donahue*, part II, p. 11.

139. This is true despite Moore's personal success at bringing his viewpoint to the attention of a wide American audience. See, for example, Ginia Bellafante, "Pranks and Populism: The director of *Roger & Me* brings his satire to prime time," in *Time*, 25 July 1994, p. 64.

140. The author's field research included an informal, nonrandom survey of over 400 Flint-area college students, which showed, among other things, that no more than 25 percent of the students had seen the film prior to its in-class screening. This estimated percentage was confirmed in the experience of colleagues as well. Also, the author interacted with Moore and, moreover, with Moore's political allies, during the 1992 presidential campaign in Flint. In this aspect of his participant observation, the author was able to note the lingering ambivalence surrounding Moore, even in his hometown, and even among his natural, and, in some cases, longtime, political allies.

141. "Michael Moore & 'Roger & Me.'" *Unity* 13, no. 1, 29 January 1990, p. 4.

142. "*Roger & Me*: Production Information," p. 2.

Chapter 6

OF MIRRORS AND WALLS

"Some Still See GM Retribution in Closing of Historic Fisher One." As a wrecking ball removes the plant's shell so it can be reborn next year as Great Lakes Technology Centre, some union officials agree that the death of Fisher One sent a loud message to Flint labor. "It was an old plant, but I'm firmly convinced the corporation hasn't forgotten the sit-down," said UAW Region 1-C Director Stan Marshall. "Anywhere you go in this country they know about that plant," said UAW Local 326 President James "Whitey" Hale.

—*Flint Journal,* Oct. 16, 1988[1]

"Groundbreaking Set Oct. 25 for Tech Center." The theme of the ceremony, "Link to the Future," will be illustrated literally. Links from chains used to pull cars' floor pans through the central part of the factory are being embedded in Lucite. More than 200 of the clear plastic blocks . . . will be given to dignitaries at the ground-breaking.

—*Flint Journal,* Oct. 16, 1988[2]

"Historic Fisher Bricks for Sale. . . ." Bricks from the former Fisher One building went on sale this morning at the hall of UAW Local 581. . . . The bricks have been cleaned and will feature brass plates stating "Historic Fisher One, Home of the Great Sit-Down of 1937."

—*Flint Journal,* Oct. 25, 1988[3]

Ideology today has sunk deeper than Marx imagined.

—Ben Agger, *Fast Capitalism*[4]

The Great Lakes Technology Centre is an important new building in Flint. Erected in 1989 over the historic site of the 1936–37 sit-down strike, Flint's Fisher One factory, the new Tech Centre complex houses several significant GM entities, including an Engineering and Development Centre and AC Rochester Division's World Headquarters. The Tech Centre's particular *cultural* significance, however, is suggested by an article (October 1991) in the *Flint Journal*, which states: "the Tech Centre still offers hope to [the] surrounding area," in part because "the transformation of the site from a shuttered auto plant to a sleek technology complex has been dramatic."[5] Furthermore, in his reelection bid a month later, Flint's mayoral incumbent courted voters with campaign literature that stated:

> Mayor Collier worked with GM, the UAW, and community leaders to turn the old Fisher One into a sparkling new automotive engineering center. Today, nearly 6,000 engineers and support staff work right here in Flint at the Great Lakes Technology Centre—one of the largest technology centers in the world.[6]

For their part, the Tech Centre's developers vividly described its origins in a brochure entitled "And the walls came tumbling down":

> Fall of 1988. Whole buildings gone. The powerhouse, stack and substation demolished . . . the walls had come tumbling down. By winter new walls were taking shape. Mechanical and electrical services were installed. That following spring, as the dust cleared, the 500,000 square foot Engineering & Development Centre emerged from the ruins.[7]

As these descriptions suggest, Flint's sleek, sparkling new technology complex is a specifically future-oriented response to Flint's experience with dependent deindustrialization. Like the Center for New Work, it is heavily encoded with a postindustrial ideology. However, looking at the Great Lakes Technology Centre as a cultural mirror reveals that Flint's hope for a phoenixlike rebirth is founded upon a mythos that exacts a high price for its promised liberation— much more, that is, than the $5 per brick charged to those seeking to recollect their memories of Flint's heroic industrial age.[8]

THE GREAT LAKES TECHNOLOGY CENTRE IN HISTORICAL CONTEXT

GM's disinvestment in Flint has had a dramatic and persistent impact on the city's landscape: plant closings and high rates of unemployment have led to small business and personal bankruptcy, population loss, declining tax revenues, and scaled-back public services. This was Daniel Zwerdling's telling description of Flint in 1982, at the nadir of the Reagan recession:

> To see what 25 percent unemployment does to a community, take a stroll down Saginaw Street to the middle of town. It used to be a

lovely place, lined with old brick buildings, with the kind of turn-of-the-century masonry you don't see much of any more. Saginaw, the main street, is paved with bricks, and the sidewalks are shaded by awnings. But there is almost nobody and nothing there. Virtually every second store is boarded up with plywood. Some businesses have fled to suburban malls, the rest of them have simply folded. Flint is a 1982 ghost town.[9]

While this account aptly reflects Flint's early dilapidation, Zwerdling was also prescient in recognizing that the truly striking changes in the city's built environment were resulting more from *new* building projects than from the neglect and decay of older structures. His article, "And then There's the Disneyland Solution," pays special attention to the development of the downtown Hyatt Regency Hotel, the New Flint North project, and the anticipation surrounding the advent of AutoWorld.

With regard to the $800,000 New Flint North project, for example, Zwerdling writes:

To see one small save-the-town strategy at work, I drove north up Saginaw Street, through the downtown, past the sprawling one-mile-long Buick complex, into the "north end"—the black side of town. Downtown Flint is dying, yes, but this looked like the rubble after a riot. I passed miles, literally miles, of abandoned stores—closed supermarkets, closed auto body shops, closed fast-food restaurants (and over it all a billboard advertising tax-free all-savers certificates).

Then suddenly, just past the boarded-up Vehicle City Golf Shop and the cemetery, a bizarre vision: for nine blocks, huge, bright orange metal tubes zigzagged along the sidewalks at waist level, ending in an orange tube sign, "New Flint North." This is Flint's version of urban renewal, high-tech style.[10]

Zwerdling also discusses the exaggerated fanfare surrounding Flint's $30 million Hyatt Regency Hotel development and notes the rising excitement for what in 1984 would become Flint's $80 million AutoWorld theme park. Flint mayor, James Rutherford, described the forthcoming AutoWorld to Zwerdling as "a combination Disneyland and automobile museum." The incredulous Zwerdling concluded that these projects constituted "the first step toward changing Flint's image from a factory town to the tourist mecca of the Middle West."[11] As early as 1982, then, Flint's surprising approach to restructuring seemed to some observers not only newsworthy, but also preposterous.

Flint's enthusiastic importation of postmodern architectural motifs ranged well beyond its "bright orange metal tubes" experimentation with street-level neon quotation and its Disneyland-style theme park construction. Advertised as a place to "relive the days when bustling villages dotted Michigan's countryside and boom towns grew up around small industries," Genesee County's Crossroads Village & Huckleberry Railroad exemplifies the area's attraction to what British cultural critic Robert Hewison calls "heritage industry" developments, whereas the 1981 downtown Windmill Place, described as "Flint's festival of international dining and shopping," added a sense of *lumpenpastiche* to the city's low-budget ethnic eateries.[12] Flint's most striking version of urban postmodernism, however, arrived in the form of its Water Street Pavilion, designed by James Rouse—a festival marketplace built in 1986 along the lines of Rouse's New York City South Street Seaport, but encoded with considerably less spectacle than the Big Apple was able to afford.[13]

Many of these downtown constructions also figure prominently in *Roger & Me*. In the film, Flint's Tourism and Convention Bureau president, Steven Wilson, describes the Hyatt Regency Hotel and the Water Street Pavilion with great optimism:

> Put a luxury hotel in the heart of our city, just like other cities with their luxury hotels, with everything from the fountains, high ceilings, the atrium lobby, to the large windows, the large plants. The quality is there, what you'd find in Chicago or Atlanta or San Francisco.
>
> [The Water Street Pavilion has] a lot of glass and steel as well as plants and different colors to make it festive and fun and exciting.[14]

Wilson's effusion suggests the allure that city planners hoped Flint would have with the erection of its new postmodern edifice. But, as *Roger & Me* emphasized, Flint's tourism and convention developments were also premised on a doubtful build-anything-anywhere-and-they-will-come theory of mass consumption. In the precise estimation of University of Michigan–Flint researchers George F. Lord and Albert C. Price, Flint received $200 million in tourist- and convention-related investment and spent an additional $400 million in tax abatement and economic redevelopment financing.[15] Despite these extraordinary expenditures, however, Flint never shed its rust-belt image; it never became a tourist mecca for the Middle West.

The Great Lakes Technology Centre appeared at this turning point in Flint's experience with deindustrialization, just as *Roger & Me*'s national audiences were shaking their heads in bewilderment at the city's failed revitalization efforts. Occupying the former site and incorporating parts of the demolished Fisher One factory, the Tech Centre was not only the city's latest flirtation with postmodern construction, it was also a new type of economic lifeline—a truly postindustrial development.

The original Fisher One factory was once the world's largest auto body factory. Built mainly of brick, construction began in 1923. The facility was greatly expanded in 1926 when Detroit's Fisher brothers, in conjunction with GM, purchased it from the failing Durant Motors Company, led by the then independent entrepreneur Billy Durant.[16] In its final form, the Fisher One factory occupied a massive 3 million square feet of floor space. By comparison, the $90–100 million Great Lakes Technology Centre is a combination of brick and metal-framed glass atria, occupying approximately 1.2 million square feet of floor space, less than half the factory it replaced. As late as October 1988, the developer's plan called for 300,000 additional square feet of floor space, but these plans were dropped because, as the developers admitted at the time, "it's almost like it's a moving target; we're designing this project as fast as we get into it."[17] Despite this rush to finish construction, several years passed before large portions of the Tech Centre were finally occupied.

Today, GM tenants occupy three of the Tech Centre's four main sections. GM's Engineering & Development Centre, the Tech Centre's first major tenant, opened its doors in 1989 (see figure 1). A part of GM's Flint Automotive Division and, hence, a part of GM's Buick-Oldsmobile-Cadillac Group, the Engineering & Development Centre employs primarily design engineers and administrative staff. GM's Regional Personnel Centre is located at the north center of the complex, occupying the former Fisher One administration building (see figures 2 and 3). The south center of the complex includes various retail and service enterprises, including a health and fitness center, two hair salons, and a restaurant named "etc...etc...," whose ambience was described by the *Flint Journal* as "high-tech industrial casual" (see figure 4).[18] GM's AC Rochester Division accounts for much of the Tech Centre's south end, where, in January 1991, it concentrated its already primarily Flint-based headquarters staff in a new World Headquarters building (see figure 5). Additional south-end office space is occupied by GM's Flint Automotive Division and GM's Electronic Data Systems subsidiary.

As the photographs depict, from north to south, the Tech Centre's exterior design moves from the use of glass atria (which break the complex's otherwise box-shaped, smooth-brick exterior surface), to the roadside personnel building (which preserves the shell of the old factory that the Tech Centre has replaced). South of this section, recessed behind a parking lot, the exterior continues with the neon-highlighted facades and signs that announce the presence of the Centre's service sector. AC Rochester's box-shaped, brick World Headquarters stands as the Centre's southern bookend. Note also that the Tech Centre's grounds include a standard green Michigan Historic Site marker describing the Great Flint Sit-Down Strike (see figure 6). Across Saginaw Street the now-defunct UAW Local 581 building is occupied by a local law firm (see figure 7). Inside the Tech Centre, wide, pastel-colored corridors and retail establishment interiors are wholly typical of recent commercial-use architecture. One apparently decorative monument, however, does stand out (see figures 8 and 9). A Norman Rockwell-like depiction of the Great Flint Sit-Down Strike hangs at the Tech Centre's northernmost end, within a secluded and quiet retail area, and is the only interior indication of the site's significance as the home of the historic strike.

Thus, it is not the Tech Centre's architectural design nor material construction that make it so significant and unique among Flint's development efforts. The physical meshing of buildings with evidently divergent cultural meanings, for example, has hardly been an isolated occurrence in Flint. For example, the construction of AutoWorld physically enveloped Flint's Industrial Mutual Association auditorium, a recognized national historical site because of the IMA's significance as an archetypal 1920s welfare-capitalist organization.[19] The Tech Centre is also not the first instance of GM investing in a structure to symbolize its commitment to Flint. As early as the 1920s, GM expanded Flint's General Motors Institute after GM founder and Flint loyalist Billy Durant was removed from the company's leadership by the DuPont family of Delaware.[20] As historian Ronald Edsforth writes:

> Recognizing the significance of Flint to the company's operations, the new management of General Motors quickly moved to reassure local investors that the corporation would sustain its commitment to the Vehicle City. Both DuPont and Sloan visited Flint, and pledged $300,000 of General Motors' financing to help erect a Durant Hotel in the downtown business district.[21]

Thus, neither its integration of already existent physical forms nor its common-sense raison d'etre as a symbol of GM's continued commitment to the city make the Tech Centre unique in Flint. Rather, the Great Lakes Technology Centre's uniqueness lies in its dual ideological function as a future-oriented response to Flint's current and unprecedented experience with dependent deindustrialization and as a beacon signaling the end of Flint's militant labor past as the price for its future relationship with GM as a scaled-down, branch-office, postindustrial city.

The building's ideology is encoded in its very name—the Great Lakes Technology Centre. There is no mention of "General Motors," even though the vast majority of the Tech Centre's space is leased to GM entities. The corporation has not, as it were, openly and publicly signed on. In the past, GM has been criticized as aloof and insensitive toward its hometown. As early as 1982, for example, the president of the Charles Stewart Mott Foundation called GM an "absentee landlord," a characterization loudly seconded by *Roger & Me*.[22] GM is thus understandably reluctant to underscore its tenant status at the Tech Centre, as its transitory relationship with the city is a chronic source of criticism. Once Flint's preeminent and acknowledged employer, builder, and landlord, GM is now a consumer of local office space in the same legal category as the Tech Centre's hair salons and restaurants; a temporary contract defines their commitment.

The Centre's name also includes Great Lakes, a regional designation. While many aspects of Flint's industrial age are accurately described in world-comparative terms, "Great Lakes" signifies the city's contemporary failure to achieve a global or even national economic status. It suggests, in other words, the merely regional scope of Flint's changing integration into the translocal economic system. Even though Flint's mayor emphasized that the Great Lakes Technology Centre is "one of the largest technology centers in the world," its $90–100 million conversion price tag and limited engineering facilities pale in comparison to both GM's massive investments in its own General Motors Technology Center in Warren, Michigan, and the Chrysler Corporation's construction of an estimated $1 billion Tech Center 40 miles southeast of Flint in Troy, Michigan. Of the "nearly 6000 engineers and support staff" that the mayor lauded in his campaign literature, only 1500 work in the "Engineering & Development Centre," the Tech Centre's chief sanctum of automotive technology development. And while the *Flint Journal* reported in October, 1991, that "one section of AC Rochester's headquarters is being used by American and Soviet engineers working on fuel systems for cars made by the Soviet Union's Volga Auto Works," the engineering of fuel systems for less-than-world-class Soviet automobiles cannot be reasonably considered cutting-edge technological research, no matter how profitable in the short run.[23]

The Tech Centre's postindustrial motif is expressed in more subtle though no less ideological terms. The abbreviation "Tech Centre," for example, allows the development to associate itself with the prestige and corporate centrality of locally well-known and truly significant tech centers, such as those cited above. Moreover, straightforward local referentiality is eschewed in the spelling of "Centre." Transposing the American spelling of Center to the European Centre accents the difference between the old and the new, and parallels the use of standardized real estate and shopping mall motifs that signify the upscale or prestigious origins of projects that might otherwise be described in such generic terms as "tract-housing subdivisions" or "retail outlets." The Engineering & Development Centre and GM Personnel Centre are also in step with this aspect of the design motif, while "etc ... etc ..." adds to its "high-tech industrial casual" ambience with a noncapitalized, abbreviated, elliptical, nonreferential name. Finally, the notion of "Centre" itself suggests the presence of an integrated community. According to the developer's literature:

> Architectural designs were still coming off the drawing boards as approximately 2.2 million square feet of the old plant was being demolished, leaving 1.25 million to be renovated into a campuslike setting of offices, automobile development and test facilities, retail shops, restaurants, and ancillary businesses.[24]

In this, the Tech Centre's motif evokes the centering idea of a "campuslike set-ting," presumably to suggest to its employees the prestige and security of their cooperative, corporative pursuit of knowledge.

Of course, the Tech Centre's motif is manifest in a variety of material forms as well. In addition to the upscale campuslike soft lighting and pastel colors of its public spaces, the Tech Centre's main exterior marquee is capped, like Philip Johnson's New York City SONY Building, with its incomplete geometric shape suggesting the scientific yet open creativity that is technological development (see figure 10). Moreover, the marquee does not list any GM divisions (GM ten-ants rate their own separate signs), perhaps because listing GM in juxtaposition to "etc ... etc ..." seemed too gross a display of the former's tenant status. The building's use of glass-enclosed atria also signals its intelligent and sculpted integration with the surrounding environment. For example, the developer's guide to the Engineering & Development Centre states:

> Highlighting the northeast corner of the state-of-the-art office facility is a dramatic atrium entrance/display area. Another feature is a three-story window wall, also skylights, which supply natural lighting to many of the 1,093 office and work stations on the first floor. There are 97 more on the second floor, which features an open hallway over-looking the first floor, and another 154 on the third floor.[25]

As with the marquee, dramatic atria, window walls, and skylights flag the inte-gration of the Centre's intelligent postindustrial motif with its construction plans and building materials.

The theme of the Great Lakes Technology Centre's opening ceremony was "Link to the Future," but what, in fact, constitutes this link? What lies behind the phoenixlike metaphors used to describe the Centre's emergence from the ruins of the Fisher One site? These questions are difficult to answer because of the dearth of available commentary on the actual technology research-and-design activities that would justify the Tech Centre's innovative, campuslike image. An exception is this statement from the Flint Automotive Division guide to its Engineering & Development Centre:

> Today, rising from old broken bricks is a model development with the capability to engineer a total automobile from concept to production. Again parking lots are filled as people make their way to this site to write a new page in the history of the automobile industry.[26]

The Great Lakes Technology Centre may well be, as this document states, a "model development," but the "capability to engineer a total automobile from concept to production," even under a single roof, is not itself a new technological achievement, nor does this necessarily entail new and significant job creation for the Flint area. In this as in all important respects, the Tech Centre has failed to deliver the postindustrial goods. Indeed, its impact on the local economy has been generally negligible.

The Tech Centre's actual employment and economic multiplier effects undermine its implicit claim to represent a rebirth of the Vehicle City. For example, Flint was already the site of AC Spark Plug's world headquarters as well as the location of most of its production facilities. Likewise, the Flint Automotive Division's Engineering & Development Centre drew nearly two-thirds of its employees from former Flint sites, with only a little over 600 employees transferring to Flint from a GM facility in Troy, Michigan.[27] According to a *Flint Journal* interview with a major local real estate company, "most of the center's professional staffers are buying houses in [the Flint suburbs of] Grand Blanc or Fenton or commuting from Oakland County [whose northern border is approximately twenty miles south of Flint]." These housing choices also lessen the Tech Centre's economic impact on Flint.[28] This same *Flint Journal* article reports that "it's simply too soon to expect major spinoffs from the converted plant" because, as the Tech Centre's vice president and general manager tersely explains, "most development doesn't go like that."[29] Indeed, the Great Lakes Technology Centre has not reemployed a single laid-off UAW member, let alone spurred a postindustrial economy in Flint.

But facts such as these do not necessarily detract from the Tech Centre as a sign of the future, at least not for Flint's boosters. The "Tech Centre" motif is embraced by city officials as a still viable symbol of future-oriented progress, much as Phil Donahue was embraced by the city's residents as a symbol of cultural recognition. Of course, the misapprehension that the Great Lakes Technology Centre is Flint's own homegrown Silicon Valley works in GM's favor. Not only did GM receive eight city tax abatements on its Tech Centre investments, it also expanded its goodwill among city officials for its having brought this new chunk of cultural capital to an area starved for attention.[30] Moreover, the Tech Centre's nonunion, white-collar work environment provides a contrast to Flint's unionized, blue-collar factories. Whereas the NDM-infested Buick complex constantly reminds Flint of the days when assembly-line production and class conflict put Flint at the center of America's industrial culture, the Great Lakes Technology Centre, in sharp contrast, signals a futuristic postindustrial utopia free from sweat and strife.

This points to the second aspect of the Tech Centre's ideological function. More than literally covering over the demolished symbol of Flint's militant labor history, the Great Lakes Technology Centre also contains and thereby reduces the cultural significance of Fisher One's symbolic import in its integration of the former structure and its history within the construction of the present complex. The people of Flint were attached to this original factory complex. According to an October, 1988, front-page article in the *Flint Journal*,

entitled "Retirees tend skeleton of memories," the demolition of the old factory
(which by that time had been renamed B-O-C Flint Body Assembly) drew regular onlookers whose sole purpose was to mourn the passing of a building in
which many had labored.

> When demolition began, in September, and it was warm, Fisher One
> retirees would sit outside on benches, watching their factory crumble
> to the ground. Now they stay in their cars, parked in small lots across
> the street from the plant. They sit, watch and think. Sometimes, there
> is only one car. Other times, six or eight.
>
> Now and then one of the drivers might recognize a face in
> another car. But usually they sit one or two to a car in vehicles lined
> up as if at a drive-in movie. Here, though, the movie is one in which
> their scenes were shown long ago.
>
> The retirees don't get teary-eyed, although they . . . are saddened
> to see the plant change so radically from what they knew.[31]

On 10 December 1987, the day that the facility officially closed, Michael
Moore's *Roger & Me* film crew was joined outside the plant by Flint-based journalist and poet Josie Kearns. In her book *Life after the Line*, she reports that
"handmade signs that hung out the shop windows said, 'Here Today, gone
tomorrow. Fisher One,' and, '1937 sit down—1987 shut down.'"[32] Kearns also
interviewed bystanders, one of whom engaged her in the following dialogue:

> I was the first vice president of Chevrolet local for about ten years.
>
> KEARNS: Why are you out here today then?
>
> Well, I'm out here today because this is really a sad event for Flint and
> I . . . I'm just surprised. They're treating it like it was a hot-dog stand
> closing. You know, I know politicians worked these plant gates for
> fifty years with their literature. I don't see one politician out here
> today and that's disgraceful. You know, not long ago we put a histor-
> ical marker here and the politicians almost crowded us out. But now
> I don't see any of them. And that's a shame. Shame on them.
>
> KEARNS: What interests me is that it's the site of the sit-down strike.
> Do you have any feelings about that?
>
> That's what makes it so sad. Whether it's international or not, who
> knows? I know they're in business to make money, so. I don't think
> they would lose any money just for that reason. But that's what makes

it so sad. You know there was a worldwide industrial revolution because of what happened right here. And you see, that's what's got me upset. Really.[33]

Whether on the day of its closing or during its actual demolition, Flint residents were drawn to witness the passing of one of the city's most recognized and powerful physical symbols, and many of these witnesses were upset, saddened, or simply nostalgic.

The cultural significance of Fisher One's physical structure was also officially recognized in the city's and UAW's joint effort to sell actual bricks from the factory walls, the proceeds of which were donated to the Displaced Workers Emergency Needs Center and the Local 581 Retirees Chapter. Flint mayor, Matthew Collier, stated at the time: "These bricks are mementos of a facility that will forever be a part of the history of our city"; UAW Region 1-C Director Stan Marshall added: "Fisher One is the birthplace of our union and it's vital that we remember and preserve our past, to help guide us in the future."[34] The developer's decision to offer dignitaries at the Tech Centre's groundbreaking ceremony clear plastic blocks containing chain links from the old factory represents a similar case in point. Comparable to owning a sliver of the Berlin Wall, these brick and chain mementos suggest the passing of factories and machines and the entire industrial era, just as pieces of the Berlin Wall symbolized the "fall of communism." They are understood as shards of a memorable history, sacred to living people who connect their experience with that which is permanently remembered in the fragment.

As we have seen, the historic Fisher One factory remains a part of the new Great Lakes Technology Centre in three specific forms. State of Michigan law provides that officially designated Historic Sites display a marker, even if the key historical structure is no longer present. While this marker ostensibly symbolizes the political-legal recognition of the site, it also consigns this historic event (and its potential contemporary meanings) to a past era. Much as with Victor Reuther's enshrinement at Flint's downtown Sit-Down Strike memorial, this Historic Site marker may help Flint's citizens "remember and preserve [the city's] past," as the UAW's Stan Marshall suggested with reference to his union, but it does little to "help guide [Flint] in the future." Even if the marker's text did not itself emphasize, as it does, that the Sit-Down Strike led to "stability for workers and company," its standardized and officially sanctioned form militates against an empathetic remembrance of the strike's radical though ultimately compromised cultural content.

The Great Lakes Technology Centre's single interior indication of the Great Sit-Down Strike only furthers the political containment of this past event. In contrast to Detroit's famous Diego Rivera murals, for example, the Tech Centre's affirmative Rockwellesque depiction of the Sit-Down Strike is barely noticeable let alone artistically noteworthy. Moreover, the Tech Centre's image of the Sit-Down Strike compares poorly with the many powerful photo-graphs of the strike scene that demand a face-to-face encounter with the gaze of real people, some of whom, like Victor Reuther, are living today (compare figure 11 with figure 9).[35] These photographs are readily available, but they are not represented in the Tech Centre. Instead, the distanced perspective of the Tech Centre wall hanging merely suggests, as it were, that among old cars and in front of a now demolished facade, people of another era once milled about. No lighting is trained on this picture, and the adjoining wall is decorated with a restaurant advertisement. This stylized, inauspicious, and perhaps even irrev-erent display signals the Tech Centre's minimal valuation of the event. That the UAW sanctioned this shrine is a telling indicator of the union's inability to affect the kind of corporate culture in which GM lives as a going concern.

The Tech Centre's incorporation of a sizable chunk of the Fisher One facil-ity (see figure 3) itself serves several ideological functions. The building's street-facing facade suggests continuity with the past as it simultaneously deflects attention from the otherwise wholesale demolition of the previous structure's productive facilities. In maintaining only the administrative building, the structure also signifies the importance of white-collar, company-salaried, paperwork over the blue-collar, union-hourly, brick-and-chain factory labor of the past. Additionally, since this administration building is now GM's Regional Personnel Centre, retired as well as current workers from the surrounding area are often compelled to visit and witness the new symbolic order that is the Great Lakes Technology Centre. Standing in the Regional Personnel Centre's main south-side parking lot, such a visitor may view the former Local 581 union hall directly across the street, while behind them the "etc . . . etc . . ." res-taurant welcomes its lunch crowd into a space once occupied by the world's largest auto body factory.

Together, these symbolic elements function to distort and conceal the cul-tural significance of Flint's Great Sit-Down Strike. While many local union leaders suspect that GM closed the Fisher One facility in retribution for the 1936–37 Sit-Down Strike, more important are the ideological distortions that the Great Lakes Technology Centre silently expresses in its edifice. These coded messages will continually signal their meaning for as long as this complex remains a part of Flint's built environment.

COMPARING TECH CENTRE AND
CENTER FOR NEW WORK IDEOLOGY

While Flint's Center for New Work stood behind its texts, the same cannot be said for GM's (virtual) authorship of the Great Lakes Technology Centre. At first glance, *sans* smokestacks and millions of square feet of floor space, the Tech Centre's low visual profile signals a lean, intelligently designed presence: a campuslike environment. Closer examination reveals, however, that this structure also occupies, contains, and distorts hallowed cultural ground. In his book *Fast Capitalism*, Ben Agger suggests that today's ideology is increasingly "dispersed" into the built environment:

> Fast capitalism speeds up the rate at which people live out the histor-
> ical possibilities presented to them. They do this by "reading" a public
> world in which deauthorized texts have been dispersed into built and
> figural environments. The books still sold at the bookstore are archaic
> remainders, not the salient texts of the time.[36]

The Tech Centre is such a deauthorized public text; a salient artifact among Flint's cultural response to its state of dependent deindustrialization. Thus, the Tech Centre's tangible form does not render the content of its postindustrial ideology any less comparable to the ideas presented in New Work's books and pamphlets; the Tech Centre's form is simply more prominent, and ominous.

As with the Center for New Work, Tech Centre ideology is antihistorical: it suppresses and distorts memory of the Great Sit-Down Strike at the same time that it fosters the illusion of GM's continuing commitment to its hometown. Because the Tech Centre is a building, however, this ideology is manifest in phys-ical, spatial terms. As noted, the Tech Centre's standardized Historic Marker entombs within contemporary standards of respectability what was in fact an oppositional, life-and-death struggle that challenged the basic institutional framework of American society. Likewise, the Tech Centre's stylized and dep-ersonalized wall hanging aestheticizes and thereby contains the Strike's political meaning. Furthermore, if the 1936–37 Great Sit-Down Strike demonstrated GM's place-specific dependency on what was then described as its Flint "citadel," then GM's contemporary tenant status at the Great Lakes Technology Centre is a symbol of its revitalization as a trans-Flint, multinational business. Contrary, then, to the GM-owes-something-to-its-hometown theme plied in *Roger & Me*, GM's Tech Centre investments in fact reassert its right to eschew place-specific values like loyalty to home or nation in favor of strict attention to profitability. The Great Lakes Technology Centre surely signals the dawn of a new symbolic order, in which Flint's historic claims on GM have been rendered as moot as the city's clinging embrace to the mythos of science and technology.

The Tech Centre's physical structure also anticipates its own form of worker and community identity. In its brick-and-chain form, the Fisher One complex signified the familiar embodied aspects of industrial manufacturing, where physical human labor augmented the mechanical processes of assembly-line production. The transformation of these symbols from old broken bricks and floor-pan chains to cleaned and Lucite-enclosed mementos suggests the sociopsychological distance between industrial manufacturing and the intelli-gent, professional, esoteric world of postindustrial design and engineering. Signifying a revolution in the material forces of production, these objects, together with the Tech Centre's postmodern architectural design, call for a sharp break in the community's once-proud industrial self-image. Furthermore, the Tech Centre's exclusive and limited employment of engineers, technicians, and administrative staff signals the coming of a postindustrial Flint stratified by new, more complex work skills, and an unprecedented and exacting degree of educational attainment. Such a place needs autotown philosophers.

Finally, the notion of a "Tech Centre" in itself signals the ascendancy of technology as the motive power behind social change, suggesting that Flint's move to postindustrial technology is a progressive and rational response to deindustrialization. In contrast to New Work ideology, however, the Tech Centre naturally bypasses recognition of the social crisis that has accompanied Flint's experience with dependent deindustrialization. The Tech Centre is meant only as a sign of capitalism's robust and progressive development.[37]

The Great Lakes Technology Centre and Center for New Work are thus similar responses to Flint's experience with dependent deindustrialization. Setting aside their obviously divergent forms in favor of a focus on their respective ideological contents shows that both the "Center" and the "Centre" reject the immanence of Flint's heroic industrial history in favor of an epic signification of Flint's potential postindustrial future. This break with the city's collective memory may mean the forced transcendence of former identities at the expense of the community's accumulated experience, where once stable identities and lives become redundant as fast as technological innovation revolutionizes the means of production. This may then leave education qua cognitive retooling as the individual's only rational response to the system's increasingly stringent specifications for its cogs. It remains to be seen whether Flint's version of postindustrial society will one day constitute a viable program of economic and social renewal. At minimum, though, the advent of Flint's Tech Centre does suggest GM's renewed hegemony. According to Professor Richard Gull, a central reason for New Work's failure lay in Flint's denial of its situation, but this is not a problem the Tech Centre confronts. In forcing itself into the community's pattern of everyday life, this building never ceases to communicate the message that some will ride the postindustrial wave, but many others will have to cope with job-free time.

NOTES

1. "Some still see GM retribution in closing of historic Fisher 1," *The Flint Journal*, 16 October 1988, Sec. A, p. 1.

2. "Groundbreaking set Oct. 25 for tech center," *The Flint Journal*, 16 October 1988, Sec. A, p. 18.

3. "Historic Fisher bricks for sale; Great Lakes to break ground," *The Flint Journal*, 25 October 1988, Sec. C, p. 1.

4. Ben Agger, *Fast Capitalism: A Critical Theory of Significance* (Urbana, IL: University of Illinois Press, 1989), p. 19.

5. "2-year-old Great Lakes Tech Centre still offers hope to surrounding area," *The Flint Journal*, 6 October 1991, Sec. F, p. 5.

6. "Ten Good Reasons . . . ," Paid for by the Friends of Mayor Collier (c. 1991 document source).

7. "Welcome to the Flint Automotive Division Engineering & Development Centre," distributed by Great Lakes Technology Centre, Inc.

8. This chapter is indebted to M. Gottdiener and Alexandros Ph. Lagopoulos, eds., *The City and the Sign: An Introduction to Urban Semiotics* (New York: Columbia University Press, 1986). Also see, M. Gottdiener, "Semiotics and Postmodernism," in David R. Dickens and Andrea Fontana, eds., *Postmodernism & Social Inquiry* (New York: The Guilford Press, 1994), pp. 155–181.

9. Daniel Zwerdling, "And Then There's the Disneyland Solution," *The Progressive*, July, 1982, pp. 34–35, 34.

10. Ibid., p. 34.

11. Ibid., p. 35.

12. See Robert Hewison, *The Heritage Industry: Britain in a Climate of Decline* (London: Methuen, 1987); "Crossroads Village & Huckleberry Railroad," brochure issued by the Genesee County Parks and Recreation Commission (c. 1991, document source); "Windmill Place: Flint's Festival of International Dining & Shopping" (document source).

13. See George F. Lord and Albert C. Price, "Growth Ideology in a Period of Decline: Deindustrialization and Restructuring, Flint Style" in *Social Problems* 39, no. 2 (May 1992): 155–169; and Michael Moore, "General Motors and Flint, Michigan," in D. Stanley Eitzen and Maxine Baca Zinn, eds., *The Reshaping of America* (Englewood Cliffs, NJ: Prentice-Hall, 1989), pp. 329–333.

14. "*Roger & Me*: A Film by Michael Moore," Dog Eat Dog Production, distributed by Warner Brothers, Inc., 1989. Also see Moore, "General Motors and Flint, Michigan."

15. See Lord and Price, pp. 158–162.

16. Ronald Edsforth, *Class Conflict and Cultural Consensus* (New Brunswick, NJ: Rutgers University Press, 1987), p. 77.

17. "Tech center's developers reduce project's size again," *The Flint Journal*, 16 October 1989, sec. A, p. 15.

18. "Varied look, menu help distinguish 'etc . . . etc . . .'" *The Flint Journal*, 26 July 1991, Sec. B, p. 4.

19. See Edsforth, pp. 98–99, 142–143. The IMA is now headquartered at The Great Lakes Technology Centre.

20. Edsforth, p. 77.

21. Ibid., p. 76.

22. Ibid., p. 225.

23. See *The Flint Journal*, 29 December 1991, Sec. F, pp. 1–12, for an interesting comparison of Flint and the city of Togliantti, "Russia's premier auto center."

24. "Welcome to the Flint Automotive Division Engineering & Development Centre."

25. Ibid.

26. Ibid.

27. See "2-year-old Great Lakes Tech Centre still offers hope to surrounding area."

28. Ibid.

29. Ibid.

30. See Lord and Price for a review of the city's tax abatement policy, including for the Great Lakes Technology Centre.

31. "Retirees tend skeleton of memories," *The Flint Journal*, 16 October 1988, Sec. A, p. 1, 15.

32. Josie Kearns, *Life after the Line* (Detroit: Wayne State University Press, 1990), p. 18.

33. Ibid., pp. 21–22.

34. See "Raising Money for the Displaced Workers," in *Headlight*, 3 November 1988.

35. Plate 11 is reproduced with kind permission from *The Flint Journal's Picture History of Flint*, ed. Lawrence R. Gustin, 3d ed. (August, 1977), p. 200.

36. Agger, pp. 20–21.

37. Given the many tax abatements extended, I hesitate to emphasize too strongly this development's "private" status.

Figure 1. The Great Lakes Technology Centre's Engineering & Development Centre (1991).

Figure 2. The Great Lakes Technology Centre's General Motors Regional Personnel Centre (1991).

Figure 3. The Fisher Body seal symbolizes the factory of old (1991).

Figure 4. etc . . . etc . . . highlights the Tech Centre's retail section (1991).

Figure 5. The Great Lakes Technology Centre's AC Rochester World Headquarters Building (1991).

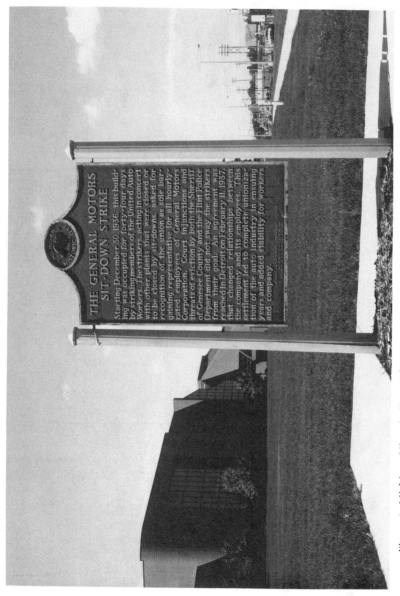

Figure 6. Michigan Historic Site marker commemorating the 1936–1937 Great Sit-Down Strike (1991).

Figure 7. Defunct UAW Local 581 building faces the Tech Centre's service sector (1991).

Figure 8. The inauspicious display of the Great Sit-Down Strike interior commemoration (1991).

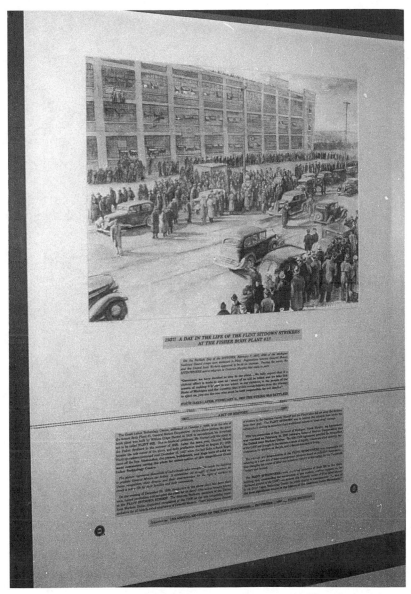

Figure 9. Close-up of the Rockwellesque depiction of the strike (1991).

Figure 10. The Great Lakes Technology Centre's marquee sans General Motors (1991).

Figure 11a. Strike sympathizers on January 17 mass in front of Fisher Body Plant 1 on S. Saginaw St., as sit-down strikers hang effigies of a "GM stool pigeon" from a third-floor window.

Figure 11b. Victor Reuther's sound truck is in the foreground of the scene on the same day at the plant.

Chapter 7

VISION THING

And what is our vision for the future? I'm intrigued that you focused on the vision because what I found is there was no vision here. Rather, we had to go create a vision, and it was among the most difficult parts of the strategic planning process to create a vision. In fact, we almost failed in achieving that vision, and I got pissed, saying, you know, "What are we gonna do here?!" And what happened was we gave it to a guy named Dallas Dort here in the community, [and] said, "Dallas, you write this shit. You're the word-smith here in town."

—Mark S. Davis,
GEAR Executive Director[1]

Mark tells me that the vision statement seems to mean something to people. I'm glad it does, but I don't see them promoting it the way I sort of wish they were. I think our morale and our self-image will be better and more productive if we believe that we're not just on an economic crusade, but [on a crusade] that has moral overtones.

—Dallas C. Dort,
GEAR Strategic Planning Committee[2]

Now Flint/Genesee County is the model. Other industrial cities around the globe are coming to see what Flint/Genesee is doing, because Flint/Genesee County has truly become the Home of the New American Dream.

—"Flint and Genesee County, 1999,
Home of the New American Dream,"
1991 GEAR Strategic Plan[3]

Blessed are the cynical, for only they have what it takes to succeed.

—C. Wright Mills,
The Power Elite[4]

Genesee Economic Area Revitalization, Inc. (GEAR) is a nonprofit economic development corporation formed in 1989 with the backing of Flint and Genesee County's business and political elite. GEAR's purpose is straightforward: "to oversee and coordinate economic development efforts in Genesee County."[5] Led by a board of directors aptly described as a "who's who" of the community's "leading lights," GEAR represents Flint's latest response to dependent deindustrialization.[6] In what is probably its most important document—the 1991 "Strategic Economic Development Plan for Flint/Genesee County" (Strategic Plan)—GEAR proffers a vision of the area's future that suggests Flint could soon become the "Home of the New American Dream." In actuality, though, GEAR's Strategic Plan is a cynical program born of enlightened false consciousness; its "vision" little more than a vision thing.

GEAR is a direct outgrowth of the dominance of GM and the C. S. Mott Foundation in Flint politics. Flint's preeminent business leaders have always played a central role in local economic planning and image management, but never before have these plans and "visions" been so openly, self-consciously, and *strategically* integrated into the city's economic development efforts. Indeed, the cultural significance of GEAR's vision thing—this reified community self-image shaped by the elite's hard-nosed reliance on instrumental rationality—extends beyond its corporate origins to suggest the ultimate fate of a culture dependent upon a crisis-ridden capitalist state. Parallel to Local PEL, then, GEAR demands that Flint acquiesce to the systemic imperatives of global capitalism.

"THE HOME OF THE NEXT AMERICAN DREAM" IN HISTORICAL CONTEXT

Official community self-images are telling creations. They often capture the reflection of the local powers that be, as well as traces of a community's integration into the wider culture. Forms of community boosterism, rationalized urban planning, and paternalistic culture management echo throughout Flint's history of documented self-representation. As a result of Flint's tight integration into dominant twentieth-century political-economic trends, these particulars regularly suggest features of twentieth-century American culture. This is certainly true of Flint's recent adoption of a self-image rooted in GEAR's strategic planning processes: the contrast with its historical antecedents indicates both a unique turn in local economic development planning and a disturbing shift in American culture as a whole.

Flint marked its fiftieth year as a city in a 1905 "Jubilee Parade" that featured a series of floats depicting the "development of the vehicle industry."[7] The Flint of 1905 was already the world's leading carriage producer. The local establishment of the Buick Motor Company in 1904 meant the city was emerging as a major auto manufacturing center as well. Events such as these help explain the optimism expressed in the commemorative volume "Fiftieth Anniversary of Flint: Golden Jubilee":

> The fiftieth anniversary of the city was signalled by the most substantial evidences of financial, intellectual and moral prosperity.
>
> The past is prophetic of the future. The influence of the pioneers persist in the pluck and energy, in the character and ability of their heirs and successors. There is every reason to believe that the one-hundredth anniversary of the city will be marked with unmistakable evidence of its progress along every line of honorable endeavor.[8]

Dedicated to celebrating Flint's "moral and religious" and "industrial development," this account emphasized the community's orientation toward the values of prosperity and progress. "Flint of Today; The Vehicle City; A City of Commercial & Industrial Progress," a 1906 document, sounds similar themes in albeit more exaggerated tones:

> The "Flint Spirit" has always been strong and binds together in one common interest the affairs of men, keeping down the petty prejudice that so often impedes the progress and narrows the minds of influential citizens. Diversified industries stimulate trade, create a fellowship in commercial circles and make the city secure against the stagnation that is so often hurtful to towns of a single idea.
>
> When other towns have vanished like bubbles and cannot be traced on the map, Flint will be like the old arrowhead, only polished and more attractive.[9]

This document evokes the "Flint Spirit" of commercial cooperation to sell the community as a stable venue for outside investment. Two years later Henry Ford produced his first Model T in Detroit and GM was founded in Flint. Boosterist blushing aside, then, prosperity and progress were in fact in the cards for the Vehicle City.

But the so-called fellowship of Flint's commercial circles was tested in the decade ahead. This was particularly the case when, in 1911, the socialist John C. Menton was elected mayor of Flint. As happened in many American communities where socialist candidates vied successfully for local office, popular political participation was met squarely by a unified and reactionary local business elite. In Flint, the young Charles Stewart Mott led a "progressive reform" program, which, in historian Ronald Edsforth's words, ultimately "undercut the appeal of municipal socialism."[10] But nothing it seems—not socialism, not even the eventual 1916 electoral defeat of Mott's business coalition politics—could stem the local business elite's enthusiasm for progress and prosperity.

The unrelenting feeling of advancement and growth was captured in the words of James A. Welch, a prominent Flint businessman, whose realty company published the 1916 brochure "Flint: Past-Present Prospective":

> The story of the growth of Flint is remarkable even in these advanced days of gigantic industrial achievements. So rapid has been the upbuilding of our city that few realize the stupendous strides that have been made in this thriving industrial metropolis. In comparison with other cities throughout the land, and from facts and figures obtained from the most reliable sources, I believe that Flint today is one of the most prosperous cities in the world.
>
> Flint's prosperity has been built on the solid rock of an immense payroll—with every man working, with jobs looking for men, and the highest salary per capita in the world. Today Flint stands second in the manufacture of automobiles for which it has the whole world as a marketplace.[11]

Envisioning the "whole world as a marketplace," the Flint of 1916 positioned itself in world-comparative terms.

Flint's rapid expansion brought chaos as well as prosperity into the city's everyday life. For this reason, the city acquired the services of the newly emerging profession of urban planning in the person of John Nolen, a planner from Cambridge, Massachusetts. The flavor of Nolen's philosophy is captured in his 1920 city plan for Flint:

> In authorizing the preparation of a comprehensive city plan, Flint has joined a notable group of progressive American cities. Heretofore cities of the United States, generally speaking, have grown with their eyes almost closed, so far as city planning is concerned. They have permitted streets to be laid out and extended either at random, or according to a gridiron pattern of deadly uniformity, and usually without even the merits of a consistent gridiron plan. One method has meant much disorder, the other drab monotony. It is difficult to say which is worse. The cost of such methods has been a heavy tax on citizenship everywhere.[12]

While Nolen elsewhere explores the aesthetic dimensions of adapting city development to its natural environment, he continues by punctuating his method's more significant social functions:

> Now comes modern city planning, with its comparatively simple and practical remedies for these evils, many of which have a direct relation

to unrest and disorder. While the discontent is widespread, it centers in industrial cities, especially those of rapid growth. An author writing on "Bridgeport and Democracy" said recently: "The factories open their doors, and a young, undisciplined crowd fills the streets, their mouths a-water like hungry hounds, for pleasure; starved for play; starved for joy and without the anchorage of a comfortable and ordered existence."[13]

Nolen's vision of orderly urban development linked the methodical rationalization of Flint's built environment to the city fathers' desire for control over Flint's working class. Instead of a "young, undisciplined crowd" and "unrest and disorder" of all types, in other words, urban planning qua social control would produce in Flint "a comfortable and ordered existence."

Noting that "its authors, and the public officials charged with [the plan's] progress, have cast their eyes ahead to the Flint of 1950," the 1920 plan also offers Flint's first vision statement:

Picture, if you please, this city in 1950. In area it will be at least as large as the area indicated by the outside boundaries on the General Plan map that forms the frontpiece of this volume. Its population, in all probability, will exceed 200,000 persons. It will be a city known not only for its industrial output, but also for its outpouring of human happiness and social content. It will be a city of schools and playgrounds, of parks and recreation facilities, of neighborliness and community centers, a city of noble architecture and spacious groupings, a city in which honest pleasure may follow worthy toil, and men and women live for something more than wages and duties.

That is the harvest; the Nolen Plan and the Arnold Transportation Plan are the seed. But between seed-time and harvest there is work to be done through all the intervening years.[14]

While Nolen stressed that "realizing the boons and benefits herein presented" will require the "steady, consistent, moral support of the plans," his "picture" or vision statement merely indicates the planner's expectation that Flint would grow demographically and geographically, that it would continue as an industrial city, and that social harmony would prevail.[15] Nolen's vision was thus little more than an appeal to stay the course.

The striking success of Flint's expanding automobile industry did, in fact, lead to continued economic growth throughout the 1920s, and the city as a whole, nurtured by its automotive elites, basked in the glow. Edsforth notes that "By the late 1920s, normalcy, the domination of political-economic decision making by Republican businessmen, appeared to be a permanent condition."[16] Judging from the effusive terms used to describe Flint in a 1929 Flint Chamber of Commerce publication, "normalcy" made boosterism an exciting business:

> Progressive Flint
> Flint—A Rapidly Growing City
> Flint—The Motor City
> A Fortunate City
> Flint—A High-Wage City
> Flint—A Prosperous City
> Flint—A Stable City   .
> The Motor Vehicle Industry—A Stable Industry
> A City of Homes.[17]

But all was not milk and honey. Perhaps in acknowledgement of the Ku Klux Klan's substantial political popularity during this period, the chamber also noted that Flint's population was 98 percent white, "and 81.6 percent native white," while under the headings "Get the Facts, Don't Be Misled" and "A Loyal Citizenry," the Chamber warned of the potential for labor unrest:

> Swarms of unemployed from all sections of the country have in cer-
> tain instances been induced to come to Flint by being told that they
> could readily secure employment at good wages, when the labor
> demands of Flint's industries were already well supplied.
>   Some of this misrepresentation has erroneously been laid to
> Flint's industries, which of course never was the case.
>   Thinking and acting collectively, realizing the interdependence
> of industrial, commercial and other interests and inspired by a glori-
> ous record of achievement, the citizens of Flint have developed a keen
> sense of loyalty and a firm confidence in the continued growth and
> prosperity of their city.[18]

While the Flint of 1929 again appeared as a prosperous and expanding city, the city's expansion was now guarded against undesirable newcomers, reflecting the mood of an increasingly polarized immigrant nation whose overall prosperity and progress would, in fact, very shortly collapse. As Edsforth writes: "In 1930, the collapse of the national automobile market began to force business-man to strip Flint's working people of the high wages and steady work that had formed the day-to-day underpinnings of normalcy."[19] The Great Depression, in other words, was at hand.

For obvious reasons, 1930s saw economic boosterism ebb in Flint, while later, during the first half of the 1940s, war making and war propaganda dominated the city's attention. Still, city planners and the C. S. Mott-led coalition of local business leaders maintained and advanced their community agendas over this period. For example, in 1937 the Flint Institute of Research and Planning, in its contribution to "A Comprehensive City Plan for Flint, Michigan," prodded the city's planning board to rationalize its traffic and thoroughfare system by emphasizing "Flint's special responsibility" "because of her notable position in the automobile industry" to lead the way on automobile-related urban development.[20] The Great Depression and subsequent decline in motor vehicle sales notwithstanding, this document outlined the prospects for a "community for the motor age" based on the "principles of controlled traffic circulation," indicating the continuity of rational urban planning even in the face of prolonged socioeconomic crisis.[21] On the other hand, researchers from the Bureau of Government at the University of Michigan (Ann Arbor) published in 1942 "An Experiment in Community Improvement," detailing the successes and wider applicability of various paternalistic C. S. Mott Foundation programs then underway in Flint.[22] These included the community schools program, initiatives in improving children's health care, and programs designed to organize the community's leisure activities. According to this report, the C. S. Mott Foundation effort "emphasizes the importance of health, education, wholesome activity, good citizenship, and the kind of democracy that comes from the intermingling of many kinds of people in their leisure time."[23]

Such programs were aimed at managing the conflicts present in Flint's Depression and Homefront society, but similar strategies continued even as World War II came to a close. In 1945, Flint's Buick Motor Division sponsored Carl Crow's book *The City of Flint Grows Up: The Success Story of an American Community*, in which Crow wrote:

> Buick is Flint and Flint is Buick. It is not far-fetched to say that the relationship between the city and the industry has been like that of a self-sacrificing father and a successful son.[24]

While this book consisted mainly of a stylized version of Flint's pioneer history, its true significance lay elsewhere. In a well-placed set of speculations on the nature of postwar Flint, Crow reassured Flint's working class that Flint's prewar depression was behind them:

> If every industrial community in America could look toward the future with the confidence enjoyed by the people of Flint, the country would have no cause for concern over the possibility of a postwar depression.[25]

In the short run, Crow's optimism seemed justified. By 1956, Flint's Chamber of Commerce again found it easy to sell the city's substantial economic successes, so much so that by this time its chief focus had turned from the stability of the city's economic infrastructure to the value and promise of its noteworthy cultural developments. The foreword of the chamber's lengthy "Flint, Michigan: The Vehicle City" stated:

> This is the story of Flint—of busy, bustling, "Fabulous Flint"—the second city of Michigan. And in a greater sense, it's the story of our country, too, for the self-same spirit that pushed, and drove, and shoved and built, that dreamed its dreams and then made them come true, is the self-same spirit that built this truly "All American" city.
>
> Mere statistics can never reveal the restless, pulsing vigor that typifies this great industrial center—nor can they reveal the warm-hearted generosity and neighborliness of its people. Flint is Flint—no other city is like it, or can ever be—for the Flint story is the story of its men who have built even better than they dreamed, and what they started still moves ahead.
>
> Flint men have built industrial might—now Flint men build beauty, and culture, and friendship, for they know that these, too, are worthy of their greatest effort.[26]

C. S. Mott again stands out among the "Flint men" whose new attention to "beauty, and culture, and friendship" contributed to Flint's "All American" status: this publication even dubs him "Mr. Flint." Confident that "any story of Flint . . . is the story of General Motors—and the General Motors story, is the story of 'Fabulous Flint,'" this report highlighted Mott Foundation programs, especially those that in 1958 culminated in Flint's still-existing College and Cultural Center.

In 1973, the year that "Mr. Flint" passed on to his reward, Flint's Chamber of Commerce offered "Frontiers Unlimited."[27] While apparently still secure in the notion that "those great pioneers of American industry had profound loyalty to their home city," Flint is now described as merely a "microcosm of midwest America," a regional designation also used to locate Flint's expanding suburban communities:

> And if the Greater Flint Community is a microcosm of midwest America, such smaller communities as Flushing, Davison, Mt. Morris, Fenton, Swartz Creek and others are miniature mirrors of the City of Flint.[28]

An additional hint of trouble is found in the introduction's last lines:

> Flint has always grown from within. Its people have been its greatest resource, providing leadership, vision, money and hard work.

As one observer declared: "We're a community characterized by many strengths and a few weaknesses, with as bright a future as any area in America."[29]

Facing white flight, the loss of Mr. Flint, and, moreover, the early signs of a faltering America's auto industry, Flint's boosters began to speak less in world-comparative terms and more in "microcosm of the midwest" analogies; less about national and global leadership, and more in terms of having "as bright a future as *any area*." Indeed, expectations concerning the city's future were hedged simply in the transformation of "Flint" into the "Greater Flint Community," which appears as an effort to reclaim a fleeing population, if only in words.

After 1973, the city's self-image production reveals a steadily falling confidence in the older notions of progress and prosperity. For example, Carter-era "malaise" characterizes the 1977 Annual Report entitled "A City in Change." Flint mayor, James Rutherford, in his introduction, for example, suggests surprisingly leveled expectations:

We may, indeed, look with pride on our accomplishments over the past year. Some of those accomplishments were:

• Award of an 8.5 Million Dollar Block Grant

• Groundbreaking for Riverfront Park

• Salmon Planted in Flint River

• "Quality of Life" Award for Sewage Control Plant[30]

After touting the city's sewage control plant, the mayor concludes: "As we go forth together, let it be known that our City—City of Flint—is very much alive and, indeed, going very well."[31] Of course, stressing that Flint "is very much alive" (i.e., not dead yet; still kicking) barely qualifies as boosterism at all.

The 1980s witnessed a rebirth of Reagan-inspired optimism in Flint as in America. This optimism materialized locally in the form of Flint's infamous tourism- and convention-related downtown revitalization projects. In "Flint: New Life," funded by the Mott Foundation and prefaced by C. S. Mott's eldest son, C. S. Harding Mott (who was acting in his capacity as chairman of the board of the Flint Area Conference, Inc.), the early 1980s downtown development strategy was trumpeted as "awakening a new confidence that is creating new plans" for a "revitalization" that "continues to create waves of new thinking for Flint and the nation."[32] Several points stand out in this self-image, which foreshadow key features of Flint's 1991 strategic plan. Flint is conceived as merely a vertical component of GM, as this document describes *Flint* as "the largest most diversified supplier in the entire GM pipeline. . . ."[33] "Flint: New Life" also emphasizes for the first time in Flint's history of official boosterism the city's "unique partnership of private and public sectors."[34] This announced blurring of political authority and economic power only increased in the ensuing years, reaching its climax, in fact, with the advent of GEAR, Inc. This document was also the first showcase for several of the late 1970s and early 1980s downtown developments, several of which ended in disaster. These included AutoWorld, the University of Michigan–Flint's downtown campus, Riverbank Park, River Village (a planned community), St. John's Industrial Park, and the Bishop Airport Airpark (an industrial park).[35] Lastly, and apparently in the thought that these numerous, ambitious developments would buffer its impact, "Flint: New Life" includes a surprisingly frank reflection upon the city's past:

> But Flint has had problems too. The decade of the 1960s found the cities everywhere reeling under the effects of urban decay, lethargy and racial conflict. Suburbia, expressways and shopping malls sped the flight from the cities. The 60s were a time of startling consciousness. Downtowns—long the hearts of the cities' vitality, the crossroads of commerce, entertainment, industry and excitement—became glum shadows of that earlier time. People seemed to have lost faith in their cities and their own ability to revitalize them. Flint was no exception.[36]

If Flint once "lost faith" in its "ability to revitalize," this document assured readers that the back-sliding was over: Flint was on a crusade in search of new life.

Sadly, though, this promised new beginning hinged upon one million tourists and conventioneers annually visiting Flint, a premise that turned out to be the plan's key flaw. The colossal failure of Flint's tourism- and convention-related economic development projects sent the community's leadership coalitions into a period of hand wringing and soul searching. According to a study conducted by University of Michigan–Flint researchers, George F. Lord and Albert C. Price, many local business elites cast blame for these failures onto their public sector leadership—especially onto the Mott Foundation—for having forced the implementation of economic development schemes against the will of the capitalist market. As one respondent in the Lord and Price study remarked: "Projects were controlled with a lot of money not a lot of good ideas; the market was distorted by the Mott Foundation's idea of what Flint should look like."[37] Poor planning was also deemed a key reason for these failures. Lord and Price cite three important statements to this effect:

> Our vision was too small, or we lacked vision. I used to ask what's next (meaning when these projects were completed), and everyone else said "What do you mean?" There was no assessment of needs. The short

coming has been no vision of what the consequences would be. Look at all of the dollars available—and we didn't do comprehensive planning.

Projects were developed without a specific goal. They failed primarily because there was not a market for what they provide—tourism. It was forced, not natural economic activity.

Poor planning, anyone could see it, it was ill-conceived.[38]

These planning failures and the reverberations they sent throughout the city's elite coalitions set the context for GEAR.

GEAR was to be strictly business centered, employing the corporate method of strategic planning to the steering problems and performances, not of a corporation, but of a city and its metropolitan area. This would be an enlightened plan, as no longer would Flint's elites directly depend upon the Mott Foundation, General Motors, or any similar benefactor. Rather, the city's continued progress and prosperity was to come from within: Flint, as a whole, would fully adapt itself to the structure of the capitalist system. In doing so, Flint would level any cultural, political, or otherwise institutionalized or normative obstacle standing in its path toward economic survival. These plans were already well established by 1989, when GEAR first emerged as a visible public entity.

In the beginning there was the Genesis Project, a glossy 1989 Price Waterhouse report commissioned for GEAR with the help of a federal Economic Development Administration (EDA) grant.[39] The Genesis Project was also aided by two separate GEAR Boards of Directors, the GEAR Oversight Committee, the Genesee County Metropolitan Planning Commission, City of Flint, and the representatives of 113 other public and private organizations. Bearing, as it did, the imprimatur of the mayor of Flint, the chairperson of the Genesee County Board of Commissioners, and representatives of the Genesee County Chapter of Township Association and the Genesee County Small Cities and Villages, the report's cover letter is to be taken seriously when it states:

Everyone should agree with the goal of building a growing, diversified economy and providing employment, training, and educational opportunities for all of our citizens. However, a fiercely competitive global economy with rapidly changing technology makes achieving this goal more challenging.

To succeed we must work together and use our resources efficiently. This requires all members of the community to unite in a coordinated approach to Genesee County's economic development.

We must have a clear vision of what we want to accomplish and an effective implementation strategy. This strategic plan provides us with that vision and coordinated strategy.

> This report is only a beginning. It should be viewed as a "living document" with visions, goals, and strategies that will evolve as we face future challenges.[40]

With these words, the Genesis Project outlines what would become GEAR's method for approaching economic development as well as, in fact, most of its eventual "strategies" and "goals."

Following the triadic strategic planning format, the Genesis Project describes Flint and Genesee County's past, current situation, and vision for the future. The latter two categories are then linked by a set of "strategic issues," or "actions for attaining our vision and goals." Applying the strategic planning format to an entire county meant not only establishing an acceptable version of reality (historical, current, and future oriented), but, equally important, an acceptable and practical plan of action. Like the GEAR Strategic Plan, then, the Genesis Project brings together means and ends in order to rationalize the community's self-image and action orientations. As the Genesis Project states:

> The plan defines the actions we must follow to secure our future. Indeed, we will need to execute thirty-one varied actions over the next five years to reach our vision by the end of this century.[41]

It is thus useful to consider the differences that separate the 1989 Genesis and 1991 GEAR Strategic Plan, especially as a gauge for measuring GEAR's developing public presentation.

In contrast to the 1991 statement, the Genesis Project's vision statement is remarkably frank in acknowledging its elite origins:

> *The Future of Genesee County: A Vision for the Year 2000*
>
> A group of key local public- and private-sector leaders joined together to describe its view for the future of Genesee County. The group developed and agreed upon the following exciting vision:
>
> "By the year 2000, the Genesee County community will have capitalized on its varied strengths and resources to build a growth-oriented, diversified economy, while providing employment and educational opportunities for all of its citizens."
>
> This picture, shared by members from across our community, provides a strong, clear signal for where we want our community to go.[42]

The Genesis vision seems to flow directly from its elite origins, for it is difficult to imagine business and community leaders who would want anything other than a "growth-oriented, diversified economy."

Genesis also declared that Flint's highest economic development priority (that is, "strategic issue 1") is "streamlining and coordinating our economic development efforts" under the "sole overall responsibility" of a "newly reorganized GEAR," new especially in that GEAR would have "private sector leadership." According to the report, "this tone *must* be emulated across the county."[43] In June 1991, in step with the Genesis timetable, the achievement of this goal was announced to the community in a *Flint Journal* article entitled "GEAR ready to accept role as major player."[44] Of course, GEAR's role as the area's primary economic development agency is no longer a part of the community's redevelopment *strategy*; as of 1991, this fact had been made an aspect of Flint's ongoing *reality*.

Genesis differs from the GEAR, lastly, in that its private-sector development strategies are presented only as vague generalities. In addition to installing GEAR at the top of the Flint/Genesee County economic development hierarchy, the five remaining Genesis "strategic issues" were: (1) "Developing the Labor Force of the Future"; (2) "Strengthening Local Business"; (3) Attracting New Business and Industries"; (4) Enhancing Opportunities for Minorities and the Disadvantaged"; and (5) "Improving the County's Internal and External Image."[45] Taking this last category as an example, the Genesis Project advocated three strategies for improving the area's "internal and external image": (a) a "coordinated, comprehensive anticrime campaign"; (b) a "redevelopment plan for downtown Flint"; and (c) a "broad-based public relations campaign that highlights the county's strengths and successes."[46] But the substance of the anticrime campaign, downtown development plan, and public relations campaign are never spelled out by Price Waterhouse or the cover-letter signatories. These proposals were suggestive of only a general course of action.

It is difficult to precisely chart the development of GEAR during 1989, or to ascertain why or even how GEAR established its Strategic Planning Committee in the spring of 1990 and charged it with "proposing a set of strategic actions that would produce a prosperous economy for the people of Flint and Genesee County."[47] Mark S. Davis, GEAR's executive director since 1990, finds GEAR's organizational origins and its method for establishing a board of directors unimportant and uninteresting:

> To be honest, I've never looked, it wasn't important, and it's not important. It's only important to academics. In the real world, what is important is what are they doing, Okay? And if we're going to get into legitimacy, and all these other sorts of stuff, I'm going to ... (pause). I don't play the game because it's bullshit.[48]

Dallas C. Dort, a Flint native and key GEAR Strategic Planning Committee member, responds in a similar vein: "It is] hard to remember, and probably not real productive to try to sort out who started what."[49] Regardless of "who started what," then, the fact remains that between March and November 1990, the GEAR Strategic Planning Committee, chaired by Flint's sitting mayor, reproduced much of the Genesis Project's recommendations as its own.[50]

In November 1990, the GEAR Strategic Planning Committee circulated its Strategic Economic Development Plan for Flint/Genesee County among community leaders, which, according to Davis, was "preliminarily adopted, subject to public participation."[51] Between November 1990 and July 1991, Davis and Charles W. Weeks, chairperson of GEAR's board of directors, presented the report on forty-four separate occasions to various groups, organizations, community gatherings, and elected officials. Their manifest purpose was the solicitation of public feedback, although, according to a separate GEAR memorandum, a second purpose was "marketing" the report.[52] Extensive revisions in the wording of the plan's Strategic Priorities and Action Agenda were made on this basis, with each change carefully documented by GEAR. The plan's final version was approved by GEAR's Board of Directors on 9 July 1991. A headline in the following day's *Flint Journal* announced: "GEAR gearing up to put finalized plans in motion."[53]

In order to assess the general cultural significance of GEAR's Strategic Plan—and in particular its vision statement—it is necessary to describe and reproduce parts of its general contents. The plan is divided into three main parts: (1) Flint and Genesee County: Past to Present; (2) Flint and Genesee County, 1999, Home of the New American Dream; and (3) Strategic Priorities and Action Agenda." This temporal organization corresponds to the strategic planning perspective.[54] The first part of the plan is further divided into three subsections: (1) An American Success Story; (2) Global Changes; and (3) Flint and Genesee County Today. In GEAR's separately published Synopsis, this section is simply labeled: Past to Present—A Shared Picture of Reality.[55]

Flint's history as "An America Success Story" is organized around a single theme: GM's centrality in Flint's economic and social development, which is presented as a good news/bad news narrative. According to this document, the good news is:

> Because of its role in creating GM, Flint/Genesee County captured the largest concentration of this new corporation's production facilities of any city/county area.
>
> For the working people of America, many of whom had migrated only recently from the poverty and rigors of rural life or from hardship and persecution abroad, the new factory jobs in Flint/Genesee County offered a chance to achieve the American Dream for themselves and for their children.[56]

This "shared picture of historical reality" directly links GM and the American Dream; however, "Even as GM's meteoric rise was lifting Flint/Genesee County to new heights of economic prosperity, there were some troubling signs."[57] The bad news, in other words, falls into three categories:

> GM's decision to be a fully integrated producer resulted in fewer supplier opportunities for area business.
>
> The relatively high salaries that GM paid made it difficult for other companies to compete for labor, and inadvertently discouraged potential entrepreneurs from taking the risks entailed in starting new businesses.
>
> Moreover, by the late 1930s Flint/Genesee County had developed a reputation for combative labor-management relations, growing out of confrontations between GM management and the United Auto Workers—a reputation that was to persist for the next fifty years.[58]

GM exacerbated Flint's already substantial GM dependency by vertically integrating most of its suppliers and by forcing the area's wage levels above the national mean. Working-class militancy, too, is singled out for critical analysis, as it clouded the local business climate even as it secured the wage levels also credited with supporting the American Dream. "Despite these disquieting developments," the plan reassures, "well into the 1950s, Flint/Genesee County remained an authentic American success story."[59]

Given the significance accorded to GM in its historical sketch of Flint, the Strategic Plan is consistent in describing the city's decline in terms of the automotive industry and, particularly, GM's various corporate decisions. Under the heading Global Changes, for example, the plan cites five main difficulties confronted by, or caused by, GM, and, by extension, difficulties confronted by, or caused by, Flint. These are: (1) the maturation of the U.S. auto industry; (2) the rise of global competition in the auto industry; (3) GM's difficulties in adjusting to global competition (resulting from (a) management being caught off guard, (b) management's initial disbelief that others could make autos better than Americans, and (c) the lack of flexibility that the history of confrontation in the company's labor-management relations had produced); (4) new technologies to improve auto industry productivity, and (5) the area's loss of final key GM decision makers.[60] Accordingly, the Strategic Plan suggests that Flint "could no longer count on a growing GM to provide the essential new jobs that would keep employment rates high and young people from leaving in search of work opportunities."[61] In other words, the link between GM and the American Dream had been broken by "global changes" that were "largely outside the control of Flint/Genesee County and its people."[62] That GM is not directly and forcefully charged with having disinvested from Flint is tempered by recognition in points 3 and 5 above of the importance of management decisions, as well as by a later comment noting the significance of "some shift of [GM] production resources to elsewhere in the U.S. and overseas."[63]

In the third section, Flint and Genesee County Today, GEAR's Strategic Plan frankly states: "The Flint/Genesee County of 1990 is a low-growth, high-unemployment, declining, manufacturing economy," which "remains heavily dependent on GM."[64] Two general points are underscored. First, GEAR's Strategic Plan is based on the assumption that "GM will only be able to offer the people of Flint/Genesee County a declining number of jobs in the future."[65] These planners also note that Flint's past dependency on GM has resulted in: (1) a lack of small- and medium-sized businesses outside of GM's control; (2) the lack of an entrepreneurial climate; (3) relatively poor rates of educational attainment; (4) a lack of community urgency due to denial of long-term changes; and (5) conflicts between city and suburbs, labor and management, and blacks and whites that have "left the community fragmented and without a common purpose and plan."[66] These factors constitute the main of Flint's "obvious and powerful competitive disadvantages."[67] If this were not an already dark enough picture of Flint and Genesee County Today, the plan points to only three positive competitive *advantages*: (1) GM is "a huge customer" for other businesses, particular "professional services, new technologies, and machine tools and parts"; (2) Flint has "a relatively strong base of institutions important for economic development, such as universities and colleges, recreational and cultural facilities, and hospitals"; and (3) Flint has "strong transportation links to other markets, through the interstate highway system and a developing airport."[68] Among Flint's strong points, then, is the fact that it sits at the juncture of several Michigan highways, has local hospitals, and a newly renovated airport.

In sum, the first part of GEAR's Strategic Plan offers a broad picture of a community that was once happily dependent upon GM but that, in the 1990s, suffers from the ill effects of such dependency. Clearly the plan is not so much concerned with the human or social impact of Flint's decline (the "very human causalities," as Davis says), as it is with the deterioration of the community's ability to effectively respond within the framework of a newly emergent global capitalist economy.[69] As we have seen, this Shared Picture of Reality is not so remarkable. Precedent for a global-comparative, progress- and prosperity-oriented self-image is well established in Flint's past community boosterism. Even GEAR's frank assessment of Flint's current situation is paralleled by both the city's own recognition that it had once lost faith in itself and the Genesis Project's description of Flint's mixed record since the 1960s and 1970s.

The second portion of GEAR's Strategic Plan is Flint's latest vision statement. The origin of this statement is as murky as the origin of GEAR overall, but it is clear that the vision statement was originally drafted by an informal group headed by Flint businessman Dallas C. Dort (whose grandfather, J. Dallas Dort, was a key business partner of GM founder Billy Durant). The membership of this group included the heads of the GM's Flint Automotive Division, AC Rochester Division, the University of Michigan–Flint, the mayor of Flint, Doug Ross, a consultant from the Corporation for Enterprise Development (whose organization was chiefly responsible for drafting GEAR's Strategic Plan), and several others who would eventually hold positions on GEAR's official Strategic Planning Committee.[70] Given such exclusive membership, it would appear that Flint's latest vision of itself is as much a product of elite planning as is the Genesis Project statement. In Dort's recollection, the group surmised that Flint had no "vision or plan"; Flint's mayor wondered aloud: "should I be doing that?"[71]

In addition to Dort's informal group of community leaders, Mark Davis credited CED's Doug Ross, stating that Ross "pushed the vision thing much more than I did. Doug ought to get a lot of credit for having pushed the vision thing so hard."[72] Dort also acknowledges Ross as a major backer and coauthor of the GEAR vision statement, or what Dort also describes as a "qualitative, visual, sensory image—a model—a visual model of life in the future."[73] The precise origins of this document aside, it was adopted in July 1991, unrevised, as part of GEAR's Strategic Plan. It thus stood as the city's and county's institutionalized image of its future. Due to its central importance, GEAR's vision statement is fully reproduced.

FLINT AND GENESEE COUNTY, 1999
HOME OF THE NEW AMERICAN DREAM

Flint/Genesee County have changed. But the change is not so much a change in our character as it is a fulfillment of our character. Our community is still committed to making things—manufacturing is still the lifeblood of the economy. But today Flint/Genesee County's technicians make things primarily with their minds and skills.

GM. General Motors is still the community's largest employer, providing thousands of high-paying union and management jobs, nearly all of them skilled or technical in nature.

Non-GM employment. The biggest change is that a broad base of new, entrepreneurial, manufacturing-related service businesses has sprung up, now employing more than 50,000 people at high skill and wage levels. Many of these businesses moved to Flint/Genesee County or were started by area residents in response to GM's growing purchases of business services during the 1990s. Because most of these firms expanded to serve customers around the world, the local economy is now more diverse. Former factory workers who saw their jobs eliminated by global competition and automation now work in the hundreds of manufacturing service businesses that have sprouted in modern brick and glass office buildings all across Flint/Genesee County.

These skilled technicians work in the engineering, design, information processing, machine tool, quality control, software, automation technology, marketing and export firms serving manufacturers around the globe—firms for which Flint/Genesee County has become famous.

The UAW. The United Auto Workers union is prospering here. It has attracted worldwide attention and respect by defining its mission as the advocate of a competitive and prosperous American work force. Businesses view the union as a constructive component of the manufacturing base.

Local G.I. Bill. Flint/Genesee County's work force is well paid and well worth it. The area's innovative local G.I. Bill for longtime local workers enabled most of these men and women to learn their new trades. In fact, Flint/Genesee County's work force has become one of the most skilled and capable in the world.

Education. Nearly all of the county's population has completed K–14 education or higher—or the equivalent, in the case of those already in the work force before 1991. All young people have an equal chance to get excellent educations and jobs. Students from the fourth grade up visit employers regularly. Starting in the tenth grade, employers sponsor them in a fashion similar to GMI, allowing for the difference in age and educational development.

As more and more Flint/Genesee County youths have demanded advanced education, GMI's student population has climbed dramatically. The UM-Flint has sophisticated interdisciplinary programs coordinated with Ann Arbor, relating to medical care and other workplace issues. These include a large and diverse master's program in career-related applied sciences as well as Ph.D.-granting programs. Mott Community College and Baker College likewise have grown, serving as the upper end of K–14, as well as in selected areas of excellence. All four colleges have shouldered the crucial task of providing continuing education for the skilled technicians and managers in Flint/Genesee County's new economy. The Michigan Industrial Development Institute continues its decade-long role of coordinating the resources of all four local colleges to provide industry with the county's nation-leading programs in applied information technology for manufacturing.

Equal opportunity. Flint/Genesee County has succeeded in realizing a healthy future in part because it has ensured that all its residents have an equal opportunity to acquire the education and skills they need to succeed in its new economy and obtain the new jobs being created locally. By insisting that the talents and energy of all of its people—black and white, male and female, young and old—be tapped, Flint/Genesee County has not only built a stronger economy, it has substantially decreased the racial polarization that hindered the community decades earlier.

Downtown. The transformation of Flint/Genesee County's economy has transformed the downtown area into a world center of industrial intelligence. Resembling a tree-shaded university campus, downtown is a collection of university facilities, research centers, finance, government and legal offices, and public parks, all clustered around the beautiful Flint Riverbank park. One frequently hears foreign languages spoken, as people from around the world come to take advantage of Flint/Genesee County's international businesses and applied technology resources.

The arts. Flint's outstanding College and Cultural Development Center has undergone a renaissance, as have the other arts organizations and activities throughout the County. As Flint/Genesee County's population has become more educated, and as people from around the world have migrated here, attendance at concerts, plays, art exhibits and museums has doubled. With an upward spiral effect, more and more top professional and managerial men and women want to move to this innovative and dynamic community.

Neighborhoods and quality of life. As the county's unemployment rate fell toward the national average, neighborhoods revived, especially the older neighborhoods. As lower-income residents gained access to good jobs, they had both the means and the will to fix up their homes and neighborhoods.

As crime rates fell, public funds were reallocated to improve public facilities and parks, education, and drug and alcohol treatment for the few who still need it. Governments now work cooperatively with neighborhood groups, the private sector, unions and schools, with the result that all neighborhoods and business zones are attractive, clean, safe and well maintained.

Summary. In short, the area's economic growth has spurred an improved quality of life for all of its people . . . and the quality of education, harmony and cooperation fostered during the 1990s has helped develop further economic growth. The people of the Flint/ Genesee County area have put themselves on a steady upward course, full of opportunity for everyone, earned and deserved as a result of the value they've learned to add in the new world economy.

Now Flint/Genesee County is the model. Other industrial cities around the globe are coming to see what Flint/Genesee is doing, because Flint/Genesee County has truly become the Home of the New American Dream.[74]

While such "visions" are not, as we have seen, unprecedented in Flint history of image production, the GEAR vision is unusual in that it is presented within the overall framework of a strategic plan (a form shared only with the Genesis Project). In content, GEAR's vision of Flint's way of life is premised upon the community's relative success at reintegrating itself by producing postindustrial "value" in the manufacturing sector of the "new world economy." In other words, Flint's survival depends on its finding a viable niche in the global capitalist system. This promises not only the return of progress and prosperity to Flint, but also the community's recouping of its lost cultural centrality through its projected status as the globally recognized "model" of the "New American Dream." With the possible exception of the new value placed on cosmopolitanism ("one frequently hears foreign languages spoken . . ."), the GEAR vision reexpresses the values present throughout Flint's ninety years of self-promoted cultural reproduction.

The third part of GEAR's Strategic Plan combines its Strategic Priorities and Action Agenda. This covers twenty of the plan's thirty-five pages and is by far the most detailed of the plan's three parts. GEAR's 24 separate strategies or Action Agenda correspond to one or more of the following four overarching goals or Strategic Priorities:

Strategic Priority 1: Develop a competitive, world-class workforce.

Strategic Priority 2: Diversify the economy by creating new non-GM manufacturing and skilled service jobs by supporting entrepreneurship and helping existing companies.

Strategic Priority 3: Make Flint/Genesee County a world center of applying information technology to manufacturing.

Strategic Priority 4: Support and complement GM, UAW, and community efforts to retain jobs by understanding and responding to changing global trends.[75]

GEAR's emphasis on technical and science-oriented education, encouraging new business formation, and supporting existing businesses (especially GM), follows not only from simple common sense but also from its Genesis Project forerunner. According to Davis, these strategic priorities followed "pretty straightforward[ly]" from GEAR's vision statement.[76]

Here it is important to underscore that only Strategic Priority 3 represents a significant departure from the earlier Genesis Project. This is the new basket into which Flint/Genesee County is placing its eggs. GEAR's Strategic Plan explains:

Every local economy must have a competitive advantage if it wishes to prosper in a global economy. In addition to the unique concentration of technically skilled workers that Flint/Genesee County proposes to create [i.e., Strategic Priority 1], the area has decided to develop a competitive advantage as a place where people know more about using information technologies and new organizational techniques in factory settings than anywhere else in the world.[77]

This goal is the key that unlocks the plan's logic. Making Flint a "world center of applying information technology to manufacturing" *requires* a locally available "world-class workforce," a diversified, non-GM "manufacturing and skilled service" economy, and a "huge customer" in the form of a scaled-down yet substantial GM presence in Flint. It is unclear whether Flint also requires a downtown area that is a "world center of industrial intelligence" resembling a "tree-shaded university campus," or whether these points simply represent garnish for the plan's main course. Nevertheless, the central economic basis behind GEAR's vision for Flint's economic and social future lies in this particular strategy for cornering a niche in the global capitalist economy.

In the past, Flint occupied an important place in the global economy merely by virtue of its special relationship with the world's largest manufacturing corporation. As the demand for GM's products increased around the world, and as worker's incomes rose through GM's collective bargaining agreements with the UAW, Flint's economic and cultural standing was thereby raised. Previous attempts to rationalize and contain Flint's internal class and cultural conflicts reflected the city elite's desire for the community to conform as much as possible to its expanding and relatively stable capitalist-industrial base. In the early stages of Flint's deindustrialization, the city first attempted to forge its own niche in America's service sector by becoming the "tourism and convention mecca of the midwest."[78] As part of this development strategy, Flint's leadership attempted to spruce up the city, embellish it with Disneyland-style attractions, and ask its residents to serve roughly one million visitors per year. Formulated in the wake of the failure of this strategy, GEAR's strategic priorities reflect Flint's second recent attempt to "create and develop a competitive advantage," this time, though, through predominantly business leadership and a manufacturing sector orientation. As a strategic response to Flint's experience with dependent deindustrialization, GEAR's Strategic Plan *itself* represents a new economic development vision for Flint.

Recognizing that Flint's former dependency relationship with GM is coming to an end as the corporation slowly withdraws from the community, but wary of anything less than a purely private-sector development strategy, such as the Mott Foundation's tourism and convention debacle, GEAR stakes out a new, more gritty, position. Davis explains:

> The economic reality of General Motors shutting down jobs during the last couple of decades has created a political environment that has many effects on the social economy, the social fabric, and other anthropological terms that I can't think of right now.
>
> But everybody in the past has been focused on the god-damned public sector, I tell you, which is not the key to understanding what's going on in our local economy.
>
> For a long time, the way things got decided in our community was people waited for GM, the UAW, and the Mott Foundation to tell them what to do. In many ways, we became and still are dependent on directions given by those three main institutions.
>
> When you have dependence, then it doesn't breed independence, does it? By definition. We are now as a community, in my judgement, having the private sector leadership assume a larger responsibility to make choices than we did in the past.
>
> The GM brass doesn't live here anymore. They come in and out of town on a monotonously regular three- to five-year basis. And that's good for GM, but in many ways it makes it kind of tough to have the kind of bold community leadership the community needs. What's happening now, though, is there are massive structural changes in the economy taking place.
>
> So, as a community, we're recognizing, in a way, the ascendancy of the private sector in economic development in a way that has never been understood before.[79]

Based on this type of thinking, GEAR envisions Flint not as an independent community, but as a community ever more intensely dependent upon the potential exchange value of its own internal resources on the global market. In other words, having established itself as the city's and county's chief economic manager, GEAR looks upon the community as a "product" in need of production for its eventual sale to potential consumers of Flint's local resources. In this, GEAR's vision integrates Flint's culture with the systemic imperatives of global capitalism. Davis explains GEAR's operating philosophy as follows:

> Here's Marx's general rule of economic development, okay? There's a technology war underway with very human casualties. Alright, the general rule is there's an innovation process, or a technology transfer, at work in society. The kinds of companies that succeed are those that are technology intensive, knowledge intensive, have new products, or new manufacturing processes. So it's product, process, technology, knowledge, okay? The best companies often have all four elements.
>
> The same can be true on a community level: there's a technology transfer, an innovation process at work, okay? There's a tendency to focus on the human casualty side of the stuff, okay? There's a tendency here in Michigan, especially here in Flint, to focus on the social service, community impact, "what's it doing to people" side of stuff. That's fine, we need to do that. But that's not the only thing that we should be doing.
>
> My message here is economic development cannot succeed unless we improve the product.
>
> A community is a product. The product is the summation of what we are. What we have to offer to a business, to an employer, to an investor, is the summation of what we are. That is our product.[80]

For Davis, as well as for GEAR as an institution, the totality or "summation" of Flint/Genesee County constitutes a commodity or "product" whose value is determined through market exchange, or "what we have to offer [or sell] to a business, to an employer, to an investor."

GEAR has thus ambitiously set out "to improve the product" by reshaping the entire community's cultural structure in accordance with the dictates set out in the 1991 strategic plan.[81] As Dort explains:

> Once we had [the] makeup of the committee, that predetermined the outcome. The outcome was, instead of coming up with a plan that became like a "sales plan," which is what everybody expected, we ended up saying that what we needed to do was define the product. So, we created this vision of what Flint could and should be and what we wanted it to be in the year 2000.
>
> [Then we asked,] Who doesn't get to buy into that? Who's getting left out of that?

What strategic or tactical things have to happen to get us there?

Actually, this becomes a community plan, which we weren't really asked to do. But we're the only community organization that brings everybody to the table, so we don't mind usurping that extra responsibility.[82]

Unlike a boosterist statement or sales plan designed to sell the community's *image* to outsiders, GEAR's vision statement is a definition of the product, the community, itself. It is a listing of the specifications for an essentially new community. In other words, GEAR's vision statement is a social engineering plan, but, unlike its 1920 predecessor, this plan focuses less on the physical and more on the cultural infrastructure of the community.

Before GEAR could begin to reshape Flint's way of life, it needed to persuade the community, as Dort put it, to "buy into" the plan. GEAR pursued three relatively broad strategies in this regard: (1) GEAR "invited representatives of academia and state government to help its members better understand the condition of the area's economy and identify development strategies that appeared to be working elsewhere";[83] (2) GEAR's executive director and chairman of the board involved themselves in the community feedback/marketing presentations noted above; and (3) GEAR ran a limited television commercial campaign featuring Davis telling viewers that "knowledge is power" and that "making it in America starts here at home."[84] However, GEAR's main effort to rally community support for its plan centered around its own formal membership. As Dort frankly admitted: "once we had the makeup of the committee, that predetermined the outcome."[85] GEAR's Strategic Planning Committee and board of directors were at this time composed of a "self-perpetuating" group, 51 percent from the private sector and 49 percent from the public sector.[86] As Davis continuously stresses: "GEAR is a public and private partnership for economic development, and *that* is the model."[87]

GEAR's own membership did not, however, include *all* of Flint and Genesee County's significant business leaders and political officialdom, many of whom were nonetheless called upon by GEAR to restructure their own organizations in line with GEAR's Strategic Plan. GEAR assigned to itself the "lead role" in implementing fourteen of the twenty-four separate points on its Action Agenda, but other groups were made responsible as well.[88] For example, The Flint Roundtable, an important local nonprofit education group, was charged with the "lead role" in producing Flint's "world-class workforce." As Davis explained:

In our strategic plan, we suggest that [The Flint Roundtable] change its name [to The Greater Flint Education Roundtable], and that, although they stay focused on the Flint [school] district, they recognize that there are indeed community-wide issues that they have a role to play in. You will also find in the strategic plan that The Flint Roundtable is the lead organization. The organization is not GEAR.

So, there is, in football terms, a handoff that has to take place between our strategic plan and the individuals and organizations that are the lead agencies, to say to them: "Hey, are you willing to accept this responsibility?"

Now, those [strategic goals] that are within the control of GEAR? Hey, we'll do our darnedest on those.

You know, I'd love . . . (pause) if I was a dictator, you know, I'd expect something different. But I'm not a dictator and I don't want to be. You either believe in freedom or you don't, and I do.[89]

GEAR thus depended upon numerous community and state organizations to aid its overall plan. In this regard, Davis saw the GEAR executive director's role as building consensus among community elites, particularly among the economic, education, and human service sectors. Indeed, given the surprising extent and depth of GEAR's planned restructuring, this cooperation and collaboration was essential.

By way of example, witness the substance of GEAR's proposed educational reforms. The strategic plan states:

Flint/Genesee County's vision of the future is one in which we become a world leader in information-based, advanced manufacturing and manufacturing services. In order for the people of Flint/Genesee County to achieve this vision, our number one priority must be to become a well-educated work force that will be the basis of that economy.

The challenge of improving our work skills is great, because it will require that every adult and youth—men and women already in the work force as well as young people still in school—acquire the learning skills, social skills and job skills to earn a middle-class living and retain and attract good jobs to Flint/Genesee County.

To meet this goal, each person must better their individual skills, and have a positive attitude about work, family and education.[90]

As part of its educational agenda, then, GEAR proposes that all Flint area residents complete a K–14 (that is, high school *plus* two years of college), "career-oriented" education; that local school systems "establish basic uniform minimum knowledge and ability standards for all students"; and that education for unemployed as well as employed adults be encouraged, for example, by various training programs and by the continuation of the GM/UAW Local PEL program for all of Flint's remaining auto workers.[91] The strategic plan even calls for a "community education program aimed at helping Flint/Genesee County leaders and institutions understand and respond to the new world economy" through the development of a program "modeled in part on the existing GM-UAW [National] Paid Education Leave Program."[92] As this documents explained:

> In essence, this would be a highly sophisticated leadership develop-
> ment program. Participants would include local political leaders, a
> diverse group of business leaders, UAW members, educational lead-
> ers, and community and civic leaders—much like the composition of
> the Strategic Planning Committee itself.[93]

This comprehensive education restructuring program was aimed at every person in the city and county, necessitating the cooperation of various educational institutions and leaders. Skillfully applying the weighty influence of its "who's who" of community leaders, GEAR hoped to overcome the difficulties inherent in this program of broad institutional restructuring and fast-paced social change.

In addition to securing political legitimation and advocating institutional change, GEAR argued for extensive sociocultural engineering as well. The introduction to GEAR's Strategic Plan states:

> Finally, but perhaps most importantly, there is the central issue of the
> human resource challenges in the Flint/Genesee County community
> that must be met if our economic future is to be bright.
>
> Unless our people are provided with the material and spiritual
> resources needed to build a healthy, safe, and prosperous commu-
> nity—one in which people are permitted to dream and make choices
> about their future—the prospect of more jobs is nothing but a hollow
> promise.
>
> Poverty, inadequate health care, poor nutrition, racial discrimi-
> nation, dysfunctional families, substandard housing, unsafe neigh-
> borhoods, drug and alcohol dependence and human despair: all are
> powerful enemies of economic development.
>
> Therefore, we are of a strong and unanimous voice in recom-
> mending to the GEAR Board that the achievement of our vision for
> Flint/Genesee County's future requires that a human resources strat-
> egy be integrated with the economic development strategy we pro-
> pose today.[94]

GEAR's Mark Davis stated the same idea more simply and directly:

> We better have a better educated work force, we better have babies
> that come to school healthy, because no amount of slick marketing on
> my part is going to succeed in attracting a company from the outside
> unless we have a product that's competitive.[95]

In other words, GEAR recognized that its "product" is initially produced by families, neighborhoods, and communities. Yet, as an economic planning organization, GEAR has little or no direct control over these spheres of life. Hence, GEAR proposed that a "human resource strategy be integrated with [its] economic development strategy" in order to encourage other, presumably better equipped, institutions to control these "variables." In effect, GEAR took the position that it couldn't easily or even readily attract jobs to Flint unless and until the people of Flint qua product were competitively engineered at all stages of socialization qua production.

GEAR's Strategic Plan also mentions the community's "spiritual resources." In fact, GEAR's vision statement was offered in part as a positive goal to be achieved, or what Davis called "the uplifting and the cohesive sort of thing."[96] For his part, Dort explained what he preferred to call the "moral thing" this way:

> I guess if I had to explain it, I guess I'd say that, number one, it wasn't really the big push. The big push was that, practically, it doesn't make any sense to try to drag on all this baggage, all these disenfranchised people.
>
> But from a moral standpoint, I guess, I don't know, I think it's sort of . . . (pause) . . . I just think it's part of America's morals. It's part of mine, it was part of everybody's on the committee. We really didn't debate it, we just said, "Wait a minute, this isn't the way we would've wanted things to go here. We're not treating people well." I don't know, this is the most I've ever talked about it.
>
> I think part of what happened is that we didn't realize there's a price, you know. Morals are nice, but when greed and need and all the rest of them get in the way, morals tend to get forgotten. They're still morals, but you're not following them.[97]

Dort thus implies that GEAR's evocation of the moral rightness of its program was originally taken for granted, and, moreover, that the absence of moralistic motivation in the community was a burden on Flint's economic development. This view—that it is costly to "drag the baggage" of "disenfranchised people"— foreshadowed the dominant approach to social problems in the 1990s.

COMPARING GEAR AND LOCAL PEL IDEOLOGY

Like Local PEL, GEAR's method for initiating change in Flint is structured as a strategic plan.[98] GEAR's temporal dimension thus contains tensions similar to those found in Local PEL. In order to legitimize its instrumental engagement with Flint's current cultural situation as well as mobilize authoritative and

material resources in pursuit of its objectives, GEAR appeals to a "shared picture" of historical reality and a "shared vision" for Flint's future. However, such
initiatives politicize the means of enacting social change, for inasmuch as Flint's
new power structure realizes its goals, it also thereby demystifies naturalistic,
evolutionary, or other similarly objectivating conceptions of social change.
What's more, GEAR also politicizes the community's values and the community's will to collectively pursue these values by publicly interpreting its history
and declaring a vision for Flint's future. In this way, GEAR's official Strategic
Plan cannot help but bring the issues of power, values, and political choice to
the fore.

Yet, the secret of the strategic plan is that it depoliticizes these same issues
by defining them as technical problems. With its raison d'etre the management
of change, the strategic form of GEAR's plan requires that the past course of
events be shaped as a teleology grounded in the status quo, and that future ends
or goals, whatever their content, conform to the limitations of presently available means to realize them in practice. There is no room in GEAR's strategic
planning approach therefore for a conception of unrealized historical possibilities that would decenter the status quo, nor is there room for a conception of
the future based in the transcendent value orientations that give particular(-
ized) human life meaning beyond itself. GEAR may need to thematize the
issues of power, values, and political choice in order to garner legitimacy and
mobilize political will for social change, but it cannot escape its self-imposed
straightjacket that requires it to rationalize Flint's historical development into
a linear and value-free procession of technical achievements.

This internal contradiction is evident in GEAR's Strategic Plan and the discourse that surrounds it. By way of example, note GEAR's inexorably twisted
interpretation of Flint's history of labor struggles, including the 1936–37 sit-
down strike:

> By the late 1930s Flint/Genesee County had developed a reputation
> for combative labor-management relations, growing out of confron-
> tations between GM management and the United Auto Workers—a
> reputation that was to persist for the next fifty years.[99]

Here, past worker struggles are rendered as negative historical residue, whose
lingering in the present day is detrimental—a "competitive disadvantage"—to
GEAR's efforts to attract capital to Flint. This reading reduces the meaning of
the American labor movement to a mere technical factor among Flint's contemporary cultural characteristics. Incredibly, GEAR defines the meaning of
the Great Flint Sit-Down Strike in terms of its cost/benefit for Flint's current
"value" to prospective businesses. While GEAR is undoubtedly correct in arguing that today's remembrance of Flint's historic working-class struggles is bad
for business, it is important also to remember that neither these struggles

themselves nor contemporary efforts to preserve their meaning were ever meant to be *good for business.*

As GEAR attempts to contain the meaning of Flint's past as a function of its present business-oriented economic development strategy, so too does it attempt to tightly manage Flint's future possibilities. For example, GEAR admits that it created Flint's now institutionalized vision for the future, and that it has actively encouraged others to "buy into" it in the hope that, with a concerted effort, the vision will be "achieved." GEAR frankly states that its posited vision is based on technically achievable goals, and that, as Davis candidly states, the vision statement is actually a more or less gratuitous product of GEAR's own organizational imagination:

> Do I have the highest degree of confidence that we're actually going to get to and achieve that image? I don't know. Probably not. Do I have a sense of direction of where we are going and why we are trying to get there? You bet. Is that image and vision widely understood by the community? No. Is it more understood than it was? Yes.[100]

Still, despite this matter-of-factness, GEAR's vision statement thematizes the issues of political power and decision (Where are we going?) as well as of values (Why are we trying to get there?), even if GEAR subsequently tries to contain possible answers within the confines of technical rationality and elite planning. GEAR may reflect a disenchanted world, but it must also struggle to perpetuate it, for, unlike Local PEL, GEAR may not simply appeal to an organization's mission statement for its orientation and legitimation; GEAR must actually create it.

And from what imaginative intellectual resources does GEAR draw inspiration for its vision-creation project? GEAR's vision document speaks only of a "fulfillment" of Flint's past "character" as a manufacturing center, in which "Flint/Genesee County's technicians [will] make things primarily with their minds and skills."[101] Naturally, GEAR is primarily, even exclusively, focused on pragmatic, material concerns. But, recognizing the transcendent logic of GEAR's sometimes lofty rhetoric, Davis adds his view that Flint's pursuit of the New American Dream transpires within a larger historical context that is singularly void of transcendent alternatives:

> The struggle that's going on today in many ways has been defined as the end of history. There's been a recent, fascinating [argument], you know: "if capitalism clearly wins, especially [if] the moral-based capitalism is clearly the winner, is there anything else left in history?"
>
> That's an interesting intellectual argument to me. I guess I think history will be a never-ending subject, but it's just absolutely clear

that extremist environmentalism, extremist socialism or Marxism, communism, simply don't work in the real world.[102]

With the "end of history" (as end of ideology), the question of future value orientations is moot. Anything other than the extension of the present "simply [doesn't] work in the real world." Flint's new vision thus appears to be as self-legitimating as it is incontestable, a testament not only to President Bush's infamous vision thing, but also to his notion of status quo plus.

But Dallas Dort adds his appreciation of what we have in this study termed "negative futurism."[103] In reference to various possible global catastrophes, Dort states that we must

> recognize that it may well be that the cosmic will is that this planet blow up anyway. What do I know? Assuming that we're all going to die, whoever is on the planet when it blows up is going to die anyway, so now we just die all together.[104]

For his part, Davis is optimistic about the future, although (or is it because?) he states: "What choice do I have?"[105] As Sloterdijk perceptively notes, in a cynical context like that created by GEAR's strategic planning in Flint, "questions of self-preservation must be approached in the same language as those of self-destruction."[106]

Similarly to Local PEL's strategic response, then, GEAR attempts to flatten Flint's historical past and its historical future by articulating them in accordance with present-oriented technical objectives. This is all that GEAR sees as a viable course of action. Its greatest cultural ally in this effort is the convergence of the so-called New American Dream and the "reality" of the ever more integrated global marketplace. Long established in Flint as the basis for the original American Dream, the secular values of prosperity and progress are in GEAR's Strategic Plan straightforwardly translated into the cynical although understandable dictum: "To be stupid and have a job, that's happiness." So taken for granted is this orientation that GEAR easily suppresses any doubts it may harbor about its historical and political legitimacy in order to pursue its plan for cultural rationalization with a zeal unparalleled even in the Local PEL program. Indeed, the meaning of history and future possibilities, as such, are as irrelevant in GEAR's strategic consciousness as are the meanings of community, equality, democracy, or other similar values that refuse easy translation into money, jobs, or success. As Davis says in a self-referential rhetorical question: "Can anybody come and help the system, the team, the coalescence of forces, to come together [in the way] that it takes for a community to win?"[107] For GEAR, the success of its historical project would mean that Flint would become a model or object lesson for other industrial cities around the globe.

This is an important part of Flint's current vision—to regain its cultural centrality by winning in the global economic arena.

Organizational self-consciousness also plays an important role in GEAR. GEAR's emphasis on collaboratively defining, improving, and ultimately selling a "world-class product" (i.e., Flint and Genesee County) parallels Local PEL's emphasis on situating and mobilizing its participants within the joint company/union framework and competitive capitalist system. For each, survival is at stake, and survival depends upon the competitiveness of their respective products (automobiles versus a people and their cultural infrastructure), their comparative market advantage over other competing firms or communities, and the political leverage available to manipulate the rules of the game and to secure surplus resources. As the tenuousness of making a living increases in Flint, GEAR contends that the free realm of everyday life must correspondingly shrink, to be replaced by the discipline, the dictates, and the requirements of what Davis approvingly invokes as the "free enterprise system." Shepherding Flint into a suitable niche in the global capitalist economy will not be easy, but GEAR is prepared to whip its product into shape in order to make it competitive, hence valuable, and thus justly rewarded. This is GEAR's "business plan" for Flint and the substance of the "dream" that it markets: "knowledge is power," says GEAR's TV spot.

As we have seen, in its ambitious yet severe discourse, GEAR's Strategic Plan recognizes no limits on its aspirations to influence and change Flint's cultural structure, even down to the level of instilling in individuals a "positive attitude about work, family, and education" and "basic abilities and values, such as personal presentation, proper attitude, and timeliness."[108] As we have seen, GEAR views the Flint area's response to its deindustrialization as a "vital experiment," even hoping to transform Flint into an "urban laboratory." GEAR's self-described sophisticated initiatives parallel Local PEL's appeals for identification with an organizational perspective on collective social action, committed individual participation within established local institutions, and hegemonic social systems. GEAR seeks so much control that it is willing to work to resolve the local manifestations and structural causes of various social problems, as they are deemed "powerful enemies of economic development," are thus unappealing to prospective capitalists, and are thus detrimental to GEAR's efforts to efficiently market its product. Social conflicts as well as individuals' attitudes and values must together be subordinated to the cost/benefit calculus of GEAR's strategic perspective. *This* is the "big push," as Dort admits. But having deemed cultural impoverishment, anomie, and individual pathologies *costly* to its systems maintenance plan, GEAR concedes that economic development with "moral overtones" can't hurt.

GEAR's Strategic Plan (or "blueprint" as it is sometimes called) projects this new discipline as the only viable course of action available—given, that is, the overwhelming reality of the global capitalist system. In this regard, note a key selection from Davis' explanation of GEAR's modus operandi in which Davis stresses the need for Flint to adopt, as Davis puts it, an "enlightened," self-consciousness, a perspective that is quite similar to Local PEL's "total systems" view:

> Publicly funded and publicly run organizations are not the modern model for economic development. One reason they're not is they tend to fail. Okay? GEAR is a public and private partnership for economic development, and that is the model.
>
> As a community, we're recognizing the ascendancy of the private sector in economic development in a way that has never been understood before.
>
> The notion that competition is healthy between communities is to me fundamental to our success as a country. There are winners and losers, however, and we have certainly been the loser, haven't we?
>
> Okay, just because we're losing, does that mean the system is flawed? I think the answer is no. I think it means the system's healthy and what we've been doing locally is flawed. Now, is that heartless? I don't think so.
>
> I believe an enlightened [inaudible], an enlightened [pause, frustrated] How do you define that? Well, you heard me pause. You know, caring and sharing and all this sort of shit, that's where I am and that's also consistent with my vision of capitalism.
>
> There are three interrelated circles: economic development, education, and human services. Before I came to town, this drawing [of overlapping circles] had never been drawn before as best as I can tell, and the folks in the education and human services segments didn't think of themselves as having relationships with economic development.
>
> They didn't view themselves as systems, first, and they certainly didn't view themselves as interacting. This was old-hat thinking fifteen years ago in Indianapolis [where Mr. Davis formally worked]. Now why Flint got stuck in the sixties politically and socially, I don't know.
>
> What is this town famous for? They're famous for high-paying, low-skilled jobs, okay? Does that sound like a good positioning strategy for a community? It *does not* sound like a good positioning strategy for a community, does it? So why are we surprised that it hasn't worked well? I'm not.[109]

These remarks illuminate Davis' idiosyncratic view of reality, but they also suggest GEAR's "enlightened" idea of what *Flint's* new shared definition of reality/identity should be. This conceptualization follows from taking the capitalist system as a community's effective Generalized Other, where "caring and sharing and all this sort of shit" is *derived from* and hence subordinated to seeing oneself first as a systemic part of the larger capitalist system. As Marx once observed, such thinking conceives society itself as an "abstract capitalist."[110]

Two main elements in GEAR's vision of capitalist society stand out, and compare easily with Local PEL's sociology. First, in general terms, Flint/Genesee County's "power structure" is understood, despite such a lofty name, to be quite incapable of altering the community's basic capitalist dependency. GEAR stresses the *reality* of GM's projected continued disinvestment; that Flint "no longer has much influence over [GM's] destiny," in other words. This conceptualization is understood as a recognition of the "ascendancy of the private sector."[111] As a result, Flint is required to develop its own "positioning strategy," a search for a viable niche in the hegemonic structure of the new world economy. This is a direct result of Flint's disintegrating relationship with GM, which heretofore had provided the city with a viable economic niche indeed. From this perspective, the meaning of "community" must be subordinated to the imperatives of various systems requirements. This is a structural outcome of changes in the larger political economy, but recognition of its meaning requires a shift in community self-consciousness toward a new self-image as a factor of production, or as a part of a system interacting in a process of self-production and self-marketing. In this regard, GEAR is merely renewing Flint's long-established tradition of viewing itself in world-comparative terms, although it is no longer a matter of taking pride in being the "world's largest" this and that, but of becoming a subordinated and reintegrated part of the whole. GEAR's version of "total systems" theory is oriented, as its name implies, to the concept of totality, where community is but a factor in the totality of capitalism.[112]

The reason GEAR regards Flint/Genesee County as a product stems from its appreciation of Flint's new relationship of dependency in the global capitalist marketplace, which, in effect, constitutes Flint's primary systems environment. As a whole, Flint must adapt to this environment because it is dependent upon it for both the sale of its projected postindustrial wares and the outside investment capital needed to produce them. Like so much else in Flint's experience with dependent deindustrialization, the *extreme* quality of this projected adaptation appears extraordinary, although, from Davis' professional perspective, it represents "old-hat thinking" in economic development circles. As we have seen, GEAR's strategic response involves managing the microprocesses of socialization and social welfare through educational and human service institutions, which are viewed as part of an emergent, locally integrated "enterprise system," defined simply as all of the "elements" or aspects of community life that come together to produce the "product."[113] In practice, then, GEAR pursues a strategy of totalization inasmuch as it seeks to form Flint's particular way of life in accordance with the structures required for full integration into the totality of the global capitalist political economy.

   C. Wright Mills concluded his famous 1956 study of the American "power elite" with an examination of what he termed "the higher immorality."[114] Unchecked by any significant public, unaccountable to any intellectual community, Mills surmised that America's national power elite acted within the structural conditions of "organized irresponsibility" and intellectual "mindlessness," and that together these factors ultimately promoted the easy institutionalization of a cultural cynicism rooted in "rationality without reason."[115] In describing the decline of the public sphere into mass society, on the one side, and the ascendancy of a new type of bureaucratic elite on the other, Mills foresaw at the national level the conditions that today obtain in Flint.

   Filling the power vacuum left by the AutoWorld debacle, GEAR has instituted an admittedly rational yet equally unreasonable program to achieve its revitalization goals. It has done so, moreover, with no formal public legitimation, nor with any especially articulate or coherent intellectual justification. Instead, GEAR has developed a strategic plan that calls for a surprisingly extensive rationalization of Flint's cultural life. GEAR's Strategic Plan is designed to reintegrate the hybrid product known as Flint/Genesee County into what amounts to a new world order. Through elite interventions into processes of local cultural reproduction (in the sphere of public education most prominently), GEAR plans to produce a manageable and efficient means/ends relationship between individual components within the product and the ultimate exchange value of the product once readied for sale. There is no going back, as GEAR recognizes, for GM, the UAW, and the Mott Foundation would appear more and more the power centers of Flint's past. Thus, GEAR has taken the reins into its own hands, and offered Flint what Davis (in an especially relaxed moment) called the "vision thing."

NOTES

   1. Interview 14, July 23, 1991.

   2. Interview 2, August 7, 1991.

   3. "Strategic Economic Development Plan For Flint/Genesee County," prepared for GEAR Strategic Planning Committee; prepared by Corporation for Enterprise Development, July 1991 (document source), p. 14.

   4. C. Wright Mills, *The Power Elite* (Oxford: Oxford University Press, 1956), p. 347.

   5. "GEAR ready to accept role as major player," *The Flint Journal*, 9 June 1991, Sec. E, p. 1, 2.

   6. The phrases "who's who" and "leading lights" are from Interview 14, July 23, 1991. For another perspective on Flint's "growth machine," see George F. Lord and

Albert C. Price, "Growth Ideology in a Period of Decline: Deindustrialization and Restructuring, Flint Style" in *Social Problems* 39, no. 2 (May 1992): 155–169.

7. "Fiftieth Anniversary of Flint: Golden Jubilee," editor unknown, 1905 (document source), pp. 256–257. This volume is available at Michigan State University, East Lansing, Michigan.

8. Ibid., pp. 1, 8.

9. "Flint of To-Day; The Vehicle City; A City of Commercial & Industrial Progress," 1905–06 (document source), available at the Genesee Historical Collections Center at The University of Michigan–Flint, Flint, Michigan, p. 4.

10. Ronald Edsforth, *Class Conflict and Cultural Consensus* (New Brunswick, NJ: Rutgers University Press, 1987), pp. 54–69, 69.

11. James A. Welch, "Prosperity Built on Solid Rock," a foreword to "Flint: Past-Present Prospective" (c. 1916, document source), available through the Genesee Historical Collections Center at The University of Michigan–Flint, Flint, Michigan.

12. John Nolen, "City Planner's Introduction," in "The City Plan of Flint, Michigan," The City Planning Board, 1920 (document source), p. 7, available through Genesee Historical Collections Center at The University of Michigan–Flint, Flint, Michigan.

13. Ibid.

14. Ibid., p. 95.

15. Ibid.

16. Edsforth, pp. 71–72.

17. "Progressive Flint," Flint Chamber of Commerce (c. 1929, document source), available through the Genesee Historical Collections Center at The University of Michigan–Flint, Flint, Michigan.

18. Ibid., p. 27.

19. See Edsforth.

20. "A Comprehensive City Plan for Flint, Michigan, Part I, Traffic Survey and Thoroughfare Plan, W.P.A. Project 25–3–1029," Flint Institute of Research and Planning, 1937 (document source), p. 9, available through the Genesee Historical Collections Center at The University of Michigan–Flint, Flint, Michigan.

21. Ibid., p. 61–62.

22. Robert S. Ford and Frances H. Miner, "An Experiment In Community Improvement," Bureau of Government, University of Michigan, Michigan Pamphlets No. 16, 1942 (document source), available through the Genesee Historical Collections Center at The University of Michigan–Flint, Flint, Michigan.

23. Ibid., p. 29.

24. Carl Crow, *The City of Flint Grows Up: The Success Story of an American Community* (New York: Harper and Brothers, 1945), p. vii.

25. Ibid., p. 211.

26. "Flint, Michigan: The Vehicle City," Flint Chamber of Commerce, foreword (c. 1956, document source), available through the Genesee Historical Collections Center at The University of Michigan–Flint, Flint, Michigan.

27. "Frontiers Unlimited: Flint & Genesee County," Flint Area Chamber of Commerce (c. 1973, document source), available at the Genesee Historical Collections Center at The University of Michigan–Flint, Flint, Michigan.

28. Ibid., p. 4.

29. Ibid., p. 5.

30. "Flint . . . : A City In Change: Annual Report," City of Flint, 1977 (document source), available through the Genesee Historical Collections Center at The University of Michigan–Flint, Flint, Michigan.

31. Ibid.

32. "Flint: New Life," with a foreword by C. S. Harding Mott, Chairman of the Board, Flint Area Conference, Inc. (c. 1982, document source), available at the Genesee Historical Collections Center at The University of Michigan–Flint, Flint, Michigan.

33. Ibid. While this may have in fact constituted a fruitful way of seeing things, the open acknowledgement of Flint's subordination to a corporate entity was ideologically risky in a society that continued to describe itself as a political democracy.

34. Ibid.

35. Ibid.

36. Ibid.

37. See Lord and Price, p. 164.

38. Ibid., p. 164.

39. "The Genesis Project: Building THE ECONOMY OF TOMORROW for GENESEE COUNTY," prepared by Price Waterhouse, Inc., under contract from the Economic Development Administration, for Genesee Economic Area Revitalization, Inc., 1989 (document source), p. 15. Note that this document is below referred to simply as "The Genesis Project."

40. Ibid. Note that this letter is addressed to "Residents of Genesee County," and thus should be considered a public document.

41. Ibid., p. 11.

42. Ibid., p. 10.

43. Ibid., p. 15, emphasis added.

44. See "GEAR ready to accept role as major player."

45. "The Genesis Report," pp. 17, 21, 27, 31, and 35.

46. Ibid., p. 36.

47. "Strategic Economic Development Plan for Flint/Genesee County," November, 1990, draft document, subject to public participation (document source), p. 2.

48. Interview 14, July 23, 1991. At this point, Mr. Davis suggested that further questioning along these lines would result in his unwillingness to continue our interview. During subsequent interviews and discussions, Mr. Davis and his colleagues were generally much more generous and forthcoming.

49. Interview 2, August 7, 1991. Mr. Dort did, however, generously agree to discuss his extensive involvement and thinking concerning the meaning of GEAR's vision statement.

50. In research conducted in June of 1992, the author was able to secure additional information concerning the origin of GEAR. These sources, however, generally wished to remain anonymous. It must be asserted, then, that GEAR is the child of the Genesee Area Focus Council, Inc., a private group of business leaders organized through the offices of the C. S. Mott Foundation. Furthermore, the reader should note that, based on estimates drawn from GEAR's own financial records for the years 1990–1993, GEAR's major contributors have been the City of Flint ($350,000); Genesee County ($278,200); Mott Foundation ($120,000); and General Motors ($120,000). Other contributors include the State of Michigan, *The Flint Journal,* Consumers Power, Citizens Bank, National Bank of Detroit, and other private businesses.

According to anonymous although well-placed sources, GEAR's purpose is to allow the Mott Foundation and General Motors to back away from a prominent, publicly visible role in the Flint area's economic development planning. This, of course, would explain Mr. Davis's and Mr. Dort's hesitancy to discuss GEAR's origins as equally well as it would these sources' desire for anonymity.

51. At any rate, Mr. Davis scrawled this disclaimer upon the photocopy of this report that he kindly offered to me during our first interview.

52. "Memorandum," 26 May 1991, to GEAR, Inc. Board of Directors, from Mark S. Davis, EXECUTIVE DIRECTOR, re GEAR STRATEGIC PLAN-MARKETING. A sampling of groups who received a presentation includes American Society of Women Accountants; Flint Rotary; Flushing Rotary; Grand Blanc Rotary; Linden Kiwanis; Grand Blanc Optimist Club; Grand Blanc Business Association; Flint Downtown Kiwanis; Sunrise Rotary at Sarvis; GM Public Affairs Committee, and other similar bodies. An additional GEAR document suggests that 228 individuals responded to a GEAR survey designed to measure community acceptance of GEAR's plan (i.e., of individuals present at various GEAR presentations). This data suggests a very positive response.

53. "GEAR gearing up to put finalized plans in motion," *The Flint Journal,* 10 July 1991, Sec. E, p. 1.

54. Interview 14, July 23, 1991.

55. "SYNOPSIS OF GEAR STRATEGIC PLAN" (c. 1991, document source).

56. "Strategic Economic Development Plan for Flint/Genesee County," July, 1991, p. 6. Hereafter this document is referred to as "Strategic Plan 1991."

57. Ibid.

58. Ibid.

59. Ibid.

60. Ibid., pp. 6–7.

61. Ibid., p. 7.

62. Ibid.

63. Ibid., p. 8.

64. Ibid., p. 7, 8.

65. Ibid., p. 8.

66. Ibid.

67. Ibid., p. 11.

68. Ibid.

69. Interview 12, July 23, 1991.

70. Interview 2, August 7, 1991. Mr. Dort also made available for this research a personal document entitled "Basic Assumptions" (dated January 17, 1990), which he and other members of this informal group used as a guide in their deliberations.

71. Interview 2, August 7, 1991. Note that these are Dort's words, and not Mayor Matthew Collier's.

72. Interview 14, July 23, 1991.

73. Interview 2, August 7, 1991.

74. "Strategic Plan 1991," pp. 12–14.

75. Ibid., pp. 15, 24, 30, and 33.

76. Interview 14, July 23, 1991.

77. "Strategic Plan 1991," p. 30.

78. See Daniel Zwerdling, "And Then There's the Disneyland Solution," in *The Progressive* (July, 1982): pp. 34–35, 35.

79. Interview 14, July 23, 1991.

80. Ibid.

81. The phrase "improve the product" is a common catchphrase used among Flint's economic development leaders.

82. Interview 2, August 7, 1991.

83. "Strategic Plan 1991," p. 2.

84. Quotations taken from field notes, 1991.

85. Interview 2, August 7, 1991.

86. Interview 14, July 23, 1991. The membership of two separate GEAR Board of Directors is listed in "The Genesis Project," p. 42. An additional GEAR document (c. 1991) also lists board members. In its 1991 manifestation, the GEAR board is composed of 21 members: two bank presidents (one, Charles W. Weeks, is chair); two GM officials (the general manager of GM-AC Rochester Division and the director of material management for the GM Service & Parts Division); the UAW Region 1-C director; the treasurer of International Brotherhood of Electrical Workers (IBEW) Local 948; seven elected officials, including Flint's mayor; the chancellor of the University of Michigan–Flint; and seven local business leaders.

87. Interview 14, July 23, 1991.

88. Information on the "Flint Roundtable" is drawn from Interview 15, June 9, 1992, and from Roundtable executive director, Patrick C. Manley's "Flint area has ability for greatness," *The Flint Journal,* 1 December 1991, Sec. C, p. 4.

89. Interview 14, July 23, 1991.

90. "Strategic Plan 1991," p. 15.

91. Ibid., pp. 15–24, 33–35.

92. Ibid., p. 33.

93. Ibid., p. 34.

94. "Strategic Plan 1991," p. 3.

95. Interview 14, July 23, 1991.

96. Interview 14, July 23, 1991.

97. Interview 2, August 2, 1991.

98. Flint's 1994 "enterprise community" program was required by the Federal government to adopt a strategic planning format, or what was described as a "Strategic Vision for Change." See "Flint Area Enterprise Community . . . *Road Map to the 21st Century*" (document source, c. 1994) and "Synopsis of Flint Area Enterprise Community Program" (document source, 6 March 1995).

99. "Strategic Plan 1991," p. 6.

100. Interview 14, July 23, 1991.

101. "Strategic Plan 1991," p. 12.

102. Interview 14, July 23, 1991.

103. Peter Sloterdijk, "Cynicism—The Twilight of False Consciousness," in *New German Critique* 33 (Fall 1984): 190–206, 198.

104. Interview 2, August 7, 1991.

105. Interview 14, July 23, 1991.

106. Peter Sloterdijk, *Critique of Cynical Reason* (Minneapolis: University of Minnesota Press, 1987), p. 8.

107. Interview 14, July 23, 1991.

108. "Strategic Plan 1991," p. 15, 18.

109. Interview 14, July 23, 1991.

110. Karl Marx, *The Economic and Philosophic Manuscripts* of 1844, ed. Dirk J. Struik (New York: International Publishers, 1964), p. 118.

111. Interview 14, July 23, 1991. Also see, "General Motors & Flint, Michigan—A Team in Transition," 19 June 1992 (document source), available from GEAR, Inc., a more optimistic portrayal of "GM's economic role in Flint," which notes, for example, GM's own estimated $5.1 billion contribution to the Flint area economy in 1990.

112. For a detailed discussion of "totality," especially in the tradition of Western Marxism, see Martin Jay, *Marxism & Totality: The Adventures of a Concept from Lukacs to Habermas* (Berkeley, CA: University of California Press, 1984).

113. Interview 2, August 7, 1991.

114. C. Wright Mills, *The Power Elite*, pp. 343–361.

115. Ibid., pp. 354, 361. The notion of "rationality without reason" is discussed in C. Wright Mills, *The Sociological Imagination* (Oxford: Oxford University Press, 1959). See p. 170.

Chapter 8

THEORETICAL
CONCLUSIONS
TO PART II

What if it were true that *Roger & Me* was just another movie, a few dollars' worth of entertainment, the Great Lakes Technology Centre simply one of many buildings on the south side of Flint, and GEAR's vision thing merely paper and words such as one would expect from local elites attempting to revitalize an economically distressed area? What if? The question posed this way suggests its own answer: the observation that all the works of Van Gogh are but canvas and paint is no less absurd. In Flint, these objects are matters of recognition, scorn, and value. They are artifacts that define a culture and shape a community. This is not to say, however, that these cultural objects fully or even willingly disclose themselves to the participant-observer, or that they exist free from entanglement with complex social relationships; if this were true, then there would be nothing to talk about. The fact is, though, that *Roger & Me*, the Tech Centre, and GEAR confront Flint's experience of dependent deindustrialization. They publicly thematize, signal, and otherwise address the issues of power, politics, and values. Therefore, they cannot be analyzed as objects for leisurely, ahistorical, value-free, decontextualized consumption; instead, they are forceful responses to changing social conditions, and this critique treats them as such.

What, then, is to be done with celluloid mirrors, urban signs, and administered visions? What are we to make of them? Perhaps the answer is again before us. The ultimate purpose of critique is to make itself useless: in effect, to render its object susceptible to thought beyond any single (always already incomplete) perspective, and thus to put itself out of business in favor of informed, collective action. In other words, culture critique encourages the public reading of purportedly shared values, symbols, and ideologies, not the imposition of additional ideological forms from on high or from without or from beyond. Ultimately, this deconstructive impulse aims at opening space for revolutionary praxis.

In this regard, note once again the cultural significance of *Roger & Me*. GEAR's Dallas Dort may have put it best:

Whether that movie was a mirror, or a joke, or an insult, or whatever
it was, it inevitably invites or compels a comparison, a reality check:
Is that true or not?[1]

Rendering *Roger & Me* as a mythic, redemptive, enlightenment-inspired, politically committed work of art in response to Flint's dependent deindustrialization may add to its already heavy baggage, but so much of the film's accumulated meaning appears as dead weight, often self-imposed. Depicting *Roger &
Me* as a conversation miscarried through the medium of the culture industry
invites further reflection on the film's meaning. Critique may demur from affir-
mation of *Roger & Me*'s moralistic logic; still, this dissenting text deserves to be
read for *what* it was talking about and not simply *how* it says what it says. Dort
was right to accord *Roger & Me* the status of a reality check.

Or consider the Great Lakes Technology Centre, one stonefaced example
of ideology among others. If the Tech Centre is Flint's link to a postindustrial
future, then why does its newspaper, *Great Lakes Technology Centre: INSIDER*,
evoke an enclosed, small-town image for Tech Centre employees?

We're sure you can appreciate—more than any outsider possibly
could—what a dynamic and growing community the Great Lakes
Technology Centre is; in fact, the Centre *is* a small town.[2]

Reading a building as a sign of the times reauthors and thus rehumanizes the
physical dimension of culture in order to meet its official interpreters on their
own ground. In effect, this study says, We're hopeful you can appreciate—more
than the *INSIDER* apparently does—what an ideological symbol this building
really is. Outsiders, beware.

Ultimately, though, GEAR's strategic vision is the most significant cultural
phenomena. GEAR's discourse represents a form of cultural manipulation *par
excellence* inasmuch as it orients Flint's latest social engineers toward the processes of cultural reproduction. As though in lock step with Jürgen Habermas'
1973 *Legitimation Crisis*, GEAR's response to Flint's economic crisis can be
understood as an instance of what Habermas calls "rationality crisis," which
refers to the inability of state administrators to resolve economic crises *within*
the confines of a inherently contradictory capitalist economic system.[3] Mark
Davis' exclamation says it all: "I mean, for god's sake, this is the town that built
AutoWorld!"[4] As Flint's business elites and city planners experience their powerlessness to effect change in the global capitalist system—as all their traditional methods for economic development prove increasingly ineffective in the
face of continuing deindustrialization—they extend their administrative powers to include more and more social variables, including the socialization of
children in families, neighborhoods, and schools, and not simply fiscal matters

like government taxation and spending. In Habermas' terms, the economic and politico-administrative systems "colonize" aspects of the "lifeworld" that were once organized independently of the strict dictates of capitalist society.

This colonization process, however, cannot proceed smoothly. According to Habermas, the systematic rationalization of a community's everyday life has the unintended and perverse effect of disrupting the "symbolic reproduction of the lifeworld," creating, in particular, the pathologies associated with the withdrawal of mass political loyalty ("legitimation crisis"), on the one hand, and the withdrawal of the desire to obtain necessary occupational skills ("motivation crisis") on the other.[5]

Habermas' perspective helps to explain GEAR's evasiveness concerning its origins and political legitimacy as well as its focus on what Davis calls the "social economy, the social fabric." After all, GEAR's advocacy for a human resource strategy and educational reforms and the reasoning behind GEAR's emphasis on the importance of Flint's "spiritual resources" stem from its need to "define the product." As the GEAR Strategic Plan states (in a rare example of cynicism): "persistent poverty breeds understandable social resentment and conflict, dividing communities and prohibiting effective common action—conditions that discourage enterprise and outside investment."[6]

GEAR is also significant because there is no effective opposition to its plans. The UAW is a case in point. A witness to the UAW's willing integration as a junior partner into GEAR's power structure and scheme, GEAR's Dallas Dort may be forgiven his jaundiced view of the once-oppositional union:

> The union (UAW) won't go away fast enough. We just can't wait for the union to die. It's having a lot of troubles, but it's not going to die in time for us to benefit by that. Furthermore, it's going to die an ugly death . . . and it's going to create a lot of problems for Flint. We'll die with it. We might grow out of its ashes, but the assumption is if we do that, we're in the ground with it.
>
> So, I've talked to Ruben [Burks, UAW Region 1-C Director] about "what's the role of the union in turning all this around?" and "what's the union's business plan?" because they're really suffering.[7]

In GEAR's view, the UAW is not only a competitive disadvantage in Flint's competition for capital investments, this labor union is also so in disarray that only a "business plan" can save it.

GEAR would, of course, disagree with this critical analysis. For example, the *Flint Journal* reported these remarks by Mark Davis:

> "There's a persistent notion in this town that we've been studied to death," [Mark Davis] said. "I get a little angry when I hear that."

"And some studies [have taken] a top-down approach, imposing findings and strategies on the community instead of seeking residents' input."[8]

GEAR *has* sought input: at one point, a consultant to GEAR even wanted to make a videotape depicting the vision of GEAR's vision statement, apparently so that the community could see what the future that it is supposed to envision—or buy into—would look like.[9] But who cannot already tell the difference between a vision and a vision thing, between a grassroots and a top-down approach, between strategic rationality and human reason?

If Flint exemplified the tendencies of one-dimensional society in its advanced industrial heyday, is this any less so now that its culture of abundance is slipping away? If the cultural consensus of old was always in part a sham and in part a managed achievement, then what separates or distinguishes current conditions? This study of the inner structure of selected cultural phenomena suggests that the answers to these questions lie in the community's apparent inability to successfully mediate its new position of peripheral dependency in the global capitalist system. One-sided retreat into either past-oriented myth or future-oriented mythos only displaces recognition of reality onto quasitranscendent grounds, while acquiescence to the force of contemporary structural change reifies history making under the banner of the end of history. Concepts are set against materiality in the latter two cases, while in the former the reverse is true. In each case, though, dialectical meditation is simply absent or distorted or both.

The general effect is a type of self-conscious hopelessness, which spans Michael Moore's it's-too-late-for-Flint rhetoric, the Tech Centre's free-floating signification of only itself, and GEAR's all too cynical vision thing. This appears as the dominant cultural trend in Flint's response to decline.[10] Only in GEAR, though, is this cultural trend wed to local institutional power. As GEAR self-consciously internalizes and then actualizes systems dependency as hegemonic local self-awareness, Flint's hope of surviving its dependent deindustrialization is directly tied to its dying as a community. The second part of this study's overall thesis is thus: powerlessness encourages a cultural cynicism bent on self-destruction disguised as survival. In other words, Flint has already cashed in its chips through its inability to successfully confront cultural distortions that deny it the power to mediate structural change. In a sense, Flint is marshalling its remaining power in a concerted effort to lose its collective mind.

This may be an understandable and perhaps even predictable outcome of the contradictions of American capitalist society. Indeed, inasmuch as the question of an alternative way of life is rendered moot by the powerlessness that motivates the question in the first place, quasitranscendent forms of consciousness become little more than artificial negativity in a culture versed in what Marcuse called "repressive desublimation."[11] Dialectical sublation is thus critique's first order of business inasmuch as cynical reason appears the only guide for reasonable action. In its dialectical negation of a positivist culture, critique hopes to be proven wrong, if only for the sake of those who are daily proven right.

A final, nagging question: Will the withdrawal of legitimation and motivation ever create the conditions for radical social change in Flint? If Habermas is correct, it is as difficult to answer this question as it is to ascertain the exact point at which an individual's or community's self-image as an administered and commodified "product" becomes unbearable, or as it is to know why or even how these conditions lead to self-debilitating and self-destructive responses, or to political revolution, or to something in between, novel, or unprecedented.

NOTES

1. Interview 2, August 7, 1991.

2. "The Inside Story: A Message from the Publisher," *Great Lakes Technology Centre: INSIDER* 1, 2 (November 1991), p. 14, emphasis in text.

3. Jürgen Habermas, *Legitimation Crisis* (Boston: Beacon Press, 1976 [1975]); *Theory of Communicative Action*, vol. 2: *A Critique of Functionalist Reason* (Boston: Beacon Press, 1987 [1984]). Also see David Held, "Crisis Tendencies, Legitimation and the State," in John B. Thompson and David Held, eds., *Habermas: Critical Debates* (Cambridge, MA: MIT Press, 1982), pp. 191–195; and Jürgen Habermas, "A Reply to My Critics," in Thompson and Held, pp. 219–293.

4. Interview 14, July 23, 1991.

5. Habermas, "A Reply to My Critics," p. 280.

6. "Strategic Economic Development Plan for Flint/Genesee County," July, 1991, p. 3.

7. Interview 2, August 7, 1991.

8. "GEAR ready to accept role as major player," *The Flint Journal*, Sec. E, p. 2.

9. The consultant was Doug Ross. See chapter 7. This information is from Interview 2, August 7, 1991.

10. This is also the conclusion reached by Don Terry in his observations of Flint after the February, 1992, announcement by General lMotors that Flint would lose an additional 4,036 UAW jobs. See his "A City Where Hope Runs on Empty," *New York Times*, Sec. A, p. 8.

11. See Herbert Marcuse, *One-Dimensional Man* (Boston: Beacon Press, 1964).

EPILOGUE

It has perhaps struck you that the train of thought that is about to be concluded presents to the writer only one demand, the demand to think, to reflect on his position in the process of production.

—Walter Benjamin, "The Author as Producer"[1]

The economy is the first cause of wretchedness, and critique, theoretical and practical, must address itself primarily to it.

—Max Horkheimer, *Critical Theory*[2]

On theoretical as well as practical grounds, the dialectical concept pronounces its own hopelessness. The human reality is its history and, in it, contradictions do not explode by themselves.

—Herbert Marcuse, *One Dimensional Man*[3]

It lies in the definition of negative dialectics that it will not come to rest in itself, as if it were total. This is its form of hope.

—Theodor W. Adorno, *Negative Dialectics*[4]

On 15 and 16 August 1991, Flint's largest sports arena was filled to its 11,000-person capacity on three separate occasions.[5] The people had come to pay witness to the miracle cures offered by the Reverend Benny Hinn, television evangelist and star of his own program, "Miracle Invasion." With the help of his crew—composed of ministers, choir, salespeople, and the holy spirit—Hinn healed with the touch of his hand and the force of his voice. Indeed, the Reverend's visit to Flint caused every available hotel, motel, and bread-and-breakfast space in the city to fill with the faithful. For this, Hinn was welcomed by a Flint area mayor and given a sympathetic, front-page treatment in Flint's only daily newspaper. Benny Hinn is no Billy Graham, but in Flint even "etc . . . etc . . ." has cultural cachet.

Fast forward to 28 February 1992, the day Flint auto workers enacted a familiar ritual when they introduced a Toyota Celica to Mr. Sledgehammer.[6] Prefaced by the Genesee County Sheriff's hearty rendition of "America the Beautiful," a group of UAW Local 598 diehards, media ghouls, and local politicos marched into a cold, windy, muddy winter day and proceeded to encircle the dreaded foreign thing. As though in tribute to Vincent Chin's assailants, the righteous sword was passed to those able to overcome their self-consciousness before the rolling cameras and anxious stares. Whack, whack, whack, the Toyota was rolled on its back. Congressman Lizzy Borden took a few swings, and was warmed by the TV lights. Flint's newly elected African American mayor made the scene, armed with a City of Flint proclamation in recognition of the days's cultural activities. "I would not lend my presence nor my name to anything that hinted of racism or bigotry," protested the mayor.[7]

These stories suggest stereotypical images of rust-belt social psychology. The headlines might as well read: Economic Cataclysm Strikes Local Community; Fear and Frustration Spread; Snake Oil for Sale; Scapegoating Expected; Officialdom Panders to Worst in Would-Be Voters. This reading, however, fails to capture the single most significant nuance of Flint's new—one is tempted to say, postmodern—cultural mood. Even the Hinn and Toyota tales would be incomplete and misleading left as deindustrialization cliches. For example, a television audience attuned to the image conveyed by these events would not realize that neither genuine fear nor robust anger were actually perceptible among the participants at these gatherings. For the many, Benny Hinn's televised extravaganza was remote bread and circuses more than a truly sacred religious gathering, and, likewise, UAW Local 598's Buy-American-Smash-a-Toyota Rally was primarily a semisophisticated staged media event. Dependent deindustrialization may have an ugly underbelly, but one would not know it from firsthand observation at these administered news spectacles.

Flint goes through the motions, it seems, because it doesn't know what else to do.[8] Levelled expectations for Flint's future stem from its unrelenting crises, including its plant closings, unemployment, and physical deterioration, as well as the failed and occasionally embarrassing politico-administrative attempts to revive the city. In this context, hope for a renewal of progress and prosperity, and, indeed, any deeply held feelings for the community at all, becomes emotionally dysfunctional. Deep emotional investment in a futile cause is irrational; systems failure, as it were, leads to disenchantment and withdrawal. This study, with its focus on organized, empowered, coherent, prominent, sustained efforts to respond to Flint's collapse, therefore avoids the mistake of accepting serial, spin-doctored performances as a community's genuine response to local crisis. Yet, as we have seen again and again, the various movements, programs, films, buildings, and plans herein examined are no more successful. Flint faces the loss of still more GM facilities, as well as the unlikelihood of attracting or generating substitute industries. *Roger & Me*'s incredulous look at Flint's world-class lint-roller production is certainly on the mark. However, if Flint's levelled expectations are grounded in a sober appreciation for political-economic fact, what, then, is to be done?[9]

Dependent deindustrialization effectively disempowers bottom-up, localist political strategies. Future sit-down strikes are improbable with so little remaining in which to sit. Furthermore, no one can justly cast aspersions against Flint for its evident preference for the safety of television and television reality over the inherent risks and bitter hard realities of protest, confrontation, and revolution. In the absence of any sustained and effective worldwide social movement to reconstruct global capitalism, it is equally difficult to blame the erstwhile progressive-minded localist for subscribing to bumpersticker, "Ben and Jerry's" politics: think globally, act locally! To such naiveté, the question must be posed: What could Flint's citizens do (that they have not already tried to do) that would switch the dynamics of capitalism (and its capital flight and corporate social irresponsibility) in their favor? The television generations and local activists are not the only groups frustrated by the barriers to action built into 1990s global capitalism. Top-down strategies and programs enacted to nurture and guide a viable local economy are increasingly ambitious, as we have seen, but also increasingly moot. In Flint, GM and the C. S. Mott Foundation are steadily withdrawing, and the mainstream UAW, as Dallas Dort suggested, simply won't die fast enough. This leaves the remaining mop-up operatives to swim against common sense: GEAR, in effect, is charged with making something out of nothing.

The study of Flint's extreme dependent deindustrialization and its responsive ideologies suggests no easy, programmatic answers. Unable to identify a viable agent for change, and thus unable to illuminate a practical path from the present state of domination to a future state of liberation, a critical theory of dependent deindustrialization must do more than ponder its own challenges and its inadequacies. This does not mean a litany of wishful policy recommendations, for the situation in Flint has gone far beyond what trickle-down, piecemeal social reform could fix. Rather, it would seem that the last best hope for liberation remains primarily vested in the critique of ideology (the effort to strip the veneer of respectability from systematic deception), and, particularly, in the old-fashioned sort that pays steady attention to economics. In this regard, we may hope, with a positive dialectician like David Harvey, that the overall "condition of postmodernity is undergoing a subtle evolution, perhaps, reaching a point of self-dissolution into something different."[10] But even when we cannot see a flicker of hope— for Flint, or for ourselves—negative dialectics remains obstinate in the world and humble before the world's objective possibilities. This is its form of hope.

NOTES

1. Walter Benjamin, "The Author as Producer," in Peter Demetz, ed., *Reflections: Essays, Aphorisms, Autobiographical Writings* (New York: Schocken Books, 1986 [1934]), pp. 220–238, 236.

2. Max Horkheimer, "Postscript," in *Critical Theory* (New York: Continuum, 1986 [1937]), pp. 244–252, 249.

3. Herbert Marcuse, *One-Dimensional Man* (Boston: Beacon Press, 1964), p. 253.

4. Theodor W. Adorno, *Negative Dialectics* (New York: Continuum, 1987 [1966]), p. 406.

5. "Faith Healing: Prayerful pack IMA in search of miracle," *The Flint Journal*, 16 August 1991, Sec. A, p. 1, 9; information is also derived from field notes.

6. Information taken from field notes, including tape-recorded interviews with Flint Mayor Woodrow Stanley and U.S. Congressman Dale E. Kildee of Flint. Also see "UAW-made pride takes swing at Japanese cars," *The Flint Journal*, 28 February 1992, Sec. A, p. 1–2; Steven Dandaneau and George Lord, "Hit or Miss for Flint," *In These Times* 16, no. 20 (April 15–21, 1992), p. 2.

7. Mayor Stanley's comments are from a tape-recorded, on-the-scene, interview. Because of the context in which this interview was conducted, it is not included in the list of formal interviews below.

8. This study has not addressed the nature of Flint's everyday life, even though it is grounded in a lifetime's experience. See David L. Harvey's, *Potter Addition: Poverty, Family, and Kinship in a Heartland Community* (Hawthorne, NY: Aldine de Gruyter, 1993) for a sensitive ethnography of poor and lower-class whites, which, such incidental personal experience suggests, well captures the oft-hidden experience of many Flint citizens who daily negotiate the extraordinary conditions wrought by dependent deindustrialization.

9. The following is particularly indebted to David Harvey, *The Condition of Post-modernity* (New York: Basil Blackwell, 1989), especially part IV, pp. 326–359. For an excellent critical examination of Harvey, also see Paul Kamolnick, "Marxism, Postmodernism, and Beyond: A Critical Analysis of David Harvey's Theory of Contemporary Culture," in *Current Perspectives in Social Theory*, vol. 14 (Greenwich, CN: JAI Press, 1994), pp. 71–88.

10. *The Condition of Postmodernity*, p. 358.

BIBLIOGRAPHY

This bibliography is divided into two parts. First is a key for cited interviews. Second, selected book, journal, and article references are listed in alphabetical order. Document, archival, and participant-observation sources are cited in endnotes.

INTERVIEWS

Interview 1. Mr. Victor G. Reuther, retiree representative, UAW-New Directions Movement, June 14, 1991, at his residence, Washington, D.C.

Interview 2. Mr. Dallas C. Dort, member, GEAR Strategic Planning Committee, August 7, 1991, at his business office, Flint, Michigan.

Interview 3. Mr. Max Grider, national trustee, UAW-New Directions Movement, member, UAW Local 599, July 17, 1991, at the Windmill Place (public area), Flint, Michigan.

Interview 4a. Mr. Dave Yettaw, national co-chair, UAW-New Directions Movement, president, UAW Local 599, May 28, 1991, at the Windmill Place (public area), Flint, Michigan.

Interview 4b. Mr. Dave Yettaw, June 5, 1991, at the Windmill Place (public area), Flint, Michigan.

Interview 4c. Mr. Dave Yettaw, January 17, 1992, at his UAW Local 599 office, Flint, Michigan.

Interview 5. Mr. Ken Scott, shop committee chairperson, UAW Local 599, June 20, 1991, at his UAW Local 599 office, Flint, Michigan.

Interview 6. Mr. Russ Cook, shop committee, UAW Local 599, July 3, 1991, at his UAW Local 599 office, Flint, Michigan.

Interview 7. Mr. Bob Roman, recording secretary, UAW Local 599, July 5, 1991, at his UAW Local 599 office, Flint, Michigan.

Interview 8. Mr. Dennis Carl, education director, UAW Local 599, July 10, 1991, at his UAW Local 599 office, Flint, Michigan.

Interview 9. Mr. James "Cap" Wheeler, financial secretary, UAW Local 599, July 26, 1991, at his UAW Local 599 office, Flint, Michigan.

Interview 10a. Professor Richard Gull, Department of Philosophy, University of Michigan–Flint, July 19, 1991, at his residence, Ann Arbor, Michigan.

Interview 10b. Professor Richard Gull, August 2, 1991, at his residence, Ann Arbor, Michigan.

Interview 11. Mr. Carl McIntire, Local Paid Educational Leave coordinator, UAW Local 651, July 25, 1991, at the University of Michigan–Flint (public area), Flint, Michigan.

Interview 12. Mr. John Grimes, education director, UAW Region 1-C, August 1, 1991, at his UAW Region 1-C office, Flint, Michigan.

Interview 13. Ms. Pat Tarver, Local Paid Educational Leave coordinator, AC Rochester Division of General Motors Corporation, July 25, 1991, at the Windmill Place (public area), Flint, Michigan.

Interview 14. Mr. Mark S. Davis, executive director, Genesee Area Economic Revitalization, Inc., July 23, 1991, at his GEAR, Inc. office, Flint, Michigan.

Interview 15. Mr. William J. Donohue, president, Genesee Area Focus Council, Inc., June 9, 1992, at his Mott Foundation Building office, Flint, Michigan.

Interview 16. The Honorable Woodrow Stanley, mayor of the City of Flint, June 9, 1992, at his City Hall office, Flint, Michigan.

Interview 17a. Mr. Charles R. Weeks, chairman of the board of directors, Genesee Economic Area Revitalization, Inc., July 23, 1992, in his Citizens Bank office, Flint, Michigan.

Interview 17b. Mr. Charles R. Weeks, July 29, 1992, at his Citizen Bank office, Flint, Michigan.

SELECTED REFERENCES

Abrams, M. H. *The Mirror and the Lamp: Romantic Theory and the Critical Tradition.* Oxford: Oxford University Press, 1971.

Adorno, Theodor W. *Minima Moralia: Reflections From a Damaged Life.* New York: Verso, 1987.

———. *Aesthetic Theory.* New York: Routledge and Kegan Paul, Inc., 1986.

———. *Negative Dialectics.* New York: Continuum, 1973.

Agger, Ben. *Critical Theory of Public Life.* London: Falmer Press, 1991.

———. *Fast Capitalism: A Critical Theory of Significance.* Urbana, IL: University of Illinois Press, 1989a.

———. *Socio(onto)logy: A Disciplinary Reading.* Urbana, IL: University of Illinois Press, 1989b.

————. "The Dialectic of Deindustrialization: An Essay on Advanced Capitalism." In *Critical Theory and Public Life*, pp. 3–21. Edited by John Forester. Cambridge, MA: MIT Press, 1985.

Benjamin, Walter. "The Author as Producer." In *Reflections: Essays, Aphorisms, Autobiographical Writings*, pp. 220–238. Peter Demetz, ed. New York: Schocken Books, 1986.

Bergmann, Frithjof. "The Future of Work." *Praxis International* 3 (October, 1983): 308–323.

————. *On Being Free*. Notre Dame, IN: University of Notre Dame, 1977.

Bernstein, J. M., ed. *The Culture Industry: Selected Essays on Mass Culture* by Theodor W. Adorno. London: Routledge, 1991.

Bluestone, Barry, and Harrison, Bennett. *The Deindustrialization of America: Plant Closings, Community Abandonment, and the Dismantling of Basic Industry*. New York: Basic, 1982.

Edsforth, Ronald. *Class Conflict and Cultural Consensus: The Making of a Mass Consumer Society in Flint, Michigan*. New Brunswick, NJ: Rutgers University Press, 1987.

Fine, Sidney. *Sit-Down: The General Motors Strike of 1936–1937*. Ann Arbor, MI: University of Michigan Press, 1969.

Forester, John, ed. *Critical Theory and Public Life*. Cambridge, MA: MIT Press, 1985.

Frankfurt School of Social Research. *Aspects of Sociology*. Boston: Beacon Press, 1972.

Habermas, Jürgen. "The New Obscurity: The Crisis of the Welfare State and the Exhaustion of Utopian Energies." *Philosophy and Social Criticism* 11, 2 (Winter, 1986): 1–18.

————. *Theory of Communicative Action*, volume 1 and 2. Boston: Beacon Press, 1984, 1987.

————. "A Reply to My Critics." In *Habermas: Critical Debates*, pp. 219–283. Edited by John B. Thompson, and David Held. Cambridge, MA: MIT Press, 1982.

————. "Modernity Versus Postmodernity." In *New German Critique* 22 (1981): 3–14.

————. *Legitimation Crisis*. Boston: Beacon Press, 1975 [1973].

Harvey, David. *The Condition of Postmodernity: An Enquiry into the Conditions of Social Change*. New York: Basil Blackwell, 1989.

Harvey, David L. *Potter Addition: Poverty, Family, and Kinship in a Heartland Community*. Hawthorne, NY: Aldine de Gruyter, 1993.

Held, David. *Introduction to Critical Theory*. Berkeley, CA: University of California Press, 1980.

Horkheimer, Max. *Critical Theory*. New York: Continuum, 1986.

Huyssen, Andreas. "The Return of Diogenes as Post-Modern Intellectual." In *Critique of Cynical Reason*, pp. ix-xxv. By Peter Sloterdijk. Minneapolis: University of Minnesota Press, 1987.

Jameson, Fredric. *Postmodernism; or, the Cultural Logic of Late Capitalism*. Durham: Duke University Press, 1991.

———. *Late Marxism: Adorno; or, The Persistence of the Dialectic*. New York: Verso, 1990.

Jay, Martin. *Marxism and Totality: The Adventures of a Concept from Lukacs to Habermas*. Berkeley, CA: University of California Press, 1984a.

———. *Adorno*. Cambridge, MA: Harvard University Press, 1984b.

———. *The Dialectical Imagination*. Boston: Little, Brown and Company, 1973.

Katz, Harry. *Shifting Gears: Changing Labor Relations in the U.S. Automobile Industry.* Cambridge, MA: MIT Press, 1985.

Kearns, Josie. *Life after the Line*. Detroit, MI: Wayne State University Press, 1990.

Kochan, Thomas A.; Katz, Harry C.; and McKersie, Robert B. *The Transformation of American Industrial Relations*. New York: Basic Books, 1986.

Kraus, Henry. *The Many and the Few: A Chronicle of the Dynamic Auto Workers*. 2d ed. Urbana, IL: University of Illinois Press, 1985.

Lord, George F., and Price, Albert C. "Growth Ideology in a Period of Decline: Deindustrialization and Restructuring, Flint Style." *Social Problems* 39, no. 2 (May 1992): 155–169.

Lynd, Robert S., and Lynd, Helen Merrell. *Middletown: A Study in Modern American Culture*. New York: Harcourt-Brace and World, 1956.

Marcuse, Herbert. *One-Dimensional Man: Studies in the Ideology of Advanced Industrial Society*. Boston: Beacon Press, 1964.

Marquart, Frank. *An Auto Worker's Journal: The UAW from Crusade to One-Party Union*. University Park, PA: Pennsylvania State University Press, 1975.

Mills, C. Wright. "On Knowledge and Power." In *Power, Politics, and People*, pp. 599–613. Irving Louis Horowitz, ed. Oxford: Oxford University Press, 1979.

———. *The Sociological Imagination*. Oxford: Oxford University Press, 1959.

———. *The Power Elite*. Oxford: Oxford University Press, 1956.

———. *The New Men of Power: America's Labor Leaders*. New York: Harcourt, Brace and Company, 1948.

Perry, David C. "The Politics of Dependency in Deindustrializing America: The Case of Buffalo, New York." In *The Capitalist City: Global Restructuring and Community Politics*, pp. 113–137. Edited by Michael Peter Smith and Joe R. Feagin. New York: Basil Blackwell, 1987.

Reuther, Victor G. "Foreword." In *Choosing Sides: Unions and the Team Concept*, pp. v–vi. By Mike Parker and Jane Slaughter. Boston: South End Press, 1988.

———. *The Brothers Reuther and the Story of the UAW*. Boston: Houghton Mifflin, 1976.

Sloterdijk, Peter. *Critique of Cynical Reason*. Minneapolis: University of Minnesota Press, 1987.

———. "Cynicism—The Twilight of False Consciousness." *New German Critique* 33 (Fall, 1984): 190–206.

Stein, Maurice R. *Eclipse of Community: An Interpretation of American Studies*. Princeton, NJ: Princeton University Press, 1960.

Terkel, Studs. *Hard Times: An Oral History of the Great Depression*. New York: Pantheon, 1970.

Van Maanen, John. *Tales of the Field*. Chicago: University of Chicago Press, 1988.

Vidich, Arthur J.; Bensman, Joseph; and Stein, Maurice R., eds. *Reflections on Community Studies*. New York: Harper and Row, 1971.

Zwerdling, Daniel. "And Then There's the Disneyland Solution." *The Progressive* (July, 1982): 34–35.

INDEX